P

F

E

C000263504

Penguin Modern Management Readings

General Editor
D. S. Pugh

Advisory Board
H. C. Edey
R. L. Edgerton
T. Kempner
T. Lupton
D. T. Marquis
B. J. McCormick
P. G. Moore
R. W. Revans
F. J. Willett

Payment Systems

Selected Readings

Edited by Tom Lupton

Penguin Books

Penguin Books Ltd, Harmondsworth,
Middlesex, England
Penguin Books Inc, 7110 Ambassador Road,
Baltimore, Md 21207, USA
Penguin Books Australia Ltd,
Ringwood, Victoria, Australia

First published 1972
This selection copyright © Tom Lupton, 1972
Introduction and notes copyright © Tom Lupton, 1972

Made and printed in Great Britain by
Richard Clay (The Chaucer Press) Ltd, Bungay, Suffolk
Set in Monotype Times

Contents

Introduction

When a person joins an organization as a paid employee, he enters into a contract. His employer will expect him to exert himself in pursuit of the purposes of the organization as he, the employer, defines them. For his part, the employee will expect to be justly rewarded for these exertions. The rewards he seeks may be monetary, or he may wish to receive the esteem or deference that high status carries, and therefore he will seek advancement or he may seek the psychological reward of doing a difficult job well, or the satisfaction of working cooperatively at a task with congenial colleagues. Whatever the desired rewards are, and they may be all of these and more, it will be difficult to set them down in detail in a formal document. Even more difficult would be the task for the employer of setting down in detail exactly what exertions he expects of the employee for the period of the contract. It is certain that for most employees the employer would not wish to be too explicit since this would limit his capacity to respond to changes in the purposes of the organization and the methods it uses to pursue them. For similar reasons, the employee will not wish to limit his own freedom of manoeuvre as the circumstances of his employment change. It is to be expected, then, that most contracts of employment will have much in them that is implied rather than explicitly stated. Therefore, the arrangements in the organization for relating effort and reward are of great importance, if both parties to the contract are to be satisfied – the employee that the rewards are just, the employer that they do call forth a will to work effectively for the organization.

At first sight, there does not seem to be much of a problem. Surely, it is merely a matter of determining what moves people to work effectively, then designing a set of rewards that are appropriate. It is probably because the problem has usually been posed in this simple, general way, however, that its solution has so far eluded the efforts of managers and university researchers alike. It begs too many questions, and it concentrates on individual motivation too much. If one takes the view, for example, that people enter employment mainly to make money, it is easy to take the further step of arguing that the promise of more money will call forth more exertion. To the extent that the promise of more cash does call forth greater effort, so will the organization prosper, making more money available for the employee and the employer. It is this kind of argument that might be used to justify a system of payment by results for manual workers. It might also be used to justify an appraisal system for managerial performance in which the annual salary rise, or the chance of promotion to a job with high pay, rests on an assessment of performance over six months or a year. And the argument rests on an unspoken assumption that since employer and employee alike share the single objective of making the firm prosperous, both can benefit. There is, on this view, no conflict of objectives, although there might be conflict as to the share of the prosperity.

There is a fascinating research literature, some readings from which are included in Part One of this book, which describes what has in fact happened to payment systems designed exclusively on these assumptions. The attempt, for example, to measure work so accurately that measured bits of it can be related to increments of cash, has foundered not only on difficulties of measurement, of which there are many, but on the complexities of technology, the difficulties of work flow control, the pressures of labour markets, the subtleties of workshop social relationships, and even the social characteristics of individuals.

The apparent record of failure of systems of payment-by-results has led to the promotion of systems of payment based mainly on other principles of motivation. It has been plausibly argued, for example, that the obligation to keep contracts freely entered into is a powerful human motive, especially if there are agreed procedures for monitoring the contract, and agreed sanctions for breach. There is no need therefore, or so it is said, to hold out a carrot in order to get people to put forth their best efforts. All that is needed is to agree what is to be done, and what will be the reward so long as it is being done. This school of thought, which is represented in Part Two by a paper of Anne Shaw's, has usually also suggested, logically enough, that the agreement should include sanctions for failure to keep the contract. It will be apparent, as I have suggested in a paper also in Part Two, that systems based upon moral obligation may not work as well as expected, and may be subjected to many of the same disturbances as payment-by-results systems. If the contract is seen by either side as unequal, or too restricting in the light of changed circumstances; if either party is dissatisfied with the procedures for monitoring the contract, as they might well be in a complex changing situation, then this also might lead to the undermining of the arrangement, and a reversion to intermittent bargaining to establish a satisfactory effort–reward relationship.

In short, it is difficult to make the contract of employment as specific as it has to be if the principle of moral obligation is to be the basis of a practical scheme of payment. As we shall see in later Readings, the contract is easier to establish and maintain in some technologies, but it will also be noted that there is a difficulty in the employer–employee relationship in establishing that the parties to the contract (which is between the individual and the firm) are equal, in the sense that their access to sanctions for breach is equal.

I do not wish to give the impression that systems of payment of wage or salary have *either* to be based on the principle that the promise of cash for effort will bring forth the effort *or* that contracts freely entered into to perform a set task regularly for a reward that is fixed and constant (and strictly monitored) will ensure the task is performed. It is possible, in fact, to negotiate a contract that specifies a rate of pay for a job, and to offer an incentive to a person who exerts himself beyond what is normally expected for that rate. Payment can also be based on the motive of *social obligation*, i.e. the expectation that people might be interested in the performance of the whole enterprise, or some definable unit, say a department, within it, and put forward their best efforts, in collaboration with others, to increase that performance; and expect rewards as a share of the proceeds. Profit sharing schemes, and schemes based on a calculation of the value added in the course of production, or some measurement of increased productivity of a firm or department, would come into this category. In Part Three I have included some Readings that refer to such schemes. Again, it is possible to include payment based on this principle in addition to the elements in pay based upon financial incentive and moral obligation. A recent book on productivity bargaining (North and Buckingham, 1969) has suggested that the pay of industrial workers should show these three elements in certain given proportions.

Individuals who work in organizations differ from each other in such particulars as skill, manual dexterity, and the capacity to take responsibility. They also differ in the physical exertion they are capable of, in the learned competences they can make available, and so on. According to the degree to which individuals differ, they will expect to be paid differently. So there must be another element in pay: the rate for the job. The comparing of jobs to establish fair pay relativities has become the subject of a great controversy that increases as one moves from the shop floor pay structures to managerial salary structures. What factor, or factors, are relevant to the comparison of diverse jobs in the same organization, and how does one measure and compare them in establishing a structure of pay relativities that will be seen to be fair? In Part Five of these Readings, I have included recent work on the comparison of managerial jobs. Job evaluation takes many forms, from agreement on simple rank ordering and grouping of jobs by persons with long experience, to very elaborate systems of ranking along a number of dimensions. No matter how elaborate the procedure for ranking, the scope for experience and judgement is wide, so there might well be anomalies of both ranking and grouping of similar jobs into grades, arising from conflicts of judgement. Therefore, the rankings and groupings will to some extent reflect the power of the parties to the procedure, and will shift as that shifts, a point discussed in Alan Fox's paper in Part Five.

All I have said so far, and indeed much of what the Readings in this book convey, suggests that however much one tries to establish a rational scheme of relating effort to reward, or a just system of pay relativities, one is likely to be defeated either by the intervention of product and labour market forces, or by the working group, or by the changing shape of power relationships in the organizations. A depressing conclusion, yet one that seems to be backed by the research literature. Nevertheless, it might be possible to find better ways of establishing job relativities so as to eliminate conflict on that score and to take account, when designing a payment system, of the forces at work in the labour market and product markets, in the technology and in work flow administration, that have to be considered when choosing what principles of motivation should be represented, in what proportions, in the pay packet, or the salary cheque. Recent advances in this direction are represented in Part Four. The attempt to find a way of selecting that combination of elements in the pay packet which is optimal in a given set of circumstances, described in the Lupton and Gowler paper in Part Four, has so far only covered shop floor workers. A paper applying the method to salaried employees' pay structures by workers at the Manchester Business School is in an advanced state of preparation and should soon be available for publication. In selecting the Readings in the final two parts, I had to indicate that different questions are now being asked than were asked hitherto, questions about 'best fit'. We have neither the data, nor the analytical apparatus, fully to answer these questions yet, but now that they have been asked, it must only be a short time before the whole subject will get, finally, on to a plane of scientific discourse, leaving behind the moralising and the home-spun psychological and sociological prejudices which hitherto have influenced too much the design of pay and salary systems.

Reference

NORTH, D. T. B., and BUCKINGHAM, G. (1969), *Productivity Agreements and Wage Systems*, Gower Press.

Part One
Cash Incentives and Limitation of Output

The Readings in Part One follow a roughly historical sequence that traces the development of a realization that human organization for production is much more than influencing individuals by dangling well-designed financial carrots and/or wielding well-designed financial sticks. The payment system is clearly just one influence amongst many on behaviour at work; of importance to be sure, but capable of being manipulated to meet ends other than those it was designed to serve. The researches reported by Roethlisberger and Dickson, Dalton, Roy, Sayles, and Lupton identify some of the more significant of these ends and influences, and thus establish the basis for better decision-making.

1 F. W. Taylor

Scientific Management: Shop Management

Excerpt from F. W. Taylor, *Scientific Management*, Harper & Row, 1964, pp. 38–46.

Of all the ordinary systems of management in use (in which no accurate scientific study of the time problem is undertaken, and no carefully measured tasks are assigned to the men which must be accomplished in a given time) the best is the plan fundamentally originated by Mr Henry R. Towne, and improved and made practical by Mr F. A. Halsey. This plan is described in papers read by Mr Towne before the American Society of Mechanical Engineers in 1886, and by Mr Halsey in 1891, and has since been criticized and ably defended in a series of articles appearing in the *American Machinist*.

The Towne–Halsey plan consists in recording the quickest time in which a job has been done, and fixing this as a standard. If the workman succeeds in doing the job in a shorter time, he is still paid his same wages per hour for the time he works on the job, and in addition is given a premium for having worked faster, consisting of from one-quarter to one-half the difference between the wages earned and the wages originally paid when the job was done in standard time. Mr Halsey recommends the payment of one-third of the difference as the best premium for most cases. The difference between this system and ordinary piece work is that the workman on piece work gets the whole of the difference between the actual time of a job and the standard time, while under the Towne–Halsey plan he gets only a fraction of this difference.

It is not unusual to hear the Towne–Halsey plan referred to as practically the same as piece work. This is far from the truth, for while the difference between the two does not appear to a casual observer to be great, and the general principles of the two seem to be the same, still we all know that success or failure in many cases hinges upon small differences.

In the writer's judgement, the Towne–Halsey plan is a great invention, and, like many other great inventions, its value lies in its simplicity.

This plan has already been successfully adopted by a large number of establishments, and has resulted in giving higher wages to many workmen, accompanied by a lower labor cost to the employer, and at the same time materially improving their relations by lessening the feeling of antagonism between the two.

This system is successful because it diminishes soldiering, and this rests entirely upon the fact that since the workman only receives say one-third of the increase in pay that he would get under corresponding conditions on piece work, there is not the same temptation for the employer to cut prices.

After this system has been in operation for a year or two, if no cuts in prices have been made, the tendency of the men to soldier on that portion of the work which is being done under the system is diminished, although it does not entirely cease. On the other hand, the tendency of the men to soldier on new work which is started, and on such portions as are still done on day work, is even greater under the Towne–Halsey plan than under piece work.

To illustrate: Workmen, like the rest of mankind, are more strongly influenced by object lessons than by theories. The effect on men of such an object lesson as the following will be apparent. Suppose that two men, named respectively Smart and Honest, are at work by the day and receive the same pay, say 20 cents per hour. Each of these men is given a new piece of work which could be done in one hour. Smart does his job in four hours (and it is by no means unusual for men to soldier to this extent). Honest does his in one and one-half hours.

Now, when these two jobs start on this basis under the Towne–Halsey plan and are ultimately done in one hour each, Smart receives for his job 20 cents per hour + a premium of $\frac{60}{3} = 20$ cents = *a total of 40 cents.* Honest receives for his job 20 cents per hour + a premium of $\frac{10}{3} = 3\frac{1}{3}$ cents = *a total of $23\frac{1}{3}$ cents.*

Most of the men in the shop will follow the example of Smart rather than that of Honest and will 'soldier' to the extent of three or four hundred per cent. if allowed to do so.

The Towne–Halsey system shares with ordinary piece work then, the greatest evil of the latter, namely that its very foundation rests upon deceit, and under both of these systems there is necessarily, as we have seen, a great lack of justice and equality in the starting-point of different jobs.

Some of the rates will have resulted from records obtained when a first-class man was working close to his maximum speed, while others will be based on the performance of a poor man at one-third or one-quarter speed.

The injustice of the very foundation of the system is thus forced upon the workman every day of his life, and no man, however kindly disposed he may be toward his employer, can fail to resent this and be seriously influenced by it in his work. These systems are, therefore, of necessity slow and irregular in their operation in reducing costs. They 'drift' gradually toward an increased output, but under them the attainment of the maximum output of a first-class man is almost impossible.

Objection has been made to the use of the word 'drifting' in this connection. It is used absolutely without any intention of slurring the Towne–Halsey system or in the least detracting from its true merit.

It appears to me, however, that 'drifting' very accurately describes it, for the reason that the management, having turned over the entire control of the speed problem to the men, the latter being influenced by their prejudices and whims, drift sometimes in one direction and sometimes in another; but on the whole, sooner or later, under the stimulus of the premium, move toward a higher rate of speed. This drifting (accompanied as it is by the irregularity and uncertainty both as to the final result which will be attained and as to how long it will take to reach this end) is in marked contrast to the distinct goal which is always kept in plain sight of both parties under task management, and the clear-cut directions which leave no doubt as to the means which are to be employed nor the time in which the work must be done. These elements constitute the fundamental difference between the two systems. Mr Halsey, in objecting to the use of the word 'drifting' as describing his system, has referred to the use of his system in England in connection with a 'rate-fixing' or planning department, and quotes as follows from his paper to show that he contemplated control of the speed of the work by the management: 'On contract work undertaken for the first time the method is the same except that the premium is based on the estimated time for the execution of the work.'

In making this claim Mr Halsey appears to have entirely lost sight of the real essence of the two plans. It is task management which is in use in England, not the Towne–Halsey system; and in the above quotation Mr Halsey describes not his system but a type of task management, in which the men are paid a premium for carrying out the directions given them by the management.

There is no doubt that there is more or less confusion in the minds of many of those who have read about the task management and the Towne–Halsey system. This extends also to those who are actually using and working under these systems. This is practically true in England, where in some cases task management is actually being used under the name of the 'Premium Plan'. It would therefore seem desirable to indicate once again and in a little different way the essential difference between the two.

The one element which the Towne–Halsey system and task management have in common is that both recognize the all-important fact that workmen cannot be induced to work extra hard without receiving extra pay. Under both systems the men who succeed are daily and automatically, as it were, paid an extra premium. The payment of this daily premium forms such a characteristic feature in both systems, and so radically differentiates these systems from those which were in use before, that people are apt to look upon this one element as the essence of both systems and so fail to recognize the more important, underlying principles upon which the success of each of them is based.

In their essence, with the one exception of the payment of a daily premium, the systems stand at the two opposite extremes in the field of management; and it is to the distinctly radical, though opposite, positions taken by them that each one owes its success; and it seems to me a matter of importance that this should be understood. In any executive work which involves the cooperation of two different men or parties, where both parties have anything like equal power or voice in its direction, there is almost sure to be a certain amount of bickering, quarreling, and vacillation, and the success of the enterprise suffers accordingly.

If, however, either one of the parties has the entire direction, the enterprise will progress consistently and probably harmoniously, even though the wrong one of the two parties may be in control.

Broadly speaking, in the field of management there are two parties – the superintendents, etc., on one side and the men on the other, and the main questions at issue are the speed and accuracy with which the work shall be done. Up to the time that task management was introduced in the Midvale Steel Works, it can be fairly said that under the old systems of management the men and the management had about equal weight in deciding how fast the work should be done. Shop records showing the quickest time in which each job had been done and more or less shrewd guessing being the means on which the management depended for bargaining with and coercing the men; and deliberate soldiering for the purpose of misinforming the management being the weapon used by the men in self-defense. Under the old system the incentive was entirely lacking which is needed to induce men to cooperate heartily with the management in increasing the speed with which work is turned out. It is chiefly due, under the old systems, to this divided control of the speed with which the work shall be done that such an amount of bickering, quarreling, and often hard feeling exists between the two sides.

The essence of task management lies in the fact that the control of the speed problem rests entirely with the management; and, on the other hand, the true strength of the Towne–Halsey system rests upon the fact that under it the question of speed is settled entirely by the men without interference on the part of the management. Thus in both cases, though from diametrically opposite causes, there is undivided control, and this is the chief element needed for harmony.

The writer has seen many jobs successfully nursed in several of our large and well-managed establishments under these drifting systems, for a term of ten to fifteen years, at from one-third to one-quarter speed. The workmen, in the meanwhile, apparently enjoyed the confidence of their employers, and in many cases the employers not only suspected the deceit, but felt quite sure of it.

The great defect, then, common to all the ordinary systems of management (including the Towne–Halsey system, the best of this class) is that their starting-point, their very foundation, rests upon ignorance and deceit, and that throughout their whole course in the one element which is most vital both to employer and workmen, namely, the speed at which work is done, they are allowed to drift instead of being intelligently directed and controlled.

The writer has found, through an experience of thirty years, covering a large variety in manufactures, as well as in the building trades, structural and engineering work, that it is not only practicable but comparatively easy to obtain, through a systematic and scientific time study, exact information as to how much of any given kind of work either a first-class or an average man can do in a day, and with this information as a foundation, he has over and over again seen the fact demonstrated that workmen of all classes are not only willing, but glad to give up all idea of soldiering, and devote all of their energies to turning out the maximum work possible, providing they are sure of a suitable permanent reward.

With accurate time knowledge as a basis, surprisingly large results can be obtained under any scheme of management from day work up; there is no question that even ordinary day work resting upon this foundation will give greater satisfaction than any of the systems in common use, standing as they do upon soldiering as a basis.

2 F. J. Roethlisberger and W. J. Dickson

Management and the Worker

Excerpts from F. J. Roethlisberger and W. J. Dickson, *Management and the Worker*, Wiley, 1964, pp. 517–35.

The relation between position in the group and output

At the end of Chapter 18 [not included here], certain puzzling questions were raised concerning the output of this group. These questions were of the following order: Why did W_3 and W_6 [W = wireman] report less output than they produced, and why did they claim less daywork than they were entitled to? Why did W_2, who ranked higher in output than W_3 or W_6, report more output than he produced, and why did he claim more daywork than he was entitled to? Finally, what accounted for the relative ranking of these operators in average hourly output? If these differences in rank were not related to differences in capacity to perform, as measured by tests of intelligence and dexterity, what were they related to? More particularly, why did W_7, W_8, and W_9, who ranked relatively high in the aptitude tests, continue to produce at a low level even though they were thereby lowering their own earnings and those of their associates?

In answering these questions, considerable reference will be made to differences in the performance of the various wiremen. Figure 1 (page 23) has been constructed to facilitate comparisons and also to show the relation between performance and position in the group. The internal organization of the group is shown at the top of the diagram. At the bottom of the diagram, directly under each wireman's number, is shown the relative size of his average hourly output, the difference between his reported and actual outputs and the amount of daywork allowance claimed. The geometric figures are drawn in proportion to the size of each person's rating. The broken circles under W_3 and W_6 indicate that their actual output exceeded their reported output.

In considering the output of the members of the group it is

necessary, first of all, to recall their general attitude toward output. It has been shown that the official 'bogey' meant nothing to the operators. In its stead they had an informal standard of a day's work which functioned for the group as a norm of conduct, as a social code. They felt that it was wrong to exceed this standard.

W_3 and W_6 in refraining from reporting all the work they produced were expressing their adherence to this code. Both of these men were good workers and both of them liked to work. Occasionally they produced too much, but instead of reporting all their output, which would have affected their standing in the group, they refrained from doing so. The fact that they claimed less daywork than they could have is explainable in the same terms. If they had claimed the daywork they were entitled to, they would have raised their reported average hourly output too high. Their adherence to the group standard also accounts for their remarkably constant output rate.

But here an apparent contradiction arises. Why, it might be asked, if these two men were so mindful of the group's sentiments regarding output, did they not occupy the same position in the group? W_3 was a member of clique A and was the best-liked person in the group, whereas W_6 was excluded from clique A and tended to associate with clique B. Unlike W_3, W_6 was subjected to sarcasm and ridicule and given such nicknames as 'Runt' and 'Shrimp'. This was in spite of the fact that he conformed to the output standards of the group and helped more people than anyone else in the group. What, then, accounts for this apparent contradiction? The answer is that output, like occupational status, was not the only determinant of position in the group. One of the things which made W_6 objectionable to clique A was his irrepressible tendency to 'horse around.' Moreover, he had no compunctions about telling another person what he thought of him. Of still more importance, however, was his striving for leadership of the group. This was an honor no one was willing to confer upon him; yet he persisted in attempting to achieve it. The result was that he became a constant source of irritation. W_6, in other words, conformed to the group's sentiments attaching to output but violated those attaching to personal conduct. This was reflected in the position assigned him in the group, which was

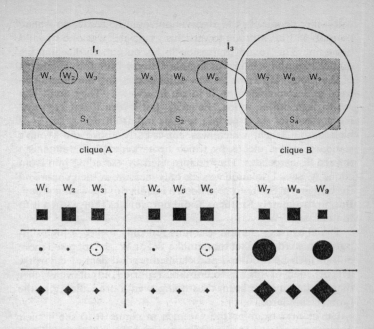

Figure 1 Bank wiring observation room: the internal organization of the group and output

Legend:

- ■ mean 'average hourly output' for entire study period
- ● difference: (reported-actual)
- ⊙ negative difference
- ◆ amount of daywork allowance claims

by no means an unfavorable one. He got along with everyone fairly well. It is quite likely that his adherence to the group's rules of output served to sustain him in the eyes of his associates. The sentiments he violated were much weaker than those attaching to output.

Let us next examine the relation between W_2's position in the group and his output. W_2, as interviews with him indicated, was not the type of person to conform to another's wishes. He was hard, enigmatic, self-reliant, and entered very little into relations with other people. In the observation room he tended to isolate himself, and his attitude toward his associates was one of mild contempt. This found expression in his output. By keeping his output high, he was expressing his disregard for the sentiments of the group. He knew he was doing something the others disliked and commented on it in his interviews. 'They don't like me to turn out so much,' he said, 'but I turn it out anyway.' He seemed to get a certain satisfaction from doing so. W_2's high output, then, which was consistently above the group's standard, was a means by which he expressed his antagonism toward his associates. They reciprocated by excluding him from clique A. Social isolation was the only measure at their command for bringing pressure to bear upon a member of the wiring group. But, unfortunately for them, it did not work as they wished it to in the case of W_2.

The above explanation accounts not only for W_2's high output but also for the fact that, unlike W_3 or W_6, he reported more output than he produced and claimed a good deal of daywork. The net effect of this was to boost his reported output even higher than it should have been, thus doing even more violence to the group's standard.

Let us next examine the wiremen in clique B to see if their output was related to the position they held in the group's informal organization. Clique B was looked down upon by clique A. The actual average hourly output rates of the members, as shown in Figure 1, were lower than the output rate of any other operator. W_7 and W_9 ranked unusually low. For this group, therefore, there was a direct correspondence between rate of output and informal standing in the group.

The same general relation held for other aspects of their performance. They tended to report more unearned output than the other wiremen. W_7 claimed more unearned output than anyone else, with W_9 a close second; W_8 ranked third. W_8's relatively good rating in this respect must be interpreted in the light of the fact that he spent a great deal of time soldering. It was less necessary for him to pad his figures in order to make a good showing because he could always use soldering as an excuse. W_7, W_8, and W_9 also claimed a great deal more daywork than any of the other wiremen. W_8 claimed an average of over 2 minutes lost time per hour. W_7 and W_9 each claimed an average of more than $3\frac{1}{2}$ minutes per hour. The most claimed by any other wireman was about 1 minute per hour. But these three not only claimed more lost time, the character of their claims differed also. Table 29 [not included here] shows that of the 160 claims entered by these three men, sixty-four were charged against their solderman and inspector. The members of clique A never once blamed a solderman or inspector for delaying them.

It may be concluded that the various performance records for the members of clique B were reflecting their position in the group. There was a clear-cut relation between their social standing and their output. But, it may be asked, did their low output determine their position in the group, or did their position in the group determine their output? The answer is that the relation worked both ways; position in the group influenced output, and output influenced position in the group. In other words, these two factors were in a relation of mutual dependence. Let us attempt to show more clearly just how this was so.

The selector wiremen, being differentiated from the connector wiremen, banded together and achieved a certain amount of solidarity among themselves. This internal solidarity resulted in increased opposition to those people who were not members of their group. Some such process usually occurs when a group becomes unified. The very process of unification entails a drawing away from those who are not members of the group. The entity retains or increases its unity by opposing other entities. In the case of the selector wiremen, opposition was expressed toward those occupational groups who stood in a relation of superordination to them; to those groups, in other words, in comparison with whom they were subordinated. These were the inspection group, represented in their case by I_3, and the connector wiremen. Their inspector, I_3, experienced the most forceful and the most personal expression of their opposition, and he eventually had to be removed from the room. The medium through which they expressed opposition to the inspector was daywork allowance claims, but with respect to the connector wiremen there was no such medium at their disposal. However, they could express their opposition to connector wiremen indirectly through output, and that is what they did. By keeping their output low, they not only lowered the earnings of the connector wiremen but at the same time they themselves managed to draw a wage quite out of proportion to their own contributions. They were, to use one of their own expressions, 'chiseling' the other wiremen. This was, of course, resented particularly by W_2, W_5, and W_6. The *bona fide* members of clique A may have been equally annoyed, but they said nothing about it. W_2, W_5, and W_6, however, time and again tried to get clique B to raise their output. For the most part, their tactics were indirect. Frequently they traded jobs with S_4 and while in that position heckled the wiremen. They bragged that they could solder for a dozen men like W_9. Sometimes they finished their soldering very quickly and then made elaborate gestures of enforced idleness. At other times they subjected the members of clique B to direct personal criticism. The interesting thing about these tactics was that they served to subordinate clique B still further and as a result to strengthen their internal solidarity still more. So, instead of increasing their output, the members of clique B kept it low, thus 'getting back' at those who were displaying their superiority.

The relation of employee to supervision as a determinant of position in the group

So far, all the operators except W_5 have been considered. He was the most disliked person in the group. Was this because he violated the output standard of the group? The answer is no. His output only rarely exceeded the standard of a day's work, and on the whole he conformed to this norm just as well as W_3 or W_6. Furthermore, he conformed to the group's practice of reporting more or less daywork and more or less output than he should have. In this area his conduct, from the standpoint of the group, was satisfactory. But in his relations with the foreman his conduct was anything but satisfactory. The operators, on the whole, were decidedly apprehensive of the higher supervisors in the department, partly because of the authority vested in them, and partly because much of their own conduct was contrary to the rules of management. It was an interesting fact that nearly all the activities by means of which the operators related themselves to one another, all their social activities in other words, were 'wrong.' They were contrary to the rules of management. Therefore, it was important that these activities be concealed from the foreman. To act as informer was an unpardonable breach of conduct. Yet this is what W_5 did, and his action explains the group's opposition to him. By 'squealing' he violated a very strong sentiment intimately connected with the relation of subordinate to superior. Here, then, is still another factor which entered into the determination of the individual's position in the group's internal organization.

Determinants of clique membership

From the foregoing analysis it is apparent that this group of operators held certain definite ideas as to the way in which an individual should conduct himself. These sentiments, which were connected chiefly with occupation, output, and supervision, may be summarized as follows:

1. You should not turn out too much work. If you do, you are a 'rate-buster'.

2. You should not turn out too little work. If you do, you are a 'chiseler'.

3. You should not tell a supervisor anything that will react to the detriment of an associate. If you do, you are a 'squealer'.

4. You should not attempt to maintain social distance or act officious. If you are an inspector, for example, you should not act like one.

It may be concluded that the individual's position in the group was in large part determined by the extent to which his behavior was in accord with these sentiments. The members of clique A, the people who held the most favored position in the group, conformed to the group's rules of behavior in all respects. Members of clique B conformed to rules (1), (3) and (4). Indeed, they attached more importance to these rules than anyone else. This is easily understood because the higher the output of their associates, the more unfavorable their own output appeared. 'Squealing' was more objectionable to them than to the others because more of their actions were wrong from the standpoint of management. Finally, they resented any show of superiority more than the others did because they were in the most subordinate position.

The function of the group's internal organization

The social organization of the bank wiremen performed a two-fold function: firstly to protect the group from internal indiscretions, and secondly to protect it from outside interference. The same mechanism sometimes served to fulfill, both functions.

The mechanisms by which internal control was exercised were varied. Perhaps the most important were sarcasm, 'binging,' and ridicule. Through such devices pressure was brought to bear upon those individuals who deviated too much from the group's norm of acceptable conduct. From this point of view, it will be seen that the great variety of activities ordinarily labeled 'restriction of output' represent attempts at social control and discipline and as such are important integrating processes. In addition to overt methods, clique membership itself may be looked upon as an instrument of control. Those persons whose behavior was most reprehensible to clique A were excluded from it. They were, in a sense, socially ostracized. This is one of the universal social processes by means of which a group chastises and brings pressure to bear upon those who transgress its codes.

The operators attempted to protect themselves from outside interference by bringing into line those outsiders, supervisors and inspectors, who stood in a position of being able to interfere in their affairs. The chief mechanism by which they attempted to control these people was that of daywork allowance claims. The manner in which this weapon was brought into play against I_3 shows how formidable it could be. The operators did not use this weapon against I_1 or the group chief because they did not have to; both of these people submitted to group control. I_3, however, refused to be assimilated, and they helped to bring about his removal by charging him with excessive amounts of daywork. This was the most effective device at their command. Interestingly enough, it was a device provided them by their wage incentive plan. The mechanism by which they sought to protect themselves from management was the maintenance of uniform output records, which could be accomplished by reporting more or less output than they produced and by claiming daywork.

It can be seen, therefore, that nearly all the activities of this group may be looked upon as methods of controlling the behavior of its members. The men had elaborated, spontaneously and quite unconsciously, an intricate social organization around their collective beliefs and sentiments. The question as to what gave rise to those sentiments and beliefs, whether they arose from actual or potential threats to their security, as the operators claimed, is an important one and will be dealt with in the following sections.

Formal *v.* informal organization

So far it has been shown that the members of the Bank Wiring Observation Room group possessed an intricate social organization in terms of which much of their conduct was determined. Restriction of output was the chief outer manifestation of this complex of interhuman relations. Let us now turn from the particularities of the bank wiring situation to a consideration of the relation of the group as an entity to the wider company organization of which it was a part.

The problem to be considered in this chapter can best be defined in terms of the external function of the bank wiremen's organization. It has been shown that the internal function of this organization was to control and regulate the behavior of its members. Externally, however, it functioned as a protective mechanism. It served to protect the group from outside interference by manifesting a strong resistance to change, or threat of change, in conditions of work and personal relations. This resistance to change not only was reflected in all the wiremen's tactics to keep output constant but also was implied in all the reasons they gave in justification of their actions. Had it been explicitly stated, their behavior could be said to have been guided by the following rule: 'Let us behave in such a way as to give management the least opportunity of interfering with us.' There is no doubt that the most pronounced over-all characteristic of the interhuman activities described was their peculiarly protective or resistive quality. The problem, therefore, becomes that of discovering those external factors which gave rise to this resistance.

When stated in these terms, a number of answers to this problem are immediately suggested. Perhaps the wiremen were apprehensive of the investigators. Did not the study situation itself encourage the type of behavior observed? Or were not the operators simply attempting to stave off the effects of the depression, which were becoming noticeable within the factory at that time? Or, finally, were they not, in restricting their output, simply attempting to protect their economic interests? Inasmuch as any of these possibilities might have accounted for the situation, they must be considered at the outset [. . .]

The effects of the depression

Did not the situation in the Bank Wiring Observation Room reflect the response of the operators to the business depression? Was this not merely their way of warding off unemployment? In part, yes. There could be no doubt that the depression and fear of layoff occupied an increasingly important place in their thoughts, particularly after the beginning of 1932. In their interviews and in their daily conversations with one another and the observer they speculated endlessly upon when the depression would end, whether they would be laid off, and what would happen to them if they were. All but one of them were in very poor financial condition and if they were unemployed could not escape public support for long.

Although this was true, the investigators believed that fear of unemployment was only one among many factors determining the situation. It is doubtful if their formation into cliques and their attitudes toward their supervision had any relation to it. As for restriction of output, it may have been related to the effects of the depression but even that is doubtful. The output figures available, which stretched back before the depression, did not reflect any major interference. Furthermore, it is fairly generally conceded that restriction in one form or another occurs in good as well as bad times. It may grow more or less pronounced, but the basic pattern remains. The interviewers had detected suggestions of this pattern even in 1929, the year in which the company reached its peak of activity. It is fair to conclude, therefore, that this was not a 'depression story', and that any conclusions derived from an analysis of such a situation might have relevance to periods of prosperity as well as to periods of depression.

Restriction of output and economic interest

Perhaps the most common way of interpreting situations like this is to argue that the employee, in acting as he does, is simply protecting his economic interests. It is argued that if he does not restrict his output at some level his piece rate will be cut, the less capable workers will be reprimanded or discharged, or some of his co-workers will be laid off. These reasons are the same as those the worker himself gives for his behavior and are taken as explanatory and self-evident. It is assumed that the worker, from a logical appraisal of his work situation or from his own past experiences, formulates a plan of action which in the long run will be to his own best interests and then acts in accordance with that plan. This theory is based upon two primary assumptions: first, that the worker is primarily motivated by economic interest; and, second, that work behavior is logical and rational. In what follows, these assumptions will be examined in the light of the facts of this study.

Let us begin by examining the reasons the employees gave for their own behavior. These reasons may be summarized in the belief the men held that if output went too high something might happen – the 'bogey' might be raised, the 'rate' might be raised, the 'rate' might be lowered, someone might be laid off, hours might be reduced, or the supervisors might reprimand the slower workers. Now one of the interesting things about these reasons is the confusion they manifest. In talking about 'rates', for example, many of the employees were not clear as to whether they were talking about piece rates, hourly rates, or rates of working. The consequences of changing a rate would vary depending upon which rate was changed; yet the operators did not discriminate. Again, raising the bogey would have none of the consequences they feared. If it induced them to increase their output, the effect would be to increase their earnings; otherwise, there would be no effect whatsoever. The result would be the opposite of cutting a piece rate; yet some of the operators felt that the result would be the same. It is clear, therefore, that their actions were not based upon a logical appraisal of their work situation.

Another important observation which supports the above conclusion is that not one of the bank wiremen had ever experienced any of the things they claimed they were guarding against. Their bogey had not been raised, their piece rates had not been lowered, nor had their hourly rates; yet they acted and talked as though they had. Their behavior, in other words, was not based upon their own concrete experience with the company. In this connection it might be pointed out that from a logical standpoint the operators should have wanted hourly rates to be flexible. They should have wanted them raised or lowered depending upon changes in the levels of an individual's efficiency, for only in that way could earnings be made to correspond with output. Yet all of them, the highest and lowest alike, were opposed to a lowering of hourly rates.

Another illustration of the nonlogical character of their behavior is found in an incident which occurred before the study began. Hours of work had been shortened from 48 to 44 per week. The supervisors told the men that if they turned out the same amount of work in the shorter time their earnings would remain the same. After a great deal of persuasion, the men agreed to try, and they were very much surprised to find that their earnings did stay the same. Not one of the men who commented upon this in an interview could see how it could be, in spite of the fact that their supervisors had tried to explain it to them.

At this point an objection might be raised. Granted that the employees did not clearly understand their payment system, were they not, nevertheless, acting in accordance with their economic interests? Even though none of them had experienced a reduction of piece rates, was it not a possibility? And were they not at least guarding against that possibility by controlling their output?

In considering this objection, let us assume for the time being that many of their fears were justified. Let us suppose that the piece rate was endangered if their output exceeded their concept of a day's work. Then what would follow from this if we assume that they were motivated primarily by economic interest? It would seem that each and every worker would push his output up to 6600 connections per day and then hold it at that point. If all of them maintained that level of output consistently, they would be securing the maximum of earnings possible without endangering the piece rate. The facts are, however, that there were wide differences in the outputs of different individuals and that some of the operators were far short of 6600 connections per day. If earnings had been their chief concern, differences in output levels should not have existed unless the operators were working at top capacity, and that was far from being the case. Furthermore, in these terms it would be impossible to account for the amount of daywork claimed. Had they been chiefly concerned with earnings, they would have seen to it that there was very little daywork. It follows that this group of operators could not be said to be acting in accordance with their economic interests even if we assume that the reasons they gave for their actions were supportable by experimental evidence, which, of course, was not the case.

Two other fallacies in the economic interpretation of restriction of output may be mentioned. One of them is the implied assumption that a fixed, unchanging piece rate is desirable on economic grounds. It is argued that a firm should maintain piece rates once they have been established, that this is the only way defensive reactions on the part of employees can be prevented. The general validity of this statement is scarcely open to question. Rapid change in piece rates is likely to undermine the workers' confidence in management and may in itself defeat the purpose of the most carefully constructed incentive plan. The justification of the fixed piece rate, however, is not so much economic as social. From a strictly economic viewpoint, it is to the advantage of the workers to have piece rates change with changes in the cost of living. The firm that takes pride in piece rates of long standing in the belief that it is thereby protecting the economic interests of the workers may be misplacing its emphasis. What it is really doing may lie more in the social than in the economic area.

The other fallacy lies in the assumption that the worker can effectively control the actions of management by acting in certain ways. Changes in piece rates, hours of work, number of people employed, and so on, frequently lie completely outside the control of the worker and even of management. Furthermore, changes in piece rates at the Western Electric Company, for example, are not based upon the earnings of the worker. The company's policy is that piece rates will not be changed unless there is a change in manufacturing process. Changes in process are made by engineers whose duty it is to reduce unit cost wherever the saving will be sufficient to justify the change. In certain instances such changes may be made irrespective of direct labor cost per unit. Again, where labor is a substantial element, increased output tends to lower unit cost and thus tends to obviate the need for a change in process. Restriction works precisely opposite. Restriction tends to increase unit costs and, instead of warding off a change in the piece rate as the worker believes, may actually induce one.

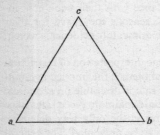

a = sentiments of the group
b = behaviour in restricting output
c = reasons given for their behaviour

Figure 2 Mutually interdependent relations between behaviour, sentiment and belief

From this analysis it may be concluded that the ideology expressed by the employees was not based upon a logical appraisal of their situation and that they were not acting strictly in accordance with their economic interests. Rather, the situation was as represented in Figure 2, in which a stands for the sentiments of the group, b for their behavior in restricting output, and c for the reasons they gave for acting as they did. The economic interest argument which we have been considering assumes a causal relation between c and b. It assumes that b follows from c. Actually, we see that for these operators b was an expression of a, the group's sentiments. Their behavior was a way of affirming those sentiments which lay at the root of their group organization. c, far from being the 'cause' of their actions, was merely the way in which they rationalized their behavior. They attempted to give logical reasons for their conduct and to make it appear as though the latter was directed toward some outside interference, whereas in fact b was primarily directed toward and expressed a.

3 Donald Roy

Quota Restriction and Goldbricking in a Machine Shop

Donald Roy, 'Quota restriction and goldbricking in a machine shop',
American Journal of Sociology, vol. 67, 1952, no. 2, pp. 427–42.

Even those sociologists who nurse a distaste for studies of industrial administration, either because the problems involved are
'practical' or because they fear managerial bias, will recognize
that study of restriction of industrial output may yield knowledge
free of both taints.[1] Systematic 'soldiering' is group activity.
One may learn about the 'human group' by studying behavior
on a production line as well as in an interracial discussion group.
And, if someone should find the knowledge useful, even for
making a little money, perhaps its scientific value will not be
completely vitiated.

I here report and analyze observations of restriction made
during eleven months of work as a radial-drill operator in the
machine shop of a steel-processing plant in 1944 and 1945. For
ten months I kept a daily record of my feelings, thoughts, experiences, and observations and of conversations with my fellow-
workers. I noted down the data from memory at the end of each
workday, only occasionally making surreptitious notes on the
job. I recorded my own production openly in the shop. I did not
reveal my research interests to either management or workers. I
remained 'one of the boys on the line', sharing the practices and
confidences of my fellows and joining them in their ceaseless war
with management, rather indifferently at first, but later whole-
heartedly.

As a member of the work group, I had access to inside talk
and activity. As a machine operator, I could put various opera-

1. In my doctoral dissertation recently accepted by the University of
Chicago I analyze the literature on this problem as well as other cases which
I studied in the role of known research man (see Bell, 1947; Blumer, 1947
and Moore, 1947).

tions under the microscope. These were great advantages, for *restrictus vulgaris* is a wary little thing. He does not like to be studied. Where groups are so sensitive and so skilled in eluding observation, participation observation can be a sensitive detector of relevant facts and relations (although the participant observer can spoil it all by over-working this method or by claiming that it is the sole means of scientific observation). I will limit this paper to the presentation of a few discriminations which break up the blanket term 'restriction' into several kinds and to a rough measuring of these restrictions in the shop where I worked.

From 9 November 1944 to 30 August 1945 I worked 1850·5 hours. 1350·9 (73 per cent) were 'production-piecework' hours.[2] The remaining 499·6 hours were taken up with time study, rework, and set-up. In 669·4 (49·6 per cent) of the production-piecework hours, I 'made out'. That is, I produced enough pieces of work to 'earn', at the piece rates for the kinds of work done, the 85-cent-per-hour 'base rate' which we received for every hour spent on the job. I thus 'earned' my 85 cents in about half the hours when there was opportunity – through completing more pieces – to earn more than that. Obversely, about half the time my 'turn in' (work done and turned in) fell below the base-rate standard.

The bimodal pattern of output

My hourly earnings on production piecework varied from $0.09 to $1.66, a range of $1.57. Table 1 shows that the spread of hourly earnings for the various jobs, or 'operations' performed, was bimodal; this distribution suggests two major types of output behavior.

About one-half of my hours of piecework 'earnings' fell on either side of the 85-cent-an-hour 'day-rate' and 'make-out' point, indicating 85 cents as an approximate median. However, this distribution by no means forms a bell-shaped curve, with 85 cents as a modal point. 'Make-out' and 'non-make-out'– piecework hours form two almost separate distributions, with 74·1 per cent of the 669·4 'make-out' hours concentrated in the $1.25–$1.34 interval, and 43·2 per cent of the 681·5 'non-make-

2. I have omitted some days of work in September 1945 because of irregularities occasioned by reorganization of the shop at that time.

Table 1 Production Piecework Hours Worked by Ten-Cent Earning Intervals

Earnings per hour (in cents)	Hours worked	Per cent
Unknown*	103·9	7·7
5–14	3·0	0·2
15–24	51·0	3·8
25–34	49·8	3·7
35–44	150·1	11·1
45–54	144·5	10·7
55–64	57·7	4·3
65–74	63·8	4·7
75–84	57·7	4·3
Total under 85 cents	681·5	50·4
85–94	51·2	3·8
95–104	19·5	1·5
105–114	17·9	1·3
115–124	83·0	6·1
125–134	496·3	36·7
165–174	1·5	0·1
Total 85 cents or more	669·4	49·6
Total	1,350·9	100·0

* All 'unknown' hourly earnings fell below the base-rate level of 85 cents per hour.

out' hours clustered in two adjacent intervals, $0.35–$0.54. Concentration of 'make-out' hours is even more marked. For 82·8 per cent fall within three 5-cent intervals, $1.20–$1.34, and 64·1 per cent fall within the one 5-cent interval, $1.25–$1.29.

That this bimodal pattern of hourly earnings for the ten-month period does not represent the joining of the 'tails' of two temporal distributions – i.e., one for an initial learning period and the other showing completely different production behavior with the acquisition of skill – is indicated by a comparison of earning distributions for two periods of four and six months, respectively. In this comparison (Table 2) the period from November through February represents one level of skill; that from March through August, a higher level. Although the proportion

Table 2 Production Piecework Hours Worked, by Ten-Cent Earning Intervals, per Two Diary Periods

Earnings per hour (in cents)	Period 1 (November through February)		Period 2 (March through August)	
	Hours worked	%	Hours worked	%
Unknown*	66·4	11·4	37·5	4·9
5–14	3·0	0·5		
15–24	13·5	2·3	37·5	4·9
25–34	37·8	6·5	12·0	1·6
35–44	93·0	16·0	57·1	7·4
45–54	74·0	12·8	70·5	9·1
55–64	43·1	7·4	14·6	1·9
65–74	36·8	6·3	27·0	3·5
75–84	49·0	8·5	8·7	1·1
Total under 85 cents	416·6	71·7	264·9	34·4
85–94	39·1	6·7	12·1	1·6
95–104	9·7	1·7	9·8	1·3
105–114	3·8	0·7	14·1	1·8
115–124	18·0	3·1	65·0	8·4
125–134	93·2	16·1	403·1	52·3
165–174			1·5	0·2
Total 85 cents or over	163·8	28·3	505·6	65·6
Total	580·4	100·0	770·5	100·0

* All 'unknown' hourly earnings fell below the base-rate level of 85 cents per hour.

of make-out hours for the second period was more than double that of the first and although concentration of make-out hours in modal earning intervals increased, the pattern was clearly bimodal in both periods. Both 'levels of skill' show the same modal earning interval of $1.25–$1.34 for make-out hours. The modal earning interval for non-make-out hours advanced but one notch, from $0.35 to $0.44 to $0.45 to $0.54.

While I did not keep a complete record of the hourly earnings of my 'day man' on the radial drill (I worked a 'second' shift), I frequently jotted down his day's run. His figures were roughly correlative with my own. References to the diary will be made to show that I was not out of line with other operators in the shop.

The bimodal pattern was the rule of the shop. An outsider might believe that it reflects the struggle of workers with two kinds of jobs, hard and easy. He might then posit any number of reasons why the jobs fall into two piles rather than into one bell-shaped heap: some peculiarity of time-study men or some change of company policy. It would indeed be difficult so to set piece rates that it would be equally easy to 'make-out' on all kinds of work. But one sophisticated in shop ways and aware of all the devices of time-study men would hardly credit them with either the ability or the will to turn up 'tight' and 'loose' piece rates in other than a single bell-shaped distribution. He would not attribute the bimodal distortion of hourly earnings to anything so improbable as bimodal distribution of hard and easy jobs. It could be that the operators, ignoring finer distinctions in job timing, sort jobs into two bins, one for 'gravy' jobs, the other for 'stinkers'.

Let us assume that the average of worker effort will be constant from job to job. Job A might be rated as 5 cents an hour 'harder' than Job B. But Job A turns out to yield 75 cents an hour less than Job B instead of the expected 5 cents an hour less. One suspects that effort has not been constant. When an operator discovers that he can earn $1.00 an hour on Job B, he will then put forth extra effort and ingenuity to make it $1.25. When, however, he finds that he can earn only 95 cents an hour on Job A, he rejects that amount and drops to a level of effort that earns only 50 cents an hour and relies upon his 85-cent base-pay rate for 'take home'. Job B has therefore become the 'gravy' job, and Job A the 'stinker'. Into the 'stinker' bin goes A, along with 90-cent jobs, 85-cent jobs, and 60-cent jobs.

The pronounced dichotomy in the production behavior of the machine operator suggests that restriction might be classified into two major types, 'quota restriction' and 'goldbricking'. The heavy concentration of hours at the $1.25–$1.34 level with no spilling-over to the next level makes 'quota restriction' appear as a limitation of effort on 'gravy' jobs in order not to exceed set maximums. It could also be inferred that 'gold-bricking' appears as a 'holding-back,' or failure to release effort, when a close approach to the quota seems unattainable.

Quota restrictions

It is 'quota restriction' which has received the most attention. The Mayo researchers observed that the bank-wiring group at Western Electric limited output to a 'quota' or 'bogey' (Roethlisberger and Dickson, 1939). Mayo inferred that this chopping-off of production was due to lack of understanding of the economic logics of management, using the following chain of reasoning: Insistence by management on purely economic logics, plus frequent changes in such logics in adaptation to technological change, result in lack of understanding on the part of the workers. Since the latter cannot understand the situation, they are unable to develop a nonlogical social code of a type that brought social cohesion to work groups prior to the Industrial Revolution. This inability to develop a Grade-A social code brings feelings of frustration. And, finally, frustration results in the development of a 'lower social code' among the workers in opposition to the economic logics of management. And one of the symptoms of this 'lower social code' is restriction of output (Mayo, 1938).

Mayo thus joins those who consider the economic man a fallacious conception. Now the operators in my shop made noises like economic men. Their talk indicated that they were canny calculators and that the dollar sign fluttered at the mast-head of every machine. Their actions were not always consistent with their words; and such inconsistency calls for further probing. But it could be precisely because they were alert to their economic interests – at least to their immediate economic interests – that the operators did not exceed their quotas. It might be inferred from their talk that they did not turn in excess earnings because they felt that to do so would result in piecework price cuts; hence the consequences would be either reduced earnings from the same amount of effort expended or increased effort to maintain the take-home level.

When I was hired, a personnel department clerk assured me that the radial-drill operators were averaging $1.25 an hour on piecework. He was using a liberal definition of the term 'averaging'. Since I had had no previous machine-shop experience and since a machine would not be available for a few days, I was advised to spend some time watching Jack Starkey, a radial-drill man of high rank in seniority and skill.

One of Starkey's first questions was, 'What have you been doing?' When I said I had worked in a Pacific Coast shipyard at a rate of pay over $1.00 an hour, Starkey exclaimed, 'Then what are you doing in this place?' When I replied that averaging $1.25 an hour wasn't bad, he exploded:

Averaging, you say! Averaging?'

'Yeah, on the average. I'm an average guy; so I ought to make my buck and a quarter. That is, after I get onto it.'

'Don't you know,' cried Starkey angrily, 'that $1.25 an hour is the *most* we can make, even when we *can* make more! And most of the time we can't even make that! Have you ever worked on piecework before?'

'No.'

'I can see that! Well, what do you suppose would happen if I turned in $1.25 an hour on these pump bodies?'

'Turned in? You mean if you actually did the work?'

'I mean if I actually did the work and turned it in!'

'They'd have to pay you, wouldn't they? Isn't that the agreement?'

'Yes! They'd pay me – once! Don't you know that if I turned in $1.50 an hour on these pump bodies tonight, the whole God-damned Methods Department would be down here tomorrow? And they'd retime this job so quick it would make your head swim! And when they retimed it, they'd cut the price in half! And I'd be working for 85 cents an hour instead of $1.25!'

From this initial exposition of Starkey's to my last day at the plant I was subject to warnings and predictions concerning price cuts. Pressure was the heaviest from Joe Mucha, day man on my machine, who shared my job repertoire and kept a close eye on my production. On 14 November, the day after my first attained quota, Mucha advised:

'Don't let it go over $1.25 an hour, or the time-study man will be right down here! And they don't waste time, either! They watch the records like a hawk! I got ahead, so I took it easy for a couple of hours.'

Joe told me that I had made $10.01 yesterday and warned me not to go over $1.25 an hour. He told me to figure the set-ups and the time on each operation very carefully so that I would not total over $10.25 in any one day.

Jack Starkey defined the quota carefully but forcefully when I turned in $10.50 for one day, or $1.31 an hour.

Jack Starkey spoke to me after Joe left. 'What's the matter? Are you trying to upset the apple cart?'

Jack explained in a friendly manner that $10.50 was too much to turn in, even on an old job.

'The turret-lathe men can turn in $1.35,' said Jack, 'but their rate is 90 cents, and ours 85 cents.'

Jack warned me that the Methods Department could lower their prices on any job, old or new, by changing the fixture slightly, or changing the size of drill. According to Jack, a couple of operators (first and second shift on the same drill) got to competing with each other to see how much they could turn in. They got up to $1.65 an hour, and the price was cut in half. And from then on they had to run that job themselves, as none of the other operators would accept the job.

According to Jack, it would be all right for us to turn in $1.28 or $1.29 an hour, when it figured out that way, but it was not all right to turn in $1.30 an hour.

Well, now I know where the maximum is – $1.29 an hour.

Starkey's beliefs concerning techniques of price-cutting were those of the shop. Leonard Bricker, an old-timer in the shop, and Willie, the stock-chaser, both affirmed that management, once bent on slashing a piecework price, would stop at nothing.

'Take these $1.25 jobs. One guy will turn in $1.30 an hour one day. Then another fellow will turn in, say, $1.31 or $1.32. Then the first fellow will go up to $1.35. First thing you know they'll be up to $1.50, and bang! They'll tear a machine to pieces to change something to cut a price!'

In the washroom, before I started work, Willie commented on my gravy job, the pedestals.

'The Methods Department is going to lower the price,' he said. 'There was some talk today about it.'

'I hope they don't cut it too much,' I said. 'I suppose they'll make some change in the jigs?'

'They'll change the tooling in some way. Don't worry, when they make up their minds to lower a price, they'll find a way to do it!'[3]

The association of quota behavior with such expressions about price-cutting does not prove a causal connection. Such a connection could be determined only by instituting changes in the work situation that would effect a substantial reduction of 'price-cut fear' and by observing the results of such changes.

Even if it should be thus indicated that there is a causal relationship, testing of alternative hypotheses would still be necessary. It may be, but it is not yet known, that 'economic determinism' may account for quota restriction in the shop investigated. It may also be, but it is not known, that factors such as Mayo's 'failure to understand the economic logics of management' are influential.

'Waste time' on quota restriction

Whatever its causes, such restriction resulted in appreciable losses of time in the shop. I have evidence of it from observation of the work behavior and talk of fellow-operators and from my own work behavior. Since ability to 'make out' early was related to skill and experience, it was some time before I found enough time wasted on quota restriction to record. But I discovered early that other operators had time to burn.

One evening Ed Sokolsky, onetime second-shift operator on Jack Starkey's drill, commented on a job that Jack was running:

'That's gravy! I worked on those, and I could turn out nine an hour. I timed myself at six minutes.'

I was surprised.

'At 35 cents apiece, that's over $3.00 an hour!'

3. John Mills (1946, p. 93) onetime research engineer in telephony and for five years engaged in personnel work for the Bell Telephone Company, has recently indicated the possibility that there were factors in the bank-wiring room situation that the Mayo group failed to detect: 'Reward is supposed to be in direct proportion to production. Well, I remember the first time I ever got behind that fiction. I was visiting the Western Electric Company, which had a reputation of never cutting a piece rate. It never did; if some manufacturing process was found to pay more than seemed right for the class of labor employed on it – if, in other words, the rate-setters had misjudged – that particular part was referred to the engineers for redesign, and then a new rate was set on the new part. Workers, in other words, were paid as a class, supposed to make about so much a week with their best efforts and, of course, less for less competent efforts.'

'And I got ten hours', said Ed. 'I used to make out in four hours and fool around the rest of the night.'

If Sokolsky reported accurately, he was 'wasting' six hours per day.

Ed claimed that he could make over $3.00 an hour on the two machines he was running, but he could turn in only $1.40 an hour or, occasionally, $1.45 or $1.50 for the two machines together. Ed said that he always makes out for ten hours by eleven o'clock, that he has nothing to do from 11:00 to 3:00, and has even left early, getting someone to punch his timecard for him.

'That's the advantage of working nights', said Ed. 'You can make out in a hurry and sit around, and nobody says anything. But you can't get away with it on day shift with all the big shots around. Jack has to take it easy on these housings to make them last eight hours, and that must be tough.'

'Old Pete,' another 'old-timer' confided in me:

'Another time when they timed me on some connecting rods, I could have made $20.00 a day, easy. I had to run them at the lowest speed on the machine to keep from making too much. I had a lot of trouble once when I was being timed, and they gave me $35.00 a hundred. Later they cut it to $19.50 a hundred, and I still made $9.50 a day.'

If Old Pete could have made $20.00 a day, he was 'wasting' four hours a day.

My own first 'spare time' came on 18 November.

Today I made out with such ease on the pedestals that I had an hour to spare. To cover the hour I had to poke along on the last operation, taking twice as much time to do 43 pieces as I ordinarily would.

But it wasn't until March, when I experienced a sudden increase in skill, that I was capable of making out early on any job but the pedestals. With this increase in skill I found the pedestals quickly fading as the supreme distributors of 'gravy'. One and one-half hours of loafing recorded on March 22 was a portent of things to come.

I stalled along tonight, turning out only 89 pieces, adding in my kitty of 40 pieces for a turn-in of 129. Joe had a kitty of 13, and I figured that the 116 pieces left would just do him tomorrow. I finished my last piece about 9:30 and started cleaning up the machine about ten o'clock. I noticed that Tony was also through early, standing around his machine.

'This is the earliest you've made out, isn't it?' he asked.

Dick Smith remarked to me, 'That's the kind of a job I like. Then I can go at it and enjoy it.'

On 7 April I was able to enjoy four hours of 'free time'.

I turned out 43 pieces in the four hours from three to seven, averaging nearly 11 an hour (or $2.085 per hour). At seven o'clock there were only 23 pieces left in the lot, and I knew there would be no point in building up a kitty for Monday if Joe punched off the job before I got to work. I could not go ahead with the next order (also a load of connecting rods) because the new ruling made presentation of a work order to the stock-chaser necessary before material could be brought up. So I was stymied and could do nothing the rest of the day. I had 43 pieces plus 11 from yesterday's kitty to turn in for a total 54.

I sat around the rest of the evening, and none of the bosses seemed to mind.

By August I was more sophisticated in the art of loafing, and complaints of being 'stymied' were not recorded.

I had good luck with the reamers and had my needed 26 pieces by six o'clock. I did 10 more for a kitty for Monday and wound up the evening's work at seven o'clock. The last four hours I sat around and talked to various operators.

I reached my peak in quota restriction on 27 June, with but three and a half hours of productive work out of the eight.

An estimate of the degree of quota restriction practiced

The amount of quota restriction practiced by operators on the drill line may be estimated from my own production behavior.

During the ten-month diary period I received approximately 75 different piecework jobs, some of which were assigned from two to six times, but the majority of which were assigned only once. On only 31 of the jobs did I ever make out.

Of the 31 make-out jobs, only 20 afforded quota earnings of $1.25 an hour or more; 5 afforded maximum earnings of from $1.20 to $1.24 an hour; 1, maximum earnings of $1.09 an hour; and 5 of the 31 yielded maximums of less than $1.00 an hour (85–99 cents). Total quota hours were 497·8, or slightly over a third of the total piecework hours.

By extending effort past quota limits to find the earning possibilities of the jobs, I discovered that on 16 of the 20 quota jobs I could have earned more than $1.30 an hour; on 4 of the 20 I was unable to exceed $1.30 per hour.

For example, on the 'NT bases,' I turned out pieces at the rate of $2.55 for a test hour, and I turned them out at the rate of $2.04 for a full eight-hour shift. On the 'G sockets,' I was able to earn $2.53 an hour; this job was touted by experienced operators to yield $3.00 an hour.

I ran 4 other jobs at a rate in excess of $2.00 an hour. Maximums on another 4 jobs came to $1.96 or better. All but 3 of the 16 'excess-quota' jobs yielded possible earnings of over $1.75 an hour.

Besides the 16 excess-quota jobs, I found 4 'nonquota-make-out' jobs (maximum earnings less than $1.25) that showed potentialities in excess of quota limits. That I did not actually achieve quota on these 4 jobs was due to slow starts; since the 4 were not assigned to me again, I could not cash in on my discoveries. If these 4 are included, the number of jobs with excess-quota potentials total 20.

Given a quota of $1.25 an hour, or $10.00 an eight-hour day, and a job that will yield $1.25 an hour but not appreciably over that rate, the operator will have to expend a full eight hours of effort to achieve the quota. But, if the job will yield earnings at the rate of $2.50 an hour, it will take the operator only four hours to earn his $10.00. A $2.50-an-hour job is thus a four-hour job, and the remaining four hours of the workday may be considered wasted time. If the operator were to extend himself for the full eight hours on a $2.50-an-hour job and were permitted to turn in the results of his effort, his earnings would be $20.00 instead of his quota of $10.00. Thus there is incurred a financial loss to the operator as well as a loss of production time to the company when the quota is observed.

Table 3 lists the twenty jobs which showed potentialities of yielding hourly earnings in excess of $1.30. Waste time and loss in earnings is computed for each job according to maximum earnings indicated in each case by actual test and according to the number of hours devoted to each job. For instance, operation 'pawls', which leads the list with 157·9 total hours worked,

Table 3 Time and Earnings (dollars) Losses on Operations with Potentialities of Yielding Hourly Earnings in Excess of $1.30 per Hour

Operation tested	Total hours worked	Maximum (per hour)	Waste time (per hour)	Total waste time (in hours)	Potential earnings	Earnings at 1.25	Loss in earnings
Pawls	157·9	1.96	0·3625	57·2	309.48	197.38	112.10
Pedestals	120·5	1.71	0·2625	31·6	206.08	150.63	55.43
NT bases	111·0	2.55	0·5125	56·9	283.05	138.75	144.30
Con rods	94·4	2.33	0·4625	43·7	219.95	118.00	101.95
Sockets	75·8	1.76	0·2875	21·8	133.41	94.75	38.66
B. housings	46·0	1.96	0·3625	16·7	90.16	57.50	32.66
Pinholes	37·7	1.87	0·3250	12·3	70.50	47.13	23.37
Casings	28·5	2.03	0·37750	10·7	57.86	35.63	22.23
Gear parts	24·0	1.83	0·3000	7·2	43.92	30.00	13.92
Replacers	19·3	2.20	0·4375	8·4	42.46	24.13	18.33
Spyglasses	18·0	1.57	0·1875	3·4	28.26	22.50	5.76
R. sockets	14·9	1.48	0·1375	2·0	22.05	18.63	3.42
Move. jaw	9·6	1.99	0·3625	3·5	19.10	12.00	7.10
Ped. $8.90	7·0	2.12	0·4000	2·8	14.84	8.75	6.09
Spot J1728	6·7	1.91	0·3375	2·3	12.80	8.38	4.42
G. sockets	4·5	2.53	0·5000	2·3	11.39	5.63	5.76
Ped. $5	4·3	1.85	0·3250	1·4	7.96	5.38	2.58
CB hubs	4·1	1.65	0·2375	1·0	6.77	5.13	1.64
SD cups	1·5	1.89	0·3250	0·5	2.84	1.88	0.96
Bolts	0·8	1.96	0·3625	0·3	1.57	1.00	0.57
Total	786·5 (98·3 days)			286·0 (35·75 days)	$1584.43	$983.18	$601.25

showed, by test, possibilities of earnings of $1.96 per hour. At potentialities of $1.96 per hour, over 36 per cent of each hour is wasted when the operator holds his turn-in to $1.25 an hour. Total waste time in the 157·9 hours expended on the pawls could then be computed at 57·2 hours, or over a third of the time actually put in. Earnings might have been, at $1.96 per hour, $309.48; whereas, at the quota level of $1.25, they would have been but $197.38 – a loss of $112.10.

Total waste time for the 20 jobs is seen to be 286 hours, or 36·4 per cent of a total 786·5 hours actually put in on them. This represents a wastage of 2·9 hours on each 8-hour day put in, or a total loss of 35·75 days out of 98·3 actually worked. With potential earnings of $1584.43 for the 98 days and with quota earnings at $983.18, the wage loss to the worker would be $601.25, or $6.12 per day, or 76½ cents per hour.

By this logic, if the worker could 'cut loose' on the 20 jobs listed, he would average $2.01 an hour instead of $1.25. And since the 786·5 hours actually put in on the 20 jobs represented 58·2 per cent of the 1,350·9 total piecework hours for the period, and 42·5 per cent of a grand total of 1,850·5 hours that included all nonpiecework activity as well, it is evident that losses resulting from quota restriction alone could represent wastage of considerable magnitude – an over-all hourly income loss for 1850·5 hours of 32½ cents an hour!

In order to generalize for the drill line from observation of my own behavior, I would have to establish that I was an 'average' performer and that my job repertoire was representative of those of other operators.

Of the men on the same shift doing my kind of work, four (McCann, Starkey, Koszyk, and Sokolsky) could turn out greater volume than I and were my betters in all-around skills. Seven were below me in these respects, of them only three (Smith, Rinky, and Dooley) worked long enough to be in the core of the group. I was about average in skill and in the work assigned me.

The maximums on which the losses are figured represent only potentialities discovered in tests of relatively short duration. Yet it is likely that had I remained in the shop long enough to allow the 20 jobs another time around, I could have routinized many of the maximums and could have raised some of them. It is also likely that if organizational changes were instituted to induce operators to abolish quota limits and 'open up' production, the writer's discovered maximums would be quickly raised to higher levels by the efforts of the group. Under adequate motivation the better operators would employ their superior skills and the results of their application would be disseminated to others. In my opinion, the production potentialities are underestimates of the output possibilities inherent in the situation. This hypothesis can be tested, of course, only through observation of experimental changes.

As a check on the foregoing appraisals, an estimate of the *actual* amount of time wasted by the writer through quota restriction may be made by reference to Table 4.

Table 4 Quota Hours Loafed, by Percentages of Total Quota Hours and Average Hours per Quota Day of Loafing (By Months, March through August, 1945)

Month	Total quota hours	Quota hours loafed	Per cent hours loafed	Hours loafed per quota day
March	69·3	7·6	11·0	0·88
April	76·3	10·35	13·6	1·09
May	69·8	5·15	7·4	0·59
June	83·5	15·2	18·2	1·46
July	84·8	21·4	25·2	2·02
August	85·9	22·2	25·8	2·06
Total	469·6	81·9	17·4	1·39

The 469·6 quota hours represented 60·9 per cent of 770·5 total piecework hours for the period, and 41·8 per cent of 1123·2 total hours worked.

With an average of 1·39 hours 'wasted' per day of 'quota piecework,' the average hours worked were 6·61; so, at quota limits of $1.25 an hour, or $10.00 per day, earnings while I was actually working on 'quota piecework' would be $1.51 per hour for the six-month period. If I had turned in 8 hours' production per day at $1.51, my daily earnings on 'quota piecework' would have been $12.08. I therefore lost $2.08 per day, or 26 cents per hour on quota piecework. Since quota piecework represented 41·8 per cent of total hours worked, the over-all loss per day due to quota restriction alone would be $0.87, approximately 11 cents an hour.

During the last two-month period, July and August, I was 'wasting' on the average over 2 hours a day while on 'quota piecework'. If my production during August may be considered indicative of my developed skill, and portentous of things to come had I stayed, then estimates of future wastages become greater. With 2·06 hours per quota-piecework day loafed, the length of the 'actual' average quota workday becomes 5·94 hours and the average earnings for 'actual' work time put in becomes $1.68 per hour. At $1.68 per hour for a full 8-hour day, the writer would earn $13.44; the daily loss would then be $3.44 and the hourly loss 43 cents. And since quota piecework for August represented 71·5 per cent of total piecework for the month, the loss per day on piecework was $2.46. And, since quota piecework represented 46 per cent of total hours worked, the over-all loss per day was $1.58 and the over-all hourly loss nearly 20 cents.

This daily loss for August would be slightly reduced if the actual quota turn-in is considered in place of the assumed $1.25 per hour. The writer actually averaged $1.27 per hour on quota piecework, raising the assumed average by 2 cents per hour, or 16 cents per day. The computed average daily and hourly losses on quota piecework would then be $3.28 and $0.41, and the over-all losses would be $1.51 and $0.19.

Piecework goldbricking

On 'gravy jobs' the operators earned a quota, then knocked off. On 'stinkers' they put forth only minimal effort; either they did not try to achieve a turn-in equal to the base wage rate or they deliberately slowed down. Jobs were defined as 'good' and 'bad' jobs, not in terms of the effort or skill necessary to making out at a bare base-rate level, but of the felt attainability of a substantial premium, i.e., 15 cents an hour or more. Earnings of $1.00 an hour in relation to a $1.25 quota and an 85-cent base rate were considered worth the effort, while earnings of 95 cents an hour were not.

The attitude basic to the goldbricking type of restriction was expressed succinctly thus: 'They're not going to get much work out of me for this pay!'

Complaints about low piecework prices were chronic and universal in the shop.

The turret lathe men discussed the matter of making out, one man stating that only half the time could a man make 84 cents day rate on a machine. It was agreed: 'What's the use of pushing when it's hard even to make day rate?'

His 50–50 estimate was almost equal to my own experience of 49·6–50·4. Pessimistic though it was, it was less so than usual statements on the subject:

I asked Jackson if he was making out, and he gave me the usual answer, 'No!'

'They ask me how I'm making out, and I always say, "O.K." As far as I'm concerned, I'm making out O.K. If they start asking me further, I'll tell them that this place stinks.

'The day man isn't making out either. We get a lot of little jobs, small lots. It's impossible to make out when you're getting small jobs all the time.'

Joe was working on a new job, time study on some small pieces tonight. I asked him, 'Something good?' and he replied, 'Nothing is good any more!'

There seemed to be no relation between a man's ability to earn and his behavior on a 'stinker'. That the men who most frequently earned the quota goldbricked like the rest on poor jobs appears in the following extracts:

Al McCann (the man who made quota most often) said that he gives a job a trial, and if it is no good he takes his time. He didn't try to make out on the chucks tonight.

Joe Mucha, my day man, said of a certain job: 'I did just one more than you did. If they don't like it they can do them themselves. To hell with them. I'm not going to bust my ass on stuff like this.'

Old Peter, the multiple drill man, said 'I ran some pieces for 25 minutes to see how many I could turn out. I turned out 20 at 1½ cents apiece (72 cents an hour). So I smoke and take it easy. I can't make out; so ———— it.'

I notice that when Ed Sokolsky, one of the better operators on the line, is working on an operation he cannot make out on, he does not go at his task with vigor. He either pokes around or leaves his machine for long periods of time; and Paul (set-up man) seems always to be looking for him. Steve (supt.) is always bellowing, 'Where in hell is Ed?' or 'Come on, Ed, let's have some production around here!' Tonight I heard him admonishing Ed again, 'Now I want you to work at that machine till three o'clock, do you understand?'

Mike Koszyk, regarded as a crack operator: The price was a poor one (a few cents a hundred) and the job tough. Mike had turned out only 9 pieces in 3 hours. When Mike takes his time, he really takes his time!

According to Al, Jack Starkey turned in 40 cents an hour today on his chuck parts. Al laughed, saying, 'I guess Jack didn't like this job'.

Gus Schmidt, regarded as the best speed-drill operator on the second shift, was timed early in the evening on a job, and given a price of $1.00 per 100 for reaming one hole, chamfering both sides of three holes, and filing burrs on one end of one hole. All that for one cent!

'To hell with them,' said Gus.

He did not try to make out.

The possibility of covering 'day rate' was ordinarily no spur to the machine operator to bestir himself on a job. A remark of Mucha's was characteristic: 'I could have made out', he said, 'but why kill yourself for day rate?'

Average hourly earnings of less or even a little more than $1.00 an hour were usually thrown into the 'day-rate' category.

Joe Mucha drilled 36 of the bases (at $8.80 per 100) today. 'The most I'll ever do until they retime this job is 40', he said. 'Do you know, they expect us to do 100? Why, I wouldn't bust my ass to do 50, for $8.00, when day rate is almost that!'

McCann was put to drilling some pieces at $6.50 per 100. I noticed him working furiously and walked over to see what he was doing. He asked me to figure out how many pieces at 6½ cents he had to turn out per hour to make $1.20. When I told him 18 or 19 he said, 'I give up', and immediately slowed down.

A few minues later I met him in the washroom, and he said, 'I wouldn't work that hard for eight or ten hours even if I could make out. I thought I'd try it for an hour or so and see what I could do.'

He figures that he was making 95 cents an hour. At lunch time he said that he had averaged $1.00 an hour for the two hours and thought maybe he would try to make out.

The slowdown

Resentment against piecework prices that were considered too low to offer possibilities of quota earnings often resulted in deliberate attempts to produce at lower rates than mere 'dogging it along' would bring. This kind of goldbricking was particularly noticeable on jobs that came relatively often and in large lots. Toward a short order of poor price that was assigned to his machine but once or twice a year, the operator's attitude was likely to be one of 'I don't give a damn,' and the result would be production below 'standard'. But toward a low-priced order assigned every month or two and in amounts that would take several shifts to a week to process, i.e., jobs that played a major part in the operator's repertoire, the attitude was likely to be, 'Just for that, you'll get as little as I can turn out and still be operating this machine!'

The hinge-base fight is an example of deliberate restriction on a major job that was regarded as poorly priced. This fight went on for at least nine months at the machine operated by Jack Starkey. During this period three men worked second shift on Jack's machine in the following sequence: Ed Sokolsky, Dooley, and Al McCann.

19 December, Ed Sokolsky and Jack Starkey have not been doing well. Ed cusses intermittently and leaves his machine for long periods of time. The foremen find the machine idle, and Steve bellows about it. Ed calls the piece he is working on a 'stinker'. I know it is, because Ed is free with his advertising of the 'gravy' he finds.

Ed seems to have constant trouble with his jig, a revolving piece attached to the side of the table. Two disks seem to stick together, and Ed is constantly (every day or so) using the crane to dismantle the jig (a very heavy one). He sands the disks and oils them, taking several hours for the cleaning operation. Steve saw the dismantled jig again tonight and bellowed, 'Again?' Steve does not like it.

Paul, the set-up man, gets concerned, too, when he finds the jig torn down and Ed away somewhere. He says, 'Where the hell's Ed?' in a provoked manner.

February, I noticed that Ed was poking along and asked him if he had a good job. He shook his head, saying that he was making but 46 cents an hour, turning out 2 pieces an hour that paid 23 cents each.

26 February, Jack Starkey told me tonight that although his job on the hinge bases was retimed, there was no raise in price. The price is still 23 cents.

I said, 'All you've got to turn out is 5 an hour to make $1.15.'

'I'd just like to see anybody turn out 5 of these an hour', said Jack, 'with a tolerance of 0·0005!'

Later, Ed Sokolsky said that he and Jack were turning out about 24 pieces in a ten-hour period (2·4 an hour), that the job had been retimed several times, but no raise in price had been given.

Ed and Jack asked for a price of 38 cents. Ed said that they could turn out 3 an hour, but, until they got a decent price, they were turning out 2 an hour.

Toward the end of the evening I noticed that Ed's machine was idle, and Ed was sitting on a box, doing nothing.

'What's the matter, did they stop the job on you?' I asked.

'I stopped it', said Ed. 'I don't feel like running it.'

March, Dooley worked on the hinge bases again tonight. He admitted that he could barely make out on the job, but 'Why bust my ass for day rate? We're doing 3 an hour or less until we get a better price!'

This 3-an-hour-or-less business has been going on several months. The price is 23 cents; so Dooley and Jack turn in 69 cents an hour (or less).

May, McCann said that Starkey was arguing all day over the price of the hinge bases. The methods men maintain that they can't raise the price 'because the jacks that the parts go on sell for $14.00 apiece'. They plan to retool the job and lower the price. According to McCann, Jack told them that if he didn't get a decent price he was going to make out on the job but scrap every one of the pieces.

'Jack fights it out with them', said McCann. 'He'll stay right with the machine and argue. I get disgusted and walk away.

'Jack turned out 28 today', McCann went on. 'That's too many, nearly 3 an hour. He'll have to watch himself if he expects to get a raise in price.'

Starkey was running the hinge bases again tonight. I remarked, 'I see you're in the gravy again.'

His reply was, 'Yeah! 69 cents an hour!'

McCann did not seem to enjoy the hinge bases either. He looked bored, tired, and disgusted all evening. His ten hours is a long stretch at day work. He cannot make out early and rest after 11 o'clock (for four hours), but has to keep on the machine until three.

14 August, Al McCann was working on the hinge bases tonight, one of the jobs that he and Jack are protesting as to price. Gil (the foreman) sat and stood behind Al for at least an hour, and I could see that Al did not like it. He worked steadily, but with deliberate slowness, and did not look at Gil or speak to him. Al and Jack have agreed to restrict production on the hinge bases until they get a better price, and Gil was probably there to see what Al could really do. I think that Al and Jack could make out on the job, but not at $1.25 an hour, and they cut production to less than 80 cents an hour.

16 August, Al told me that they had won a price raise on the hinge bases, from 23 to 28 cents, and another raise to 31 cents.

'But it's still not high enough. As it is now we can make exactly 94 cents an hour. We're trying to get 35 cents. We can turn out 1 in exactly 16 minutes. That's not 4 an hour. We've been giving them 3 an hour.'

An attempt to estimate the degree of piecework goldbricking

I failed to earn the base rate of 85 cents for slightly over half my piecework hours, but I cannot claim that I failed in spite of a maximum effort. There were only a few occasions when I tried to 'make out', but could not, and did not let failure diminish my efforts. Normally, I behaved in the manner of my fellow-operators; I 'tried out' a job for a short sampling period of an hour, more or less, and slowed my pace to a restrictive one if the job did not show 'possibilities'. There were numerous occasions when even 'trial runs' were not attempted, when I was forewarned that the job was a 'stinker'. Since possible output was not determined, the amount of restriction cannot be computed.

There were times when the words of various operators indicated that they could have 'covered' day rate if they had tried; the expression, 'Why bust my ass for day rate?' was considered adequate explanation for failure to press on to the maximum attainable. If claims of ability to achieve the scorned 'day rate' could be accepted as indicative of the true possibilities inherent in a job, it is clear that the man who turned in 42·5 cents an hour for a day's average hourly earnings, and who says that he could have made 85 cents an hour, has accomplished but 4 hours' work in 8. A man who turned in 21·25 cents an hour, instead of a possible 85 cents, has done 2 hours' work in 8, and has 'wasted' 6 hours. That an operator has turned in 42·5 cents an hour, or 21 cents, or 10 cents may be determined easily enough; the difficulty lies in inability to test his claims of what he could have done.

Recorded observations do allow some objective estimate of

losses incurred by goldbricking in isolated cases. For instance, the four operators assigned to Jack Starkey's machine made it a practise to restrict production on the hinge bases to from 2 to 3 pieces an hour. To this restriction were attributed two price increases, from 25 cents to 28 cents to 31 cents per piece. Thus, at the 31-cent price in effect in August, and at the output rate of 3 pieces per hour, the men were turning in 93 cents per hour, or $7.44 per 8-hour day. Since their special base rate, as experienced operators on a machine handling heavy fixtures, was $1.10 per hour, they were earning 17 cents an hour less than they were paid. One of the operators involved, Al McCann, claimed that by test they could turn out 1 piece in exactly 16 minutes. At this rate they could have turned in 3·75 pieces per hour for earnings of $1.16 per hour, or $9.28 per day. 'Waste' time could be computed at 1·6 production-hours, and the loss in 'earnings' at 23 cents per hour.

McCann's estimate of the job's possibilities proved to be low, however; for, a few weeks later, upon abandoning hope for a further increase in piecework price, he 'made out easily in 6 hours.'

Al said tonight that he was making out on the hinge bases, that he got disgusted Friday, speeded up the tools, and turned in 31 pieces for earnings of $9.60 (3¾ pieces per hour, or $1.20 per hour earnings).

'It was easy, just as easy as the frames. Now I'm kicking myself all over for not doing it before. All I did was to change the speed from 95 to 130. I was sick of stalling around all evening, and I got mad and decided to make out and let the tools burn up. But they made it all right, for 8 hours. What's the use of turning in 93 cents an hour when you can turn in $1.25 just as easy? They'd never raise a price you could make 93 cents on anyhow. Now maybe they'll cut it back.'

Tonight Al made out easily in 6 hours, though he stretched the last few pieces to carry him until 10:30.

Since McCann reported a turn-in of 31 pieces for earnings of $9.60, or $1.20 an hour on the previous workday, his first day of 'making out,' it was likely that his 'making out' at the 6 hours involved regular quota earnings of $1.25 an hour. A turn-in of 32 pieces would net $9.92 per day, or $1.24 an hour; accomplished in 6 hours, such output would mean that McCann earned $1.65 an hour while working and was now 'wasting' 2 hours a shift on quota restriction. And the $1.65-per-hour earnings meant, when compared to previous earnings of 93 cents an hour while goldbricking, that McCann had been 'wasting' 3·5 hours a day each time the hinge bases were assigned to his machine; his former earnings loss had been 72 cents an hour, or $5.76 per day. (Actually less than this if 'earnings' be defined as 'take-home' and not as 'turn-in', for McCann's 'day rate' had been raised to $1.10 an hour. His personal loss would thus have been 17 cents less per hour – 55 cents an hour, or $4.40 per day.)

McCann, engaged in goldbricking, estimated that he could turn out a piece every 16 minutes; this means that he saw production possibilities to be 3·75 pieces per hour and earning possibilities to be $1.16 per hour. But under piecework incentive he actually turned out 5·33 pieces per hour and earned $1.65 per hour while working. If the difference between his estimated and his achieved production can be taken as indicative of such differences in general, then the man who claims that he could have covered his day rate of 85 cents an hour but did not try to do so could have boosted his earnings to $1.21 an hour. In other words, if an operator can see day-rate earnings in a job, he can make quota earnings. My experience would seem to bear this out. If I found that I could make out on a job at day rate, such a discovery motivated me to 'wring the neck' of the particular operation for quota earnings. The bimodal pattern production would suggest this; my total quota-piecework hours were 75 per cent of my total make-out–piecework hours, and the latter included short runs of once-assigned jobs that did not receive adequate 'test'. Though the words of fellow-operators indicated the 'pour-it-on' point to be $1.00 an hour, it is possible that energetic performance on 85-cent-an-hour jobs would yield the desired quota.

By the foregoing logic a worker who limits his output to 68 cents an hour, when he thinks he can make 85 cents an hour, is 'potentially' limiting output by 44 per cent instead of by the assumed 20 per cent.

Daywork goldbricking

Operators on 'nonpiecework,' or 'daywork' jobs, followed almost uniformly a pattern of restriction of the goldbricking type. They kept in mind rough estimates of output that they felt would fall appreciably below 'day-rate' standards if and when the 'non-piecework' jobs were timed and priced.

Nonpiecework jobs in the shop were of two kinds: 'time study' and 'rework'. 'Time-study' operations were those that either were so newly established that they were not yet timed and priced or were jobs whose price had been 'removed'. In either case, timing procedures and a piecework price were expected in the immediate future.

'Rework' was the reprocessing of defective pieces that were considered salvageable. Rework carried no premium pay and no expectations of it, but rough standards of output limitation were applied.

I worked 300 hours at time study and 53 hours at rework, 16 per cent and 3 per cent of total hours put in. Thus, roughly, one-fifth of my time was employed at nonpiecework production, and for this one-fifth the operator could be counted upon, without fail, to be goldbricking. A concise bit of advice, offered by Mc-Cann, then set-up man and wise in the ways of production lines, stated the common attitude:

It was a time-study operation, drilling and tapping a set-screw hole in some sprockets.

'Take it easy,' advised McCann.

This advice I, already of five months' shop experience, considered unnecessary. By no stretch of the imagination could my accustomed pace on time study be regarded as other than 'easy.' But, under McCann's expert tutelage, I discovered that there were degrees of goldbricking, and that for time study, a mere 'punking along' exceeded worker standards.

McCann started me out at 95 speed on the drill and spot-facer, and 70 on chamfer and taps.

'Isn't that too slow for the drill?' I asked.

'It's fast enough on this tough stuff for time study. Run it that way till they speed you up. If you go too fast today, you won't get a good price when it's timed.'

Even this slow pace looked too fast for Gus Schmidt, who watched from the next machine.

Later in the evening Schmidt said to me, 'Aren't you going too fast with that time study?'

I did not think I was going very fast and told him so.

'Well, maybe it just looks fast because you're going so steady at it. You've got to slow down on time study or you won't get a good price. They look at the record of what you do today and compare it with the timing speed when it's timed. Those time-study men are sharp!'

Toward the end of the evening I raised the speeds of the taps and chamfer to 95. It was going too slow for me and actually tired me out standing around waiting for the taps to go through. My legs were tired at the end of the day; yet I had not worked hard.

Goldbricking on time study may be indistinguishable, even to a fellow-operator, from 'quota restriction'. On one occasion I noticed that Tony, the speed-drill man, was 'fooling around', and asked him if he had made out already. Only through information supplied by Tony did I become aware that my neighbor was goldbricking on a time-study job and not relaxing his efforts after achieving quota. In order to classify operator behavior when an operator is 'doing nothing', one must have access to additional facts not provided by casual observation. There are times when an operator may be mistaken in classification of his own restriction of output. He may think he is loafing on time study when he is in reality loafing on piecework.

I discovered, when I came to work, that yesterday's job on the pedestals had been timed.

Joe said, 'I see you didn't make out yesterday'.

I had turned in 60 pieces, price $4.90, for a day's earnings of less than $3.00. I was glad I didn't know the job was timed, with a price like that.

Rework restriction

I received advice on 'rework' that led to the same productive results on time-study operation.

Joe finished the gears, and I spent a slow evening on time study and rework. The first job was 15 gear brackets, a time-study job. The next was the reworking of 1 jack shell.

Said Al, when I told him I was on rework, 'Well, you've got all night to turn it out. When they give you a rework job, that's a sign they've got nothing for you to do.'

'You mean they expect me to take all night at it?'

McCann was hesitant. 'No, I don't mean that. But you can take your time.'

About ten o'clock Paul (set-up man) suggested that we 'take it easy.' 'We're doing too much as it is, on this rework', he said.

When Ed Sokolsky heard that we had done 4, he was surprised. 'I wouldn't have done that many', he said.

An attempt to estimate the degree of nonpiecework restriction

An indication of the amount of restriction practiced on non-piecework operations can be obtained in a comparison of the writer's output on a job before it was timed and priced, and his output on the same job after a piecework price was set.

One day some gear parts were assigned as time study. I accepted the advice to take it easy proffered by the set-up man, McCann, and by a fellow-operator, Schmidt, and turned in a total of 64 pieces for the day's work. The next day I came to work to discover that the job had been timed at $7.95 a hundred. Joe Mucha reported the job a good one, but I was dubious.

'It's a good job', he said. 'They timed me for $1.20 an hour, and it worked out just that. You can do 16 an hour. But watch yourself, now, and don't turn in too many!'

'Don't worry, I probably won't get 100,' I assured him.

Yesterday's 64 had given me the feeling that I would have to push very hard to turn out 100 ($1.00 per hour).

I had underestimated the job. My effort reached a peak of $1.83 per hour, or 23 pieces per hour, and I completed 150 pieces in 7·5 hours for average earnings of $1.59 an hour for the time worked.

After lunch I decided to try to see how many I could turn out. I did manage to complete 12 in half an hour but never got higher than 23 for the whole hour. The speeds were set at 225 for drilling and 95 for the other tools, just as I finished yesterday. At 10:30 I had completed 150 pieces.

At a price of $7.95 per 100, the 64 pieces turned out on time study would have represented average earnings of about 64 cents an hour. Since I expected to turn out no more than 100 pieces with full effort on piecework, my assumed restriction on time study was 36 per cent, with a 'loss' of 36 cents an hour, or $2.86 a day, and with a time 'waste' of 2·9 hours.

But with an actual subsequent output of 20 per hour for 7·5

hours, a rate of 160 per day, restriction the first day turned out to be 60 per cent, with a loss of 95 cents an hour, or $7.63 per day, and a time 'waste' of 4·8 hours a day. And with a 'potential' output of 23 per hour, a rate of 184 per day, restriction the first day turned out to be 65 per cent, with a 'loss' of $9.55 a day, or $1.19 an hour, and a time 'waste' of 5·2 hours a day.

Summary and conclusion

These appraisals of output limitation can be accepted only as suggestive of the amount of time wasted by operatives in piece-work machine shops. Certainly, the 'waste' is great.

I have indicated that the time 'wasted' on my own quota restriction for a six-month period was 1·39 hours out of every 8. I was 83 per cent 'efficient' for the 469·6 quota piecework-hours put in, by my own standards of performance, and thus could have increased production by 21 per cent by abandoning quota limitations. If my wastage of 2 hours a day on quota restriction during the last two months of employment is accepted as charac-teristic of the behavior of more seasoned operators, efficiency would be 75 per cent, with immediate possibilities for a 33·3 per cent increase in production on quota jobs.

Also, by experimenting with twenty jobs which represented 58 per cent of the total piecework hours put in during a ten-month period, and which offered earning possibilities beyond quota limits, I derived an estimate of 'potential quota restriction' of 2·9 hours a day. This restriction represented an efficiency of 64 per cent, with possibilities for a 57 per cent increase in pro-duction.

Furthermore, from observations of the work behavior of fellow-operators, I was able to speculate with some objective evidence on the degree of slowdown goldbricking practiced on non-make-out piecework. It was pointed out that four drill operators had been restricting production at a rate of 3·5 'waste' hours out of 8, as indicated by the output achieved by one of the four men when he ceased goldbricking. Efficiency had been 56 per cent, with immediate possibilities for a 78 per cent production increase. Renunciation of goldbricking did not, in this particular case, mean fulfilment of possibilities, however; for the conversion was to quota restriction with stabilization at 75 per cent efficiency.

In addition, I essayed an estimate on daywork goldbricking, first cousin to piecework goldbricking and easily mistaken for the latter. This estimate was obtained by comparing output on a job before and after it was timed. The 'before' efficiency was determined to be at least as low as 40 per cent, possibly 35 per cent, with 150 per cent improvement in production a 'cinch' and 186 per cent improvement an immediate possibility. But like the case of piecework goldbricking just cited, the switch was to quota restriction; so possibilities were never realized.

Since these appraisals were confined to the behavior of machine operators, the loss of time accountable to the sometimes remarkable restraint exercised by the 'service' employees, such as stock-chasers, tool-crib attendants, and inspectors, was not considered. Likewise unmentioned were the various defections of shop supervisors. A more complete record might also include the 'work' of members of management at higher levels, whose series of new rules, regulations, orders, and pronunciamentos designed for purposes of expediting production processes actually operated to reduce the effectiveness of the work force.

Confining scrutiny to the behavior of machine operators, the observer sees output restriction of such magnitude that the 'phenomenal' results of the organizational innovations tried in the steel industry under the guiding genius of Joe Scanlon (see also Chamberlain, 1946 and Davenport, 1950) do not seem at all surprising. The concept of 'cultural drag' might be more descriptive than 'cultural lag' in depicting the trailing of some of our industrial practices behind technological advance. Our organization of people for work is in general so primitive that anthropologists need not attempt to justify their interest in the 'modern' industrial scene.

References

BELL, D. (1947). 'Exploring factory life', *Commentary*.

BLUMER, H. (1947), 'Sociological theory: industrial relations', *Amer. soc. Rev.*, vol. 12, pp. 271–8.

CHAMBERLAIN, J. (1946), 'Every man a capitalist', *Life Magazine*.

DAVENPORT, R. W. (1950), 'Enterprise for everyman', *Fortune*, vol. 55.

MAYO, E. (1938), *Human Problems of an Industrial Civilization*, Macmillan Co.

MILLS, J. (1946), *The Engineer in Society*, Van Nostrand.

MOORE, W. (1947), 'Current issues in industrial sociology', *Amer. soc. Rev.*, vol. 12, pp. 651–7.

ROETHLISBERGER, F., and DICKSON, J. (1939), *Management and the Worker*, Harvard University Press.

4 Melville Dalton

The Industrial 'Rate-Buster': a Characterization

Melville Dalton, 'The industrial "rate-buster": a characterization',
Applied Anthropology, Winter 1948, pp. 5–18.

Under present-day industrial conditions in America, 'a day's work' is a concept much used by both industrial management and workers in connection with wage incentives. Management of course uses wage incentives to get increased production from the worker. Work groups, however, among other reactions, usually fear that the rate will be cut if they produce too much. Hence they reach an informal agreement among themselves not to produce beyond a certain point. Such a point will be the ceiling or upper limit of a day's work. This level of production varies with the time, the technology, and the industry. Whatever the point is, however, workers feel that their observance of it will protect them from rate cuts and still allow them to make some bonus. But in every work group there is nearly always a very small minority of individuals who refuse to be held back and insist on making as much bonus as they like, or are able to. In current American industrial literature such workers are referred to as 'rate-busters' (e.g. see Gardner, 1945, p. 154 and Roethlisberger and Dickson, 1939, p. 522). The aim of this paper is to study the social backgrounds of rate-busters and to seek the reasons for their behavior. To defy as they do the expectations of groups in which they make their living and spend nearly a third of their time, is an unusual procedure. Rate-busters are interesting also because they usually are the only workers who respond to wage incentives as management expects.

To get actual cases of rate-busters for study, the writer drew on his experience with the application of a wage incentive system in a large Middlewestern manufacturing plant during the recent war. Over 300 skilled machinists were employed in the shops of this plant. From these a sample of eighty-four men were taken for a study of disparities in response to the incentive plan. The results of this study have been reported elsewhere (see Dalton, 1946 and 1947). In these reports production data were taken for the years 1942–45. Data for the present study are from the same shops for the year 1946, and deal with all men in the total group of 300 who exceeded the informal production ceiling of 150 per cent.[1] There were only nine such men. As was to be expected, they were the same men who ignored the production limit in the preceding years. Their production levels with standard deviations and their respective names[2] are given in Table 1.

Table 1 Performances and Deviations of Rate-Busters

Machinist	Mean performance	Standard deviation
Watson	225±3·39	16·25±2·38
Keith	212±2·11	10·11±1·49
Shane	207±1·46	7·29±1·03
Bellini	195±4·66	21·85±3·30
Reid	193±2·86	13·44±2·03
Paine	189±4·45	22·26±3·15
Rylander	182±3·88	16·90±2·74
Richter	160±2·86	13·10±2·02
Funkhauser	158±3·57	15·55±2·52

Following will be given life sketches of the nine rate-busters which will include such characteristics as age, politics, religion, education, home tenure, hobbies, social activities, and relations with the work group. Data were collected by participant observation and free interviewing.

Fritz Funkhauser

At sixty-two Fritz is the oldest of the rate-busters. He was born and lived on a Middle Western farm till he was nine. At that time his father died and his mother moved to the city to live with her

1. Performance in all cases was determined by dividing the time required to do a job into the time allowed for the job. The percentages given in the table represent in each case the mean performance of the individual for the entire year of 1946. While the standard deviations and the standard errors probably have little significance, they may aid in answering the statistical questions of some readers.

2. Names are fictitious but ethnically correct.

relatives. Throughout his childhood and adolescence Fritz had many disputes that ended in fist-fights. He graduated from high school but took no part in school activities. He regarded girls with contempt, and was too pugnacious to get along with the boys. In his early twenties, however, Fritz married a young widow with two small children. He has been a machinist or shop foreman since his apprenticeship following high school. He boasted of having owned his home free of mortgage by the time he was thirty.

Fritz belongs to no organization but the Congress of Industrial Organisations (CIO) which he dislikes intensely but automatically became a member of.[3] He goes to no church but is nominally a Protestant.

Fritz is a strong Republican, and reads the *Chicago Tribune* which, he says, 'is the only American paper left since Roosevelt tried to make this country a Russian stooge.' His spare time at home Fritz spends tinkering with his car, a Ford, which he keeps running perfectly despite the 200,000 miles it has travelled.

On the job Fritz has almost no relations with other workers. He is disliked because 'he runs so high'. He in turn dislikes most workers because they are Democrats 'and too damn lazy and weak to stand on their own feet! Do you know what a Democrat is? – anybody that wants a hand-out! All the damned bums in the country are Democrats!'

Fritz especially dislikes workers from Southern Europe. He refers to them as 'hunkies'. His next greatest dislike is for Jews. So far as the writer knows, none of the industrial engineers who devised the incentive system under which Fritz works, were Jewish, but once when Fritz believed his bonus on a certain job would be relatively low, he exclaimed, 'The whole goddamn incentive bunch are all Jews! That's why the company hired them – to beat the workin' man. You never saw a goddamn Jew out here in the shop getting his hands dirty, did you? No, by God, and you won't!'

Fritz has twice been a shop foreman but each time gave up the job. A departmental superintendent said of him, 'He can't get along with men. He's so damned overbearing and domineering

3. Dislike of, and membership in, the CIO is true of all the rate-busters. Dues are paid by the check-off system.

that he couldn't get along with Jesus Christ himself! He treated his men like dogs, and tried to treat his superiors the same way. There's nothing he can't do on a lathe, though. We couldn't replace him.'

Peter Richter

Peter is fifty-nine. His father was a German farmer who came to New York State before he was twenty and became a huckster. Peter went only to the eighth grade in school. He started his apprenticeship at fourteen. Peter married early and had three children. He has never attended church since he was a boy. He owns his home but has no hobbies or social activities. He votes Republican, and reads the *Chicago Tribune*.

In addition to his high production, Peter is also disliked for his boast that he is the best machinist in the shop.

Perky Adams, who disapproves of Peter's high performance, remarked, 'Look at Richter over there! He's so damned worried about how much bonus he's going to get that he can't act like a human being. I wouldn't be in the shape he is for an extra thousand a year.'

Peter is indifferent to what the workers think of him but is concerned about the engineers. He says, 'If dey let me make de bonus, I can do 400 per cent. I can beat any man in de shops. I can turn out more and better work dan anybody! Dese guys in here try to stop me, but dey don't bodder me! But I don't want to kill a good ting. De company has to have its profits you know, and if I get too much dey cut me down.'[4]

Peter's wife died recently of cancer. During the last two weeks she was expected to die at any moment. Peter works from 3 p.m. to 11 p.m. Other machinists expressed surprise among themselves to see him at his machine regularly. When a telephone call at 6 p.m. of the last day announced her death to Peter, he shut his machine down and left the shop. All the other machines in the area of Peter's also stopped. The machinists gathered to discuss

4. In another situation, one of the engineers told the writer: 'There's no such thing as cutting a rate because all the rates are guaranteed to the union. The boys in the shop all know that. It stands to reason though that there's just so much work to do. When that's all out for a given period, it's a cinch the company can't pay men to stand around with their hands folded. The old axe has to fall someplace.'

him. One of the men remarked that 'only a damned heartless skunk would let his wife die like that. He'd rape his grandmother for a five spot.'

For the last year Peter and Funkhauser have worked on the same machine. Recently Fritz, who relieves Peter, accused Peter of 'laying down on the job', which would, of course have lowered the bonus of both men. Peter said the charge was a lie. Fritz knocked him down, then struck him again as he got to his feet. Other workers stopped the fight. Everyone knew informally of the clash but formal recognition would have meant discharge for both machinists. Management remained formally ignorant, because both men were 'good workers and near retirement anyhow'.

Though disliking both men, the other machinists sided with Fritz, who said; 'If that son-of-a-bitch ever calls me a liar again, by God I'll kill him!' Peter refused to comment on the incident.

Olaf Rylander

Olaf was born in Sweden fifty-nine years ago, the son of a shipping manager in the paper industry. Olaf's father wished to send him to college, but Olaf completed only high school when he married. He has since been a machinist. He has two children, owns his home, has no hobbies, but is a member of the Odd Fellows, a conservation club, and the Swedish Lutheran Church, reads the *Chicago Tribune* and is a Republican. Olaf dislikes the CIO, the *Chicago Sun* and Russia. He says, 'If de unions keep on, America will be yust like Russia – nobody can speak his mind or get what he has coming for his work. Efen now dese fellows try to stop you from making what you can – and papers like de *Chicago Sun* back dem up. But dey don't stop me! I haf a good yob and dis is a free country and I'm being paid to vork, so I vork hard!'

Olaf is probably the least disliked of all the rate-busters. This is apparently due to his being less grimly defiant than the others.

Ray Paine

Ray is fifty-six. He was born and lived on an eastern farm till he was thirteen. He attended high school two years. Ray is taciturn and difficult to draw into a conversation.[5] His neighbors say he loves children but that his wife, to whom he has been married for thirty-three years, is unable to bear children. When he is approached for donations to the Red Cross and Community Chest he denounces them and equates charity with graft. Ray once held a rather high supervisory job in another company but for some unknown reason was demoted to a machinist. During the depression following 1929 he lost a home worth $15,000.

Ray owns his home, belongs to nothing,[6] has no hobbies, reads the *Chicago Tribune*, is a Republican, and sporadically attends the Presbyterian Church. He works in an isolated area of the shop and avoids everyone. His standard deviation of 22·3 is the most erratic of that of any of the rate-busters. When he gets a job that he feels pays too little he 'gets even' with the engineers by 'taking his time'.

Though not interacting with people in the shop, Ray has been sufficiently amenable as a teacher of shop in the local night schools that he has held this position for several years.

Ray's strong political consciousness and status-feeling have caused him much suffering. To his demotion, his losses during the depression, and his frustration at having no children, he added hatred of the late President Roosevelt. Having to work among men he considered inferior to himself, men who were Democratic becoming more strongly unionized each year, caused Ray to become more acrid with each election that the Republicans failed to win.

Walter Reid

Walter is fifty-three and lived on a farm till he was fifteen. His father was a building contractor as well as a farmer. Walter attended high school only one year. He early became interested in handicrafts and learned furniture-making. From his mother, who was a sempstress, he learned sewing. Walter married a school teacher by whom he had five sons. Today he spends time in sewing for his family and in making furniture which he sells.

5. Data on his private life are from his neighbors and two intimates.
6. Pressure by members of the CIO to collect dues from Ray was futile before the check-off was installed.

Walter belongs to no social organizations. He is an inactive Protestant, a Republican, and reads the *Chicago Tribune*,

After Paine, no machinist is so disliked by the incentive appliers as Walter. While detesting unions, he is quick to call the union if he has any reason to believe an upward revision of his bonus could be obtained. He allows no one to interrupt his work. If he feels that his rights are imposed on, however, he will put the shop in an uproar until he has satisfaction.

His view of his role is clear-cut. 'I'm not out here for my health or a good time. I'm out here to make money. If any of these damn loafers think they can stop me, let them try it. I keep my bills paid and I don't owe anybody a damn cent. I mind my own business and look after my job. I'm always on time. I never sneak out early. The company can count on me, so why should I care what a bunch of damn snoopy bums think of me?'

Paul Bellini

Paul is different from all the other rate-busters in that he is the youngest (age thirty-one), is single, was born of Roman Catholic parents, is of South European descent, and talks considerably. His talking, however, is made up largely of banter, wise-cracking, and 'razzing'. Furthermore, it occurs only when he is far ahead of his production goal for the day.

Paul is a Republican, reads the *Chicago Tribune*, has no hobbies, and belongs to nothing. Though he graduated from high school in a city of 100,000, Paul has lived outside the city with his parents on their farm all his life. Though born a Catholic, he never attends church, nor donates, nor does his Easter Duty. He said, however, that he would go to the Catholic Church if he attended any.

On the job Paul watches the performances of workers near him very closely. He is quick to suspect collusion between machinists and the incentive men, and several times he has caused severe disturbances between staff and line by his investigations and charges. He flouts all attempts to restrain him. Bad feelings exist between him and nearly all the other workers, who are usually older. This age difference may aggravate his relations with others. 'I like to get these guys sore', he says. 'They think they're so damn smart!' Paul talks freely of his plans and his life outside the plant.

'I'm going to retire at fifty. I've really made the bucks since they put in this incentive. It's the best thing that ever happened in here. They may take it out one of these times. If they do while I'm working, I'll sure stop putting out. They're going to be laying off men one of these times, so I'm getting mine while the getting's good.

'I'm laying by the bucks. One of these times I'll be taking it easy doing nothing while a lot of these sour pusses around here'll be taking it easy working like hell!

'I don't need a lot. All I've got to have to keep me going is three cokes a day and a long-legged whore twice a week. That and the old lady's [his mother] eats keeps me fit.'

During the war, there was much complaint in the shop about Paul's not being drafted. Fathers with sons in the service were incensed. They were all glad when Paul was finally put in 1-A. But Paul layed off work the week before he was to leave for his first examination, and spent it carousing. He went without sleep, and divided his time between taverns and brothels. He boasted that he would beat the draft by being found in poor physical condition. 'Only damned fools get drafted', he said. 'Why the hell should a guy get his head shot off for thirty dollars a month when he can stay at home for better than three hundred?'

Paul was found to have a bad heart, and was rejected. On his return he maintained that his heart was sound and that the findings of the army doctors were due to his carousal.

Pat Shane

Pat is forty-five. His father was a Texas village barber. In his teens Pat spent considerable time in the cotton fields of his future father-in-law, but completed two years in the local high school. Though of Irish descent, Pat is an inactive Protestant and rarely goes to church. He doubts the value of religion for himself, but believes that it is helpful to many people.

Pat is singular among the rate-busters in that he is a Democrat and does not read the Tribune. His home and family – which he rules – take all his time. He says, 'I don't belong to a damn thing but the CIO, and I wouldn't belong to that if they didn't take dues out of my check every pay. I don't like unions, and I don't give a damn who knows it. I've never been a meeting in the five years I've been paying money in. I wouldn't want to go even if it wasn't a union meeting. Most of the people up North are damned crooks anyhow. They're out to skin everybody they can. They talk a lot about how the South mistreats the niggers. Hell, I ain't seen anybody around here moving in with niggers. And you don't see them teaching the niggers to run machines around here, do you?

The people up North ain't nearly as friendly as in Texas. I've lived next door to people for six years and one of them was in my house twice.'

Pat feels very moral about his work. If supervision makes last minute changes in a job that will cut his pay, he reports this at once to the person who figures his bonus. Asked why he is so careful to report these changes, he answered, 'By God, I don't have to make my money that way. A lot of these damn crooks around here lie to a new green checker [worker who figures bonus time] to raise the time on their jobs, and then raise hell because I run high. Well, by God I'm honest, and I don't have to kiss anybody's ass to get my money.'

Pat is much talked about. Alfons Schmidt, a machinist near him, said, 'Pat is killing himself. He said during the war that he was working hard because of his two sons in the service. That's a damn lie. Look at him now – still working like hell! And did you ever see the kind of work he turns out? He can't do a decent job. I wouldn't be guilty of finishing work the way he does.'[7]

Sammy Johnson, who strives to maintain a point just under the ceiling, said of Shane, 'The way that son-of-a-bitch jumps around, the company would be money ahead if they'd run a broom handle up his ass so he could sweep the floor at the same time. By God I could run 200 per cent, too, if I'd throw my ass around the way he does! He's just another Texas hillbilly. They ought to disfranchise the whole goddamn South. They're no better than the goddamn niggers they lay around with.'[8]

7. To the writer's knowledge Pat had not had any work rejected because of faulty finish during the last two years.
8. Facility in the use of the tabooed Anglo-Saxon words is almost a condition of membership in the work group.

Jock Keith

Jock was born in Dundee, Scotland, in 1901, the son of a sanitary engineer and contractor. He had two years of engineering in the University of Edinburgh. He votes Republican and reads the *Chicago Tribune*. In the shop Jock has time only for his job, but outside the plant he divides his time between a hobby and lodge activities. His hobby is model-making, especially boats, with which he has won numerous prizes. At least five nights a week he is active as a Mason. He belongs to all bodies of that order. Twenty-two years ago in Scotland, he was Past Master of the Royal Order of Ancient Shepherds. He has been Illustrious Master of the Royal and Select Masters, and Commander of Knights Templar. At present he is a member of the Grand Council of De Molay.

There is much talk in the shop of Jock's fondness for women and those who dislike him (which includes most of the shop) say that he is a lecher. However this may be, he married two years ago and took his wife into the home where he had lived with his widowed mother for years. In a few months he and his mother were having difficulties which developed into a law suit. Nearly everyone in the shop followed the case closely and charged that Jock forced his mother out of her home. Whether this was the whole truth or not, Jock was condemned by nearly all the machinists.

The opinion of Jock in the shop is well expressed by John Burns. Burns was criticizing wage incentives to the writer when he looked about for an example of their effect. He said,

Now you take that son-of-a-bitch over there [nodding toward Jock] – the incentive system made him what he is. He's got a bad principle and the system brought it out. He'd cut the working man's throat for a nickel. I've told him to stay the hell away from my machine and not to speak to me because I'd feel insulted. I value my fellow worker's opinion above the dollar.

Here is what Jock thinks of the group:

These guys lay down at 150 per cent because they have the idea in the back of their minds to make this a group incentive. When they do that, my performance is going down to 66 per cent.[9]

9. The point at which bonus payment begins.

There are three classes of men: (1) Those who can and will; (2) those who can't and are envious; (3) those who can and won't – they're nuts!

To show you how dumb people are – there was a Chicago Tribune reporter who stood on a corner with one hundred ten-dollar bills in his hand offering them for fifty cents each. One woman bought one and came back fifteen minutes later and demanded her fifty cents back! He couldn't sell them!

Do you know that there are plants in this country where the union fines men if they go beyond 130 per cent or so? They're dumb! They don't know that if they produce more they won't run out of jobs but will actually increase demand. Some of these dummies here in the shop would rather make ten pieces for five dollars than they would one hundred pieces for ten dollars – even if it was easier to make the hundred! They think the company'll cut the rate. All the squabbling in here is over nothing but money! Hell! The company would be a damn fool to cut the rates. If anything, they ought to raise them.

Jim Watson

Now fifty, Watson lived with his father on the farm till he was twenty-one. Since then he has had his own farm and has been a machinist. Jim was one of seventeen children, but his father owned nearly a section of land, so was able to do fairly well by his family. Jim chose to leave high school at the end of his second year.

Both Watson's father and mother were preachers as were also four of his uncles. They had little formal education and shifted about considerably among the three faiths of Baptist, Methodist, and Church of God. All had large families. Watson himself has eight children, six of whom are still dependent.[10]

Watson's reading includes the *Chicago Tribune. The Country Gentleman*, and *The Progressive Farmer*. He is a Republican.

Watson always hurries to the box where bonus slips[11] are filed (as they are completed) to get his reports before others can see them and estimate his income for the pay period. His shoes

10. As noted in the paper 'Worker and social background', responsibility for dependent children is not necessarily a factor in response to wage incentive.

11. Slips recording each man's bonus as earned under the incentive.

show mud from the farm and he wears bibbed overalls and a 'jumper'. These badges of his rural life seem to aggravate the group resentment that is always high. Inspectors envy, and report, his high performance,[12] while rumors go about the shop of his profits from eggs and chickens sold directly to customers in the city as he drives to the job and on his days off.

Jim knows much of what the feelings are toward him. He says,

When them sons-of-bitches start buyin' my groceries they can tell me how much bonus to make. Until then, I'll make as much as I can. I want to send my girl to school, and as long as I can make the money to do it, I'm not lettin' a damn union stop me. A lotta these guys think a union will get them big money for doin' nothing. Well, I joined to shut them up, so I'll make as much as I can.[13] They're always puttin' pressure on the inspectors to get my work rejected, but I'll get by.

Sometimes I think this is the damnedest country in the world. If you need a little help, everybody runs from you; if you make a little money, everybody's down on you. Well, they can stay down on me. If I can run 400 per cent, by God, I'll do it.

Summary of characteristics
Politics and newspaper

Eight of the nine rate-busters were Republican. Shane was the one Democrat, but this distinction was more nominal than real. Reared in Texas, he was a traditional Democrat with a political philosophy as individualistic as that of the 'states' rights' Southerners, and Republicans of the North.

12. The rate-busters each earned from $4500 to $6000 in each of the years 1944–45. Shane, Keith, Rylander, Reid, and Paine, each bought at least $4000 in war bonds between 1942 and 1946. Shane and Keith vied with each other to keep their names at the top of the honor roll for bond purchases. Both, however, bought more bonds at the bank than from the plant, because 'you lose interest buying them here in the plant – you have to wait two weeks after they're paid for till they're made out and you start drawing interest.'

13. Over a two-year period, as recorded in the M.A. thesis cited above, Watson had a mean performance of 168 per cent. During these two years he shared much of his work with a machinist who observed the ceiling of 150 per cent and thus obscured Watson's real behavior toward the incentive. Jim now works alone and has the highest performance of any man in the shops.

When the nine rate-busters were compared with the other seventy-five men in the sample of eighty-four, the significance of being Republican became clearer. Nearly seventy per cent of the eighty-four men were Democrats. Of the three hundred machinists from which the sample was drawn, four out of five were Democrats; while from those workers performing below 100 per cent (sometimes called 'restricters' in industrial literature), 90 per cent were Democrats.[14]

There was a close relation between the rate-buster's political thinking and his newspaper preference. He supports a party and reads a paper that stress private enterprise and individualism, which accords with his own thinking, and his behavior in the shop. Eight of the group were Republican and read the *Chicago Tribune*, a paper that is strongly laissez-faire and isolationist, and has been consistently opposed to the New Deal. Shane is the only non-*Tribune* reader of the group. This newspaper choice of the rate-busters emphasized the preference of all Republicans in the shop and contrasted with the choice of Democrats. That is, 72 per cent of all Republicans preferred the Tribune as compared with only 24 per cent of all Democrats. Most of the latter read instead the *Chicago Sun* and *Times*, which they regarded as papers 'that stand up for the working man'.

Education

Where Democrats of the original sample has a median educational level of eight years as against nine for all Republicans, the rate-busters had a median of ten years' schooling.

Ethnic and class origin

Excepting Bellini, who was of Italian descent, the rate-busters were all of northwest European lineage – Germany, Sweden, and

14. As noted in the earlier paper, all workers, Democrats and Republicans alike, had a performance level beyond which they hesitated to go. This was true also of the rate-busters. Richter has said so, while Shane has admitted confidentially that he is 'afraid to go much over 200 per cent because they might think I'm making too much money.' There is little doubt, however, that 200 per cent or so, as the rate was set up in this plant, was near the limit of what man, cutters, and machine could maintain.

the British Isles.[15] And all came from middle-class families.[16] Seven of them are sons of large farm owners, supervisors, or small businessmen. Such origins contrast with those of most machinists in the shop, whose fathers were usually unskilled urban industrial workers, renters, and without financial and material resources. Where there were forty-two renters (fifty per cent) in the original sample, all the rate-busters but Bellini (who is single) own their homes, and only Reid does not own a car.[17]

Religion

Bellini is the only rate-buster born in a Catholic family. As noted above, however, he has neither standing as a Catholic nor interest in acquiring such status. The other rate-busters are largely nominal Protestants. Richter and Funkhauser have not been in a church since they were boys. Reid enters a church only when he attends a traditional funeral. Watson sometimes goes to church 'because so many of my family are preachers'. Keith confesses that when he goes to church it is for social reasons only, since he is an agnostic. Shane believes that religion is useful, but not to him. Paine is an agnostic, despite his occasional church attendance. Only Rylander goes to church with any regularity; he attends the Swedish Lutheran Church on the Sunday mornings that he does not work.

The question of religion[18] is raised because none of the ninety-eight Catholics among the three hundred machinists of the sample climbed above the performance ceiling, though many had the necessary skill, as they have had the rank and pay of A-machinists for years.

15. In the original sample of eighty-four men, the machinists came from fifteen of the United States, from two countries of the New World outside of the United States, and from thirteen countries of the Old World.
16. They agreed on at least the three points of difference betraying a middleclass origin: (1) their having greater material and occupational resources, (2) having a stronger moral feeling about private ownership and work as a gauge of merit, and (3) having more upperclass conservatism. The rate-busters' higher educational level is also an indication of a different status of their families of origin.
17. He recently sold his four-year old – but excellently kept – Buick for nearly double the price he gave for it new.
18. The only indication of management's awareness of religious differences was shown by the employee personnel form, which contained a space for religion that the employee was free to ignore.

Hobbies

If a hobby is defined as a recreational, integrating, non-profitable, and irregularly followed activity, then Keith is the only rate-buster having a hobby. Reid's making of furniture, and sewing, have a practical value: he sells the furniture and cabinets he makes, and the sewing is for his family.

The absence of hobbies among the rate-busters differs sharply from their presence among the lower-scoring performers. The latter always had hobbies and sometimes had two or three hobbies. Such hobbies ranged from the making of trinkets and the breaking and training of saddle horses through engine-modeling, photography, microscopy, and the collecting of coins, guns, stamps, and fine tools.

Social participation

Only Keith and Rylander engage in formal social activities. Funkhauser once applied to become a Mason but withdrew his application when he learned that a man he disliked very much was a member. Shane was twice invited to attend meetings for installation of officers in the Masonic Order.[19] He declined the invitations and remarked later to the writer that 'When I have to belong to the Masons to keep my job, they can shove it up their asses.'

With this characteristic, as with hobbies, the least responsible workers were the ones most often belonging to lodges, clubs, associations, and so on.

Analysis

Before discussing the significance of the rate-buster's characteristics it is well for comparative purposes first to note briefly the behavior of the whole group toward wage incentive. On the basis of such behavior the group may be divided roughly into three sections: (1) the restricters, or those who for various reasons withdrew from the incentive; (2) the middle performers, whose rate of production lay roughly between 100 and 150 per cent, and (3) the rate-busters, the top performers.

Individual conflicts over whether to be loyal to the group when working under incentive, or to follow one's real wishes,

19. Such invitations are said to be equivalent to an invitation to join, though formally the order proffers membership to no one.

were chiefly responsible for this division.[20] The process of breaking up into informal groups on the basis of response to the incentive was of course unconscious and unguided. There was both individual and cooperative experiment to see what was possible in the way of output. Machinists felt each other out with statements of 'where we ought to stop'. Such remarks were sincere only in varying degrees and were seldom accepted at face value. Instead, machinists watched each other to keep score of one another's output and conferred with the incentive checkers about it. Checkers were forbidden to discuss the performance or bonus of one man with another, but they did so nevertheless. The few workers who took no part in this scoring of each other were the potential rate-busters.

From seventy to eighty per cent of the whole group thus fell into the middle performers, who were torn incessantly with indecision and mental conflict over their performances. This condition will be discussed below. The remainder of the group, restricters and rate-busters, together constituted nearly all of the machinists who had resolved their conflicting feelings about the incentive. The restricters felt that the incentive destroyed friendships and made the group a pawn of management. They shunned the incentive by holding their production to a level paying little or no bonus but yet high enough to let them escape trouble with supervisors.[21] The rate-busters of course chose the other

20. This is not to say that skill had no part in the division, but that it was minor. E.g., in the group of twenty-five restricters, fifteen of them were A-machinists. (A-rating is given only to machinists who can competently handle any machine in the shop. All the men in the original sample of eighty-four men had had at least five years of experience on the type of machine they were operating at the outset of the study.)

21. Actually, a few of the restricters were bitter and reduced output in a feeling of revenge, but they were exceptional. Perky Adams, whose mean performance over a period of two years was 97 per cent, is a typical restricter. Admitting that money is essential, he says: 'But I've too many problems to be bothered as long as I have enough to get by on. If I didn't have *any* money I'd probably worry. You wouldn't want me to get up and yell and fight like some of these guys would you? I've seen some of these guys grab their bonus slips and run through them as though they had ten thousand dollars. They go out of here all fagged out. It's not worth it. Hell, I'm going to get by. I always have. I got by about as well before the system came in. And if I've got to have a fight or make somebody sore to get a few cents more on the turn, I don't give a damn if I never make any bonus.'

extreme of response to the incentive. Feeling no allegiance to the group, they suffered no conflict over their rate of production under the incentive.

While most of the middle performers were like the restricters to a degree, in wishing to avoid conflict, they nevertheless felt that a considerable amount of bonus could be made without harm to group solidarity: the danger point was production beyond the rate of 150 per cent.[22]

To return to the restricters. As shown earlier,[23] back of the restricters' avoidance of the incentive lay a high degree of socialization. Most of them were reared in middle-sized or large cities where they had acquired a skill in, and a need of, social activity. Hobbies were also important socializing factors. Their pursuit led to social interaction with others and often, also, to a considerable and continuing outlay of money. For example, Perky Adams dominates a cinema club and constantly enlarges his circle of friends by his hobby of colored movies. Jean Desmoulins will lose a night's sleep (and the next day's work) demonstrating the patterns and trinkets that he can form with his home-made welding set. Hobbies in most cases amounted to a positive interest leading away from the potential conflict and social isolation of

22. One hundred and fifty per cent was also regarded by most of the middle group as a point at which the process of diminishing returns sets in. Some of their informal leaders argued that the machinist receives proportionately less for additional effort beyond that point than he does before, and, hence, they said, workers producing above 150 per cent are not only 'suckers', but they are also hurting the rest of the group by putting out additional work for what amounts to less pay. Some of the engineers confidentially agreed that this thinking is mathematically sound but others denied it. Whether true or not, as long as the machinist believes it to be, conduct of the work group is strongly affected by the belief.

Jerry Bates, a leader in the shop, views the matter like this: 'The incentive is just a trick to beat the working man. They didn't put it in here to make us rich. We know that. That's why we try to stick together – so we can use them some while they're using us. . . . This slowing up is just like holding back butter and shirts to get high prices. You know yourself that the big factories, farmers, and producers of all kinds always lay down when prices begin to fall or when they see a chance to push 'em up. Well, in a way, we're doing the same damn thing – and we got just as much right to do it. That way some of the boys can make a little extra without hurting anybody. That's the way things are run in this country – while you're shaking a man's hand, be thinking how you can beat him.'

23. See the M.A. thesis cited above.

individual concentration on bonus. Related to the factor of hobbies was the social activity of the restricters both in the shop and the community. In short, love of social pleasures, combined with a variety of socializing interests, made the restricter dislike conflict. And since higher income by means of wage incentive involved him in conflict, he ignored the lure of increased pay even though his easy and genial way of living might threaten to push his expenses above his income.

In theory we may say that the restricter and the rate-buster are opposite in their conduct toward wage incentive, and that attending these contrary behaviors are also pertinent social and political differences.[24] Related to the conduct of each is a distinctive set of experiences, broadly social on the one hand and narrowly social on the other. The restricter and the rate-buster are 'ideal types' of the two extremes of response to money incentive. Their characteristics blend in workers of the middle group, where the lower and upper performers grade off in social traits in similarity to the restricter and the rate-buster respectively.

Rural origin was an important experience among the rate-busters. There solitude, hard work, and production were essentials of life (see Kolb and Brunner, 1940, pp. 8–9; Whyte, 1944). Every meal was a conference on private enterprise. Success was equated with production. All the family worked, and the husband and father was final authority. To check production was criminal, because work and private enterprise were indivisible. Social activities were fitted into the production unit – the family. Seven of the rate-busters reflect this early training, both in the shop and at home. The other two, Keith and Rylander, were reared in urban middle-class families where they learned the respectability of getting up in the world. They matured in homes having the social as well as the material symbols of success. Their goal of

24. While the rate-busters were Republican and individualistic, and the restricters were Democrat and collectivistic, there were a few exceptional cases in the shop, both Democrats and Republicans, who lacked a policy toward the incentive and could not explain their choice of party. That most machinists were so specific politically may be due partly to the median age of forty-eight years (sample of 84 men). Most of the men had clear memories of the period following 1929, which appeared to stimulate greatly their political consciousness one way or the other.

achieving or maintaining a higher style of life called for greater income. They identified themselves with groups outside the shop which their fellow machinists could rarely, if ever, enter. Instead of loyalty, they felt a class contempt for most of the work group with its 'radicalism', its 'immoral' views toward work, and its concern for only the present. Rural and urban alike, the rate-busters had this conservative temper. In addition to their earlier experiences, there are other factors that may well check participation in community life by the rate-busters. First, their hard work leaves them little energy for such activity; second, since they wish to possess at least the material symbols of success,[25] they may avoid social activity because of the expense it incurs;[26] and third, the rapid social change of recent times with its attendant uncertainties for the individual may cause the rate-buster (who is vigorous and skilled) to count more on what he can accumulate[27] than on having friends.

Concerning religion, much has been written on the economic implications of the so-called Protestant ethic. Active membership in a Protestant Church, in the shops where this study was made, appeared to have no significance.[28] Among the rate-busters, only

25. Some of the rate-busters have referred to the factory as 'a hell of a place to work' and have expressed a desire 'to be my own boss', and to 'go into business for myself'. In many cases machinists of the other groups have felt that it is no longer possible for an individual to achieve success in business 'because things are just too big for one man to handle. You just don't stand a chance any more. It costs too much to go into business. And if you go broke, then where are you?'

26. In discussing Pat Shane, Jerry Bates said: 'Pat's a funny guy. He don't go no place. For a long time I didn't know what to think of it. Now I'm sure it's because he don't want to spend anything. When I tell him of a good restaurant, he wants to know how much a meal costs. When I tell him, he says "Hell no meal's worth that. You're a damn fool to pay that much!"'

27. Three of the rate-busters have remarked that 'the guys who raise hell about me running high wouldn't help me out if I went broke.' All of this small group dislike the thought of borrowing or owing money, or of being dependent on others.

28. It is admitted that ancestors of all the rate-busters but Bellini came from countries that have been Protestant for centuries. However, even if Protestantism were a factor in the rise of capitalism, both have undergone such changes in the last century that to say the hollow Protestantism of the rate-buster determines his *Wirtschatsethik* is to look too casually at the matter.

Rylander could be called an active Protestant. The others, at best, were only nominally Protestant. Considering their indifference toward formal Christianity, they could as well be referred to as non-Catholics. Roman Catholicism, however, appeared to play a role. All of the ninety-eight Catholics conformed to the group aim of holding production below the 150 per cent level. Regardless of his ability, no Catholic presumed to exceed the informal limit. To some extent this lack of individualism may be due to the social as well as the religious experiences which Catholics have. The faithful Catholic, as was noted earlier (Dalton, 1947), from childhood on engages in group activity of a kind that is likely to prevent or subdue individualistic tendencies. This is an experience that the non-Catholic, or at least the nominal Protestants, may very well not have.

In addition to participation in group activities of the Church, emphasis here is also on positive socializing[29] influences such as the psychological[30] effects of the confessional.

29. If willingness to give to charitable organizations is a mark of socialization, then Catholics and rate-busters in the shop were strikingly different in that respect. Jerry Bates, the shop steward, said: 'When I was working for the Red Cross and Community Chest drives, Reid, Shane, Keith, and Richter was all tight as hell to get anything from. I went to them first because I knew them was makin' a hell of a lot of bonus, but they just didn't want to give. Then when I'd make the rounds to Jean (Catholic) and Carl (Catholic), an' guys like that, I'd always get the quota an' I didn't have to drag it out of them. That's a funny thing, too – when them guys hit a hundred per cent, it's somethin' to write home about.'

Another indication of anti-individualism in the Catholics was the fact that twenty-four of the twenty-seven (sample of eighty-four men) Catholics were New Deal Democrats. The other three were Republicans. This is not to imply that Catholics and New Deal Democrats are never individualistic, or that Republicans and non-Catholics are necessarily non-charitable. There are naturally thousands of people in these categories who are there not from personal choice but from chance, and who have little awareness of the implications of their affiliation. However, in the shop there exists a keen political consciousness. It is admitted that conclusions presented here on Catholicism as a factor are speculative in nature, but in the shop studied here at least, they are supported by data. Wider research might point to other conclusions and precipitate such problems as, what constitutes a good Catholic? and what is the relation, if any, between socioeconomic status and individualistic behavior among Catholics?

30. It is difficult to conceive of such men as Keith, Shane, and Funkhauser ever bringing themselves to the emotional state normally needed for

Wage incentive encourages individualism.[31] Each man is told by the management that he is free to make as much bonus as he can. Furthermore, in such a situation a worker's income is not dependent on good relations with others as in many occupations and professions. A worker may even come to regard his bonus as a compensation for poor working conditions or lack of good social relationships.

Actually, wage incentive only abets what our culture implants in the worker. Probably more than any other society ever has, we urge success, which is largely a matter of social status and economic resources with the former dictating to the latter the appropriate level and style of emulation to be used in a career of 'conspicuous consumption'. For those not born in situations favorable to the easy obtaining of success, struggle is necessary. Competition and individual effort are the mainstays of our social heritage. As we all know, the urbane utilization of others to win success is approved in some areas of our society. But not by the rate-buster. His mode of attaining success is actuated by an unbending morality. While he disregards the rights of others in the shop, he feels no need of pretending concern about their welfare. He detests lip-service. To such men as Shane, Reid, Watson, and Funkhauser, the use of 'connections' to gain an end is to be a 'suckass'; and to fail to 'speak your mind' in any situation is to be hypocritical and cowardly. Success won by any means other than one's own efforts would not be success, but indebtedness. The rate-buster believes that success is attainable only by hard work and attentiveness to his own affairs.[32] Success and his family are his only interests.

While the few rate-busters were the only machinists who worked as management expected, neither this fact, their being Republican,

---

the confessional, just as an individual habitually engaging in such practice would probably never be able to persist in behavior year after year that caused dozens of men about him to show by their conduct that they regarded him as an enemy, when all that he would need to do to have their friendship would be to work less hard!

31. In some industries there are 'group' incentives in which this is less true.

32. This naturally is less true of Keith. His experiences with the Masons and other associates outside the plant show his skill in outside social relationships.

nor their individualism toward the work group necessarily meant that they identified themselves completely with their employer. Actually, the rate-buster will behave individualistically toward anyone who threatens his goal of 'getting ahead'. Since he is powerless as an individual to engage his employer in an open economic struggle when they have differences, he will instead reduce his production so sharply that there is no doubt of his using the curtailment as an economic weapon to gain his end. And, paradoxically, he will suffer a great loss of bonus rather than surrender once he has taken a stand.

Keith is an example. His remarks suggest that he saw eye to eye with management, and his behavior during a sit-down strike supported his words. The strike was against the employment of a certain incentive official in that area of the plant. Keith was the only man who remained on the job.[33] Despite this apparent loyalty, he has several times had bitter struggles with management. Some months ago incentive officials allowed Keith a machinability[34] factor of 1·24 for a given job. He insisted on a factor of 1·53. With the factor of 1·24 the job per piece allowed him 1·6 hours; with the higher factor, 1·8 hours, a difference of about twelve minutes, which is considered small. When he was denied the larger factor, he for two weeks produced only three units per turn of eight hours, which made his performance only 61 per cent for that period, and allowed him no bonus at all. Keith is also opposed to unions, but in this case he went to the union and filed a grievance. After two weeks,[35] the factor was raised to 1·53, but the job was nearly done. Keith immediately started turning out fourteen pieces in eight hours at a performance of 322 per cent or an increase of over 500 per cent. For the two-week period of restriction he made his regular hourly pay totalling about $12 per turn. With his new pace he was making $25 per turn, but he received this for only the two remaining turns of the job. If he had worked at the same rate with the lower

33. And also the only rate-buster in that shop on that turn.

34. For relative difficulty in machining a given metal because of varying contents of the 'tough' elements, chromium, manganese, vanadium, etc. The higher the factor, the greater the time allowed for the job.

35. The union 'taking its time' because of Keith's well-known anti-union bias.

factor he would have made nearly $23 per turn, which means that he lost $110 for the two-week period.

Keith was not unique in this behavior toward management. Watson has shut his machine down and gone 'over the heads' of his superiors directly to the remote and aloof office of the engineers to announce that he would continue his work only when they gave him the 'time' (which had been unavoidably delayed) for the job. Rylander also has shut his machine down for the same reason. Both Reid and Bellini react to similar situations by seeking to aggravate already tenuous relations between line and staff.

There is a softer side to the rate-buster's behavior that is never seen in the shop. For instance, during the last eight years Keith has made many gifts such as toy houses, boats and other objects in his shop for his next door neighbor's small daughter. And Jock's recent marriage was to a widow, with children whom he must support. Funkhauser also married a widow with two small children and has had two children of his own by her. Mrs Funkhauser has told her neighbors that though Fritz 'rules the roost' at home, he has never made any distinction in treatment of his own children and his step-children.

The case of Paine is also significant. Having practically no relations with people in the shop, his students in the night school where he teaches say that he jokes with them and is very considerate of their errors. As mentioned above, though Paine loves children, he is apparently not embittered toward his wife because of her inability to bear them.

Related to these traits is the rate-buster's attachment to marriage and family life. Excepting Bellini who is single (but prefers remaining with his parents), and Keith who just recently married, all the rate-busters wed early and have never divorced.[36]

Despite his outbursts of individualism, management has given more than verbal proof of liking[37] the rate-buster. For example,

36. To some extent this may be due to the rural backgrounds of several of the rate-busters. (See Kolb and Brunner, 1940, pp. 25–26.)

37. It should be mentioned that these were maintenance shops, that is, their function was to replace and/or repair broken or worn parts of the plant equipment. This meant that breakdowns created a demand for immediate replacement of parts so that production in the disrupted area or unit could

recently both Shane and Keith had temporarily completed all work that was on hand for the turn. In another part of the shop, the saw and bolt-threader man was sawing the rods from which he was to thread two hundred stud bolts. He could have done the entire job in three days at a cost of about $30. However, after he had cut the studs and was preparing to thread them, they were taken from him and delivered to the machines of Shane and Keith to be threaded. Because of the differential between 'production' and 'special' rates, the job 'payed so well' that both men had to 'slow down' to keep from 'killing it', which might have brought the engineers around for an explanation. Instead of three turns at a cost of $30 for the complete job, the work of threading alone required eight turns and a cost of $160.

Possibly the rate-buster's personal organization and adjustment should be questioned. It is clear that he fails to shape his behavior in terms of the work group. If he can be said to show an excessive desire for security, he might, in terms of W. I. Thomas' four-wish pattern (Thomas, 1923), be thought maladjusted. Surely the case of Paine is that of a man suffering from some degree of maladjustment. However, he is hardly representative. It is probably more correct to think of the rate-buster as well-integrated. His aim and standard are the same. Regardless of how he appears to the work group, or of how damaging his conduct may be to their unity, or of how disloyal to the employer he may be said to be, he has a set of norms valid to himself. In the shop he fulfils his function of high production, and, though restricted to his family for the most part, he has specific social relationships. These facts are uncommon in our shifting and unstable world. However blameworthy his lack of social consciousness may be from some viewpoints, his contempt and indignation for the work group's 'pegging of production' show his integration. Though the restricters also escape conflict, because their interest in money is dominated by other interests, in most cases only the rate-buster accepts and pursues our pecuniary

be resumed. Since no one equalled the rate-busters' speed of output, supervision's regard of him is understandable. There may well be industrial situations, however, in which the presence of rate-busters would be regarded by management as more harmful than helpful.

and economic success values without conflict. In terms of the competition versus humility behavior pattern of our society (see Elliott and Merrill, 1941, p. 535) the rate-busters have chosen competition, the restricters humility, and the middle performers have attempted to reconcile the two. And the latter – or most workers under incentive – are the ones who suffer from conflicts. Daily in the shop it is apparent that members of the central group suffer from two very real sets of conflicts: first the desire for a 'good' job and the fear and uncertainty of not getting it, or the envy of someone who does get it; and second frustration of the desire to get as much as possible out of a good job by the necessity of remaining below the production ceiling.

In connection with the increasing attention given by psychiatry to the relation of mental conflicts and stomach ulcers, it may be noteworthy that none of the restricters or rate-busters had such ulcers, but that nine of the fifty middle performers[38] (sample of eighty-four men) were being treated for this ailment.

Implications

From a sample of only nine men it would be ridiculous to suggest that 'conclusions' could be drawn enabling one to 'predict'

38. This paper is not intended as an attack on wage incentive systems, but since rate-busters and incentive systems are inseparable, the latter unavoidably enter the discussion in an unfavorable light because of remarks against the rate-busters. The impression may have been given that all workers but the rate-busters disliked the incentive, and that *all* machinists of the central group were emotionally upset by it. There are two exceptional cases among the middle performers that should be noted. Both were men well liked by the work group, and both were Catholics and Democrats. To the writer's knowledge, neither ever displayed irritation over the incentive, or used abusive language in referring to others.

Fred Williamson, the first, remarked concerning the incentive:

'When we didn't have the incentive we still had pressure. All the foremen had some idea in mind of what a day's work is. If you didn't put out that much, you caught hell. I'm really under less pressure now than I was then.

'A lot of these fellows give the incentive hell. That's because they let it get their goat. The only way you can stand up under this kind of a system is to forget about what the other guy's doing. And when a job don't pay, forget that too. If it does pay, be glad.

'The real fault of incentive systems is the job distribution, but that's supervision. There's pets in every shop that get favors the other men don't. There's one thing that has to be said for incentive systems. They bring out new methods. If a worker can find some way to get a job done sooner, he'll the behavior of workers under wage incentive. It would also be unfair. For a supervisor in an operating situation to assume – on such slight evidence – that to increase his production he need only employ Republicans, good family men, non-joiners, non-church-goers, and so on, would be as foolish as a labor leader's selecting only Democrats and joiners to assure thereby solidarity in the ranks of his union!

The paucity of rate-busters makes the gathering of a sample large enough to warrant conclusions so difficult that the effort of the task might very well outweigh the worth of the findings. Rather than as conclusions, therefore, we should think of the following summary of characteristics as hypotheses on the type of worker who responds most strongly to wage incentive.

Regarded in this way, we may say that the rate-buster is likely to come from a family of higher socioeconomic level than that of other members of the work group, or, if he does not, he is trying to reach such a level. He is ambitious and his immediate goal is money. Later he may convert his savings into some form of security and/or prestige. For the present he is often content to possess middle-class material symbols and to ignore present social experience of enjoyment. Often, too, the rate-buster is of rural origin, having a personality organization well-adapted to individualistic behavior at work. He is much more likely to be a nominal Protestant who rarely if ever goes to church than he is to be a Catholic. Ethnically he will probably be an Anglo-American or an immigrant from one of the countries of Northwestern Europe. Politically the rate-buster will usually be a Republican and will read a conservative newspaper. He dislikes labor unions

---

do it in spite of what's considered proper. Without incentive he'd go along with the old methods and never care.'

The other machinist, Larry Shaw, says:

'I don't work any harder now than I did before the incentive came in. I just work steadier. Now I never leave the machine for more than a couple of minutes at a time. Maybe I get a little tireder, but not much.

'If I wasn't on incentive I couldn't get by. I'm only getting B-rate and I don't have the connections to get A-rate. That's the good thing about incentive: it lets a low rate man get by. Sometimes I make $25 more on the pay. Of course, sometimes I don't make anything much. But then I'm not killing myself like Shane and Watson and some of the other fools around here.'

and regards their function as essentially immoral. He is insensible of the struggle for power between management and labor and of his role in it.

The rate-buster is a 'family-man'. He marries early and does not divorce. His marriage, however, is not of a modern equalitarian type. Instead, he practices the traditional Puritan virtues of a good provider and a home-lover and avoids the Puritan-abhorred vices of drink and gambling.

He prides himself on keeping out of debt, minding his own business, speaking forthrightly, and not being dependent on others. He is master in the home and makes all decisions of consequence. If he does not marry he is likely to show strong family attachment by living with his parents or close relatives. His preoccupation with his family is to great that he is likely to have little social activity outside it. He regards such activity as frivolous and costly, and is inclined to prefer material things like real estate, a car, and luxuries in the home. He is also likely to consider hobbies as impractical and expensive. His familial devotion is accompanied by a relative indifference to the community at large, as shown by his reluctance to aid charitable organizations. In this he is unlike the civic-minded middle classes whom he apes materially. Despite his restricted social life and extremely individualistic behavior, the rate-buster is not personally disorganized. He has a set of standards valid to himself. His adherence to them may make him a problem to the work group, but not to himself. He rebels against authority of the work group, but not that of the social order, the competitively derived success values of which are the same as his own. There is no uncertainty or confusion in his behavior. His impulses are channelized and guided by clear-cut images and goals. He is maladjusted only in the sense that he is a microcosm of laissez-faire thought in occupational contact with workers of a collectivistic outlook. Any disjointing he may suffer from this experience is healed by his knowledge of sympathy from groups with whom he identifies himself.

His social world has remained so small and manageable that he finds laissez-faire more workable than do its great proponents in the entangled spheres of commerce. Feeling no need of the workers about him, he ignores their demands on him. In his aspirations and mode of life the rate-buster represents one of the nearest possible approaches to the concept of an 'economic man'.

References

DALTON, M. (1946), 'Wage incentive and social behaviour' unpublished M.A. thesis, University of Chicago.

DALTON, M. (1947), 'Worker response and social background', *J. polit. Econ.*, vol. 55, pp. 323–32.

ELLIOTT, M. A., and MERRILL, F. E. (1941), *Social Disorganisation*, Harper & Row.

GARDNER, B. B. (1945), *Human Relations in Industry*, Irwin.

KOLB, J. H., and BRUNNER, E. (1940), *A Study of Rural Society*, Houghton Mifflin.

ROETHLISBERGER, F. J., and DICKSON, W. J. (1939), *Management and the Worker*, Harvard University Press.

THOMAS, W. I. (1923), *The Unadjusted Girl*, Little, Brown & Co.

WHYTE, W. F. (1944), 'Who goes union and why', *Personn. J.*, vol. 23, pp. 221–2.

5 Leonard Sayles

The Impact of Incentives on Inter-Group Work Relations

Leonard Sayles, 'The impact of incentives on inter group work relations', *Personnel*, vol. 28, no. 5, 1957.

It is becoming increasingly important for management to re-assess its incentive programs. The productivity demands of a defense economy plus the pressures for higher wages place added emphasis on adequate incentive plan development. This study presents field research data on some aspects of the impact of incentives on *plant-level* human relations.

In the past decade management has become aware that job incentives are complicated by imposing human problems. Industrial relations researchers have drawn attention primarily to two types of 'human relations problems' surrounding the application of these formulas. The first is concerned with informal restrictions of output on the part of the work group itself. These are presumably motivated by fears of rate-cutting on the part of management or excessive daily production quotas. They have shown, as well, the perilous position of the 'rate-buster' who ignores the group 'bogey'. The second type stresses the importance of gaining union acceptance of incentive changes through advance consultation with union leaders and educational programs.

But we have failed to concentrate sufficient attention on the impact of incentives on inter-group relations at the worker level. Certainly the reactions of the men who must work under a given incentive plan, and those of their union leaders, are important factors in its success or failure. Equally vital, however, are the responses of other work groups and departments in the plant who feel themselves in one way or another affected by the incentive plan.

How does an incentive for one work group affect other workers in the plant? Perhaps one of the clearest ways of illustrating these interdepartmental and inter-group relationships is to examine the pressures on local union leaders. When one group or another in an organized plant feels it is being treated unjustly, it will make its grievance known to the union. The attempts of the officers to settle the case and the rank-and-file's evaluation of their efforts provide a significant influence on plant morale and productivity.

Let us now turn to a series of 'incentive cases' in which inter-group differences played a prominent role in determining union action.

Differences between incentive and 'daywork' earnings

Most personnel administrators are familiar with the feelings that separate 'day workers' and 'incentive workers'. Often there is a distinct differential between the average earnings of these two groups that favors the incentive workers in the plant. Union officials are in a position of constantly having to justify such differences. The problem becomes an especially acute one for the union during negotiations when the decision must be made: How much of a wage increase should we ask? 'How much' means, in fact, how much should we give one group and not give another; for a majority of union leaders recognize that management has limited resources just as the union has limited bargaining power

Many day workers refuse to recognize that the piece worker actually earns all his extra wages. Although they themselves may be unwilling, or at least not anxious to accept an incentive plan for their own job, they look at the incentive earnings of others as 'pure gravy'. In turn they may expect the union to get them additional hourly benefits to compensate for these incentive earnings.

In one recent case in a medium-size plant the union was able to work out a negotiation formula with management that apparently satisfied both the day workers and incentive workers. The wage increase afforded the day workers somewhat greater benefits, presumably because of an existing inequity between these two large groups. All went well until the question of retroactive pay came into the picture. Management was willing to grant as an effective date for the wage increase the contract expiration date. A strike and the delay imposed by the Wage Stabilization Board finally resulted in a 'sizeable pie' to be divided among the membership. The union then discovered that the incentive workers were not satisfied with the wage settlement and felt the least that could be done would be for the day workers to consent to an equal sharing of all back pay.

The union meeting at which this proposal was discussed provides considerable insight into the feelings of these two groups toward one another. Several day workers got up to say, 'These high paid piece workers never offered to split their wages with a day worker before and so why should we split our wage increase? In most of these negotiations we day workers have always taken a beating and we're certainly not going to give up any money that's coming to us now.' A former union president who was an incentive worker replied, 'As far back as I can remember, and I've participated in a lot of negotiations, the union always went out of its way to see that the day worker got a better break because the union realized that the day worker didn't share in the incentive bonus.'

A maintenance man shouted him down: 'Sure the union officers always have good intentions but they don't mean a damn. The day worker still has always been very underpaid in this plant.'

He was answered by another rank-and-file member who worked on an incentive job: 'Maybe they're paid a little less because they do a little less work!'

A long argument then raged as to what group out-worked the other until finally the president had to call an end to the debate.

After talking with the members one had the feeling that their attitude toward the wage increase itself would be conditioned by the outcome of this dispute between incentive workers and day workers. Thus, how workers interpreted the value of management's wage concession was related to the relative earnings of the two groups.

Differences within the rank-and-file group over incentives are not restricted to negotiations. These are of course the most striking examples of inter-group problems resulting from the existence of different types of wage payment systems in the same plant. During the contract period, itself, union officers have a multitude of decisions requiring them to *choose between* various work groups. As we shall see, many of these do not directly involve grievances against management, although indirectly plant morale and in turn productivity may be affected. In these cases union leaders are faced with the problem of deciding whether or not one group should be placated at the expense of another.

Conflict with adjacent day worker groups

When management introduces an attractive incentive plan that is successful in promoting increased production, some groups of workers feel that their best interests are hurt. These are often the men on day-rated jobs who are just *above* or just *below* the incentive workers in the line of production. If the men on incentive speed up significantly, more material must be handled to supply them or in the finishing stages following their production operation. The day worker laments 'those guys get paid for every little bit extra, but we've got to handle all that increased production at the same old hourly wage rate'.

In one case, for example, a day worker group became so incensed that they attempted to pressure their union leaders into 'inducing' the incentive workers to cut down on production. This presumably would alleviate their sense of injustice.

Day worker groups can respond in other ways as well. In many instances they may demand an incentive plan of their own. Often they believe they should be included in the incentive plan that has affected their work loads, particularly if this is a group bonus system. However, management may not always be aware of this demand, or at least may not be in a position to bargain effectively with the union. There are situations in which the present participants in a group incentive plan have no desire to broaden the base of the plan and include adjacent work groups. They believe, often mistakenly, that the inclusion of more workers diminishes their own share of the incentive, and they encourage their officers to block any attempts at widening the group.

An even more serious conflict is often faced by union leaders. Where there is some question of who is entitled to work on a desirable incentive job, that is, where there is a seniority question complicating the picture, emotions may run high.

Here is an example of another case that caused serious interdepartmental jealousies.

In Department X there were several different types of stamping machines side by side. The 'old stampers', as the men referred to them, were the machines that turned out the bulk of the department's quality product. These were also considered the best day work jobs in the department and paid the highest hourly rate. Understandably, most of the men with top seniority worked on these machines. In recent years the company has been experimenting with a new stamping machine that produced the exact same product as the 'old stampers'. To encourage greater production the company and the union have negotiated an incentive plan for these 'new stampers'. In the eyes of the company and union the plan has been a success. The men have found the rate highly satisfactory and, although their job is evaluated as being in a lower job grade than the 'old stampers', their average weekly earnings exceed those of the top seniority men in the department by about 20 to 25 dollars a week. These men who have the seniority are up in arms claiming that the union should force management to give them the incentive jobs on the 'new stampers'. They have in fact decreased production to enforce their protests that they are not being protected by the contract's seniority clause as the 'oldest men'.

The union has a ticklish problem on its hands. In time the company has promised to develop an incentive plan for the old stamping machines, but in the meantime the men are dissatisfied and out to make trouble. Really what has happened here is that the incentive formula has upset the established social equilibrium of the department. The men on the 'old stampers', being the oldest in the department and having the best jobs, were at the top of the 'social hierarchy', or, as the sociologist would say, they had the highest *status* in the department. The incentive earnings of the new group has thrown all this out of the window. This disruption of normal inter-worker relationships naturally affects productivity.

A similar problem occurs when promotions are involved. The men in the 'stock cleaning room' of a large manufacturing plant had a lucrative incentive plan. When an opening occurred for the job of inspector in that same department, the company was hard pressed to find candidates who would accept, although departmental seniority prevailed. Not only were the inspectors who were on day work bitter that their higher rated job paid *less* than the cleaners, but the men on cleaning rebelled whenever their union officials asked them to 'promote' according to seniority.

Conflict among non-adjacent work areas

Above a case was cited in which two different types of machines were interchangeable on the same operation within a department. There are also situations in which two or more departments are capable of doing roughly the same work. In one large plant that produced a diversity of products a highly skilled 'tool room department' was often called upon to produce the same article turned out by one of the production departments. The latter had an incentive plan. When the plant's general level of production declined, management shifted production of the product in question to the incentive department. The tool room vigorously complained to the union that they were being discriminated against because of a difference in costs. The union was unable to bargain with the company on this question. In the first place satisfying the complaint of the tool room would only hurt the production department. Second, this was a decision involving management prerogatives.

Although the tool room legitimately could not file a grievance to have the work relocated, they proceeded to threaten to strike unless all labor grades in their department were raised! This apparently was a reaction to their frustration over losing important work, but the grievance was processed in terms of 'job changes that had not resulted in new evaluated rates'. Both the union and the company faced the difficult problem of placating the tool room. Their operations were essential to the maintenance of the plant's productivity, and management eventually gave in and granted a new rate schedule. Here day worker–piece worker comparisons affected plant morale and production costs.

Most managements are aware that a 'loose' incentive rate can throw the rate structure completely out of line.[1] The union, too, can have its own 'internal structure' disrupted by rates that are too 'loose' or too 'tight'. Union officers are, of course, more reticent about making this generalization.

In this area of day worker–incentive worker differences we have seen one case in which a lucrative incentive rate upset the normal earnings relationship and, as a result, social relations between two

1. An incentive rate on a particular job is referred to as 'loose' when the workers can easily earn a more than average bonus.

groups in a single department. The same holds true for individual departments. When a 'loose rate' appears in one section of a shop it is not unusual for men in other parts of the plant to begin to worry about what will happen when their jobs are studied for new incentive plans. They reason as the men in Department Y did: 'Those guys over there are killing the job. The union beat its brains out to get the company to give in a little on the incentive, and now the men are going to show it up so when the company gets around to putting an incentive on this job, it'll really be a tight one.'

This rank-and-file logic as to the company's reaction to high earnings in one department working under a given incentive plan may or may not have been correct. More important, however, was the response of these day workers in their union.

Union officers were told in no uncertain terms that they had better 'get those guys in Department X to cut down on their production'. The argument that they were jeopardizing potential incentive earnings in other parts of the plant was bolstered, because indeed the union had struggled with the company to attain this particular rate for the job.

One situation was a classic example of inter-departmental differences. There had actually been a wildcat strike. The men had obtained union support to force the company to improve a particular incentive plan. When management consented to a compromise proposal and the men went back to work, production and earnings soared in the department that had walked out first. Shortly after one could hear murmurings throughout the plant: 'And to think we walked out for those guys. Look what they're earning now! You can be sure it'll never happen again. They're working the rest of us to death.'

Production in that department felt these pressures.

Conflicts among incentive groups

It might be expected that if day-worker groups compare their earnings and efforts with incentive-worker groups, even closer comparisons are made by other incentive workers. If their jobs bear any similarity to those of other incentive workers in the plant they expect to have the same relative 'bonus earnings'.

The most flagrant frustration of these expectations occurred in a defense plant. Management was anxious to secure high out-put in a department that had recently secured an important government contract. They had made many concessions to the union negotiating team and wound up with what many knew was an easy rate to beat. Although this department contained some of the lowest-rated jobs in the plant, the new incentive plan permitted earnings that far exceeded those of other depart-ments. Long-service employees were bristling that young men who had been in the plant for less than a year were earning sub-stantially more than they. One worker, a former union officer, summed up their sentiments: 'Can you imagine how I feel walking into a bar and getting my check cashed next to some youngster who has only been in the plant a few months? He maybe gets thirty dollars more than I do and I've been around here for fifteen years.'

Throughout the plant there were demands that all incentive rates be renegotiated. At the time the company was attempting to establish a new system that would provide better cost control. For many months their efforts to gain union acceptance were fruitless as the men refused to cooperate in the new program.

Of course there were also rank-and-file pressures on union officers to permit the older men to leave their regular jobs and 'bump' some of the young men with the exceptional earnings. In fact, the union faced a whole series of internal squabbles on seniority questions related to such moves as men competed with one another for the right to move into that department. This in turn threatened the company with the loss of many experienced workers who were requesting transfers from other departments.

Several months after these 'loose' rates had gone into effect, the plant was shut down by an unexpected month-long strike. The issues presumably concerned a general wage increase under a contract reopening clause. Nevertheless, some of the hostility aroused during this period of internal unrest contributed to the feelings expressed during the strike.

Obviously in those departments where the incentive rates appear 'tight' in comparison to plant averages, morale is low and men are not motivated to produce at an incentive pace. Such a rate may be considerably worse than having no incentive as the men constantly agitate for a change.

It is well known that various shifts on an incentive job closely compare their daily earning records. As one worker from a shift 'on the high side' expressed it, 'Oh! you know they (the men on the other shift) always think you're hungry, that's all. They're jealous of anything. They think you're killing yourself to turn out all this stuff.'

The case of Department Z in a large mill is a good example of the type of disagreements that occur among shift crews. Three shifts had been turning out about the same quantity until this incident occurred, as described by one of the men in the department, 'On the first shift we put out a little bit more. In fact one day we unexpectedly hit 225. Well, then, the third shift got really sore – they figured we were trying to break the line. So they cut their production even lower than it had been the next day. In fact they got really mad and started producing so little that the company began to complain.'

It was rumored among the workers that management purposely had inflated the first shift's production record to cause trouble and break an informal production limit set by the men. Internal jealousies magnified the third shift's reaction. In time social pressure forced the first shift to reduce its production in line with the other shifts. The level reached was lower than it had been before the incident, for the men had grown increasingly antagonistic toward the company over the 'mistake', and the inter-shift differences this had generated. The rumor may have been false, but the effect was substantial.

Internal conflicts among shifts resulting from a comparison of earnings can have just the opposite effect, at least temporarily. A feud between night and day shifts caused the night shift to *increase* its daily output, in a casting department. This increase was a means of expressing their contempt for the day shift. Since earnings and of course production are recorded by management, this group thought it could embarrass the day shift by a substantial increase in its earnings and production. Management obviously benefited by this dispute.

Such benefits, however, are usually of short-run duration for the instability of such situations leads eventually to an unpleasant aftermath. In this case, for example, resentment built up until the shifts subtly began sabotaging each other's efforts.

Finally, there are those cases in which one incentive department initiates a *slowdown* that affects another group. Here an attempt by one department to exert pressure on management, because of some dissatisfaction over incentive payments, decreases the amount of materials available for another incentive group. This in turn hurts its opportunity to earn a satisfactory bonus. Where the two departments are not in agreement over the objectives involved, the one which feels unjustly deprived of its bonus is likely to request the union to settle the case as quickly as possible. Sometimes this might even involve 'calling the whole plant out'.

Maintaining relative earnings

These examples of inter-group comparisons in the area of incentives illustrate two principles. In the first place, relative earnings are as important if not more important than the absolute level of earnings. Work groups within a plant – whether they comprise men on the same machine or shift or in the same department – are always comparing their working conditions, their hours, and earnings with other workers in the same plant. Where for one reason or another the results are unfavorable, or the activities of one group pose a threat to another, there is usually an immediate reaction. Management often feels this reaction, in terms of changes in the level of productivity, quality or costs, even when it is not familiar with the cause.

Secondly, management retains the responsibility for maintaining equitable 'earnings relationships' among various work groups in the plants. This is not because management prerogatives are involved, nor because union officials are unwilling to exercise the requisite leadership.

Often, in fact, the union does face a situation in which two or more groups within its own ranks are in conflict over incentives. No written grievance can be directed against the company, for the issue is essentially between the members themselves and the problem posed for the union is a difficult one.

Management can take the attitude: 'If the union officers were sufficiently courageous they would come right out and take a stand on some of these things themselves, even if some workers did get hurt!' The implication is that the union is too politically oriented. What must be remembered, however, is that the union leader is a 'politician' insofar as he represents the entire bargaining unit. In such a position of responsibility it is difficult to express a judgement which says that one group is right and one is wrong.

Management people may think they have enough problems of their own without worrying about those of their local union. Nevertheless, they need to consider the internal stability of the union organization in the development of incentives, for, as we have seen, social disequilibrium at the rank-and-file level may result in irrational grievances and strikes.

It seems apparent that management must take the initiative in maintaining a relationship among the weekly earnings levels for various jobs that will be seen as equitable by the men in the shop. Over time, workers come to expect a certain relationship, and if this is drastically altered by incentive bonuses, the results may be less favorable than could be predicted by evaluating the mechanics of the plan. As Professors Pigors and Myers have concluded:

Wage differentials are a mark of social status in the factory organization. If they do not correspond with the relative significance of jobs as employees view them, the workers' sense of justice is outraged (Pigors and Myers, 1950, p. 255).

Further where incentive earnings are obviously out of line, this may be an advance signal of a potential sore spot in the plant's industrial relations.

Even when management is concerned about the general problem of employee communications, it can be assured that earnings are quickly transmitted throughout the shop. In developing incentive proposals for a particular job, then, the entire plant must be considered a social unit.

Reference

PIGORS, P., and MYERS, C. A. (1950), *Personnel Administration*, McGraw-Hill, 2nd edn.

6 William Foote Whyte

Economic Incentives and Human Relations

William Foote Whyte, ' Economic incentives and human relations',
Harvard Business Review, vol. 30, no. 2, 1952.

How can a system of economic incentives be made to pay off in
higher productivity?

Executives, personnel men, and industrial engineers are coming
increasingly to recognize that money is not the sole answer to the
problem of worker motivation.[1] As the economic man theory is
discarded, there may be a tendency to go to the other extreme, to
assume that human relations is *the* thing, that money hardly
counts at all.

Many people are arguing the question today: Which is more
important to workers, economic incentives or human relations?
In that form the question is meaningless and unanswerable. Men
are interested in money. They are also concerned about their relations with other men. Offer them a financial reward for behavior
that damages their relations with other men, and you can hardly
expect them to respond with enthusiasm.

The issue then is not: economic incentives or human relations.
The problem is to fit economic incentives and human relations
effectively together, to *integrate* them. In other words, the pulling
power of the money reward will be strongly affected by the pattern of human relations into which it is introduced.

Human relations in rate administration

The problems of applying incentive rates in my complex factory
are so many and difficult that we cannot weigh the effect of economic incentives without giving serious consideration to problems of administering the incentive system. A review of some of
the common problems in this area will show that practically every

1. Roethlisberger and Dickson (1939) have provided the classic study
which, among other things, lays low *economic man*.

rate-setting problem has an important human relations aspect.

How are rates set in the first place? It is now well recognized that rate setting at best is a combination of some measurement and some judgement or guesswork. Where judgement enters in, we are necessarily looking at the relations among people.

We are all familiar with the allowances for fatigue and personal time that are estimated for incentive jobs, and we recognize that these are based more on traditional concepts than on any scientific standards.

When we consider allowances for percentage of efficiency of the operator who is being measured, we run into more serious difficulty. In many plants such allowances are made. The time-and-motion-study man observes a worker for a period of time. He checks the amount of production and the time spent, but then he asks himself: Is this worker producing at about the average speed that should be expected of a man on this job? Perhaps the time-and-motion-study man concludes that the worker is not trying as hard as he should, or is even deliberately holding back, and accordingly estimates an efficiency of 80 or 90 per cent. The rate will then be set not on what the worker has actually produced but on the basis of what he should have produced had he been working at 100 per cent.

In one plant I studied, the workers were convinced that management never rated their time-study performance at 100 per cent but was always making allowances that would justify an expectation of higher performance. In still another plant covered in an unpublished study by Donald Roy, the workers firmly believed that it was impossible to make a bonus on a job unless they had been timed on that job at slower feeds and speeds than they would be able to use after the rate was set.

Where these beliefs prevail, the workers make every possible effort to slow down and add unnecessary motions while they are being studied. The rate setters who know that the workers are trying to fool them must then seek to make an allowance for the amount that they are being fooled. The question then is: Can the worker fool the time-study man more than he thinks he is being fooled? Or as the workers in one plant put it, 'You've got to screw him, or he'll screw you'.

This problem of allowances for efficiency would be serious

enough even if the time-and-motion-study people had unlimited time in which to make their studies. In practice we usually find that, while there may be certain jobs which will be run for a long period and thus afford the time-and-motion-study men ample opportunity to make their studies, there are many jobs which involve such short runs that extensive studies are too costly to undertake, as well as not being feasible in the time allowed. Rates set for such jobs are particularly likely to be subject to the distortions of worker efforts to fool the rate setter and rate-setter efforts to compensate for the fooling process.

Problem of rate changes

The problem of rate changing must be recognized as a very real one and not simply the result of worker misunderstandings.

Workers expect management to revise upward a rate that has been proved to be too tight. Can managers similarly expect workers to accept the downward adjustment in a rate that has been set too loose? The *Supervisor's Guide to General Electric Job Information* is interesting on this point. Note the following paragraphs:

The fact that rate setters sometimes have been wrong and rates have had to be cut should be faced squarely by the supervisors.

No rate setter is perfect. However, it must be pointed out that these occasional mistakes are made on the up side as well as on the down side. No employee thinks it is wrong to adjust a rate upward when a mistake on the down side has been made.

There should be just as fair recognition of the necessity and right to make a downward adjustment in a rate as an upward adjustment [p. 51].

This statement has an eminently fair and reasonable sound. It certainly seems just as fair to change rates set too high as it is to change rates set too low. But in practice how does management discover that a 'mistake' has been made in rate setting? Workers have the impression that this discovery will take place only if they turn out exceptionally high earnings on the job. In fact, I know of cases where the industrial engineers were under instructions to take a new look at any job showing earnings over a certain figure. As to whether rate changes were then put into effect the record is not clear, that the regular appearance of these incentive engineers to check unusually high earnings could hardly have failed to create the impression that it was dangerous to go beyond a certain quota.

If we move from possible 'mistakes' in the rate-setting process to consider changes in job methods and content, the picture becomes still more complicated. Most union contracts provide for changes in rates based on changes in job methods and/or content. But we usually find the qualifying adjective of 'substantial' or 'major' describing the change. It seems generally agreed that management should not be allowed to change a rate on the basis of a trivial change in the job. If this were allowed then management could make some trifling change in any job as an excuse for setting a new rate. In fact, I have heard workers in some plants charge that this was exactly the excuse that management manufactured and used.

If we pass over a few cases of sharp practice where changes seem clearly to be introduced in order to justify rate cutting, we still come face to face with major questions of judgement. When does a change become a 'major' or a 'substantial' change? It is obvious that two men of equal goodwill and sincerity can hold different opinions on this point for many cases.

There is the further troublesome problem of a series of minor changes. It often happens in industry that a job will be modified step by step over a period of months or even years. No single change in itself would qualify as 'major' or 'substantial', and yet the sum total of these modifications might change a rate that was average in earnings to one that was very loose. At what point in the series of minor changes should management be allowed to intervene with a new rate?

Even if all parties agree that the change in the job is so substantial that a new rate must be set, the problem is still far from a solution. Let us assume that the old job was yielding incentive earnings of 50 per cent over base pay. Let us assume that the average earnings figure on other incentive jobs is only 30 per cent above base. In setting the new rate for this group of workers, should the rate setter aim at a 30 per cent or a 50 per cent bonus?

The workers on the job and their union officers will naturally argue that the new rate should provide earnings equivalent to those under the old one. The management may well feel that the old rate was out of line with the general plant picture and that earnings on the new rate of 30 per cent above base are quite adequate. So even if we assume that the rate setter would be able to predict accurately the earnings possibilities of the job – and we have seen how risky this assumption is – there is no easy answer to the question of what earnings he should aim to make possible.

Worker sentiment and rate acceptance

If X argues that a certain desk is three feet long and Y argues that it is four feet long, it is a simple matter to test the statement of each by the operation of measurement with a ruler. We can then tell whether X or Y is correct or by how much each of them is in error. We can do this because the question is purely a factual one and the operation for determining the answer is one that is universally accepted in our culture. We recognize that it is futile to argue such differences of opinion when the measuring operation provides the answer.

Some incentive engineers wish that people would accept their measuring operations in the same way. But more sophisticated engineers, and others who are familiar with these problems, recognize that the operation of measuring the length of a desk and the operation of measuring work performance for rate setting present drastically different problems. In the rate-setting case, we operate with a ruler that is flexibly adjusted to a variety of allowances, and we find little agreement as to what this ruler is and how it shall be used. At almost every point in the rate-setting process, we come upon elements of personal judgement that cannot be disguised as simple questions of fact.

This does not mean that the labor–management conflict on rates is insoluble. We need not conclude that judgements and opinions can never be accepted as a basis for people's working together. In fact, in any sort of organization people must learn to adjust themselves to the opinions and judgements of others. We must ask, however, under what conditions the judgements of one party in labor–management relations will be accorded reasonable acceptance by the other party.

If we put the problem in this way, it becomes clear that conflict over incentives cannot be resolved simply through better training and skill in the rate-setting process. The elements of judgement are so large that, where there is mistrust between the parties, it inevitably follows that the union officers and workers will not accept rates set by management as having been figured in good faith.

It is unrealistic to expect a condition of such skill on the part of rate setters and such mutual trust that all of the rates set by management will be accepted as reasonable by the workers. But unless there is a widespread feeling through the plant that most of the rates are fair, we cannot expect the workers to go out and produce at anything approximating their abilities. When they distrust management, they will hold back at a certain safe quota point on loose rates, and they will hold back much further on tight rates in order to fight against management for a change in rates.

Worker response to the incentive system thus depends not only upon the actual financial rewards but upon the setting of interpersonal sentiments in which these rewards are offered. Where mistrust between the parties persists, worker response to financial incentive will be halfhearted.

Illustrative cases

The relationship between worker–management sentiments and response to the incentive system may be illustrated from an actual case[2] the main points of which can be briefly summarized as follows:

The case came up at a time of intense antagonism between management and union in the Inland Steel Container Company's Chicago plant.

It involved a grievance concerning a change in rates on two jobs on a particular punch press. This punch press blanked out covers from sheets of steel to be used on the pail line. When the job was first run, there was a tendency for the cover pieces to stick to the machine; the operator then had to tap them loose, which slowed up the machine considerably. One of the workers on the job connected an air hose to a compressed-air connection so that the hose would blow air upon the covers from above to push them loose onto an inclined plane out of the machine.

This change had been in effect for some time without any change in rates when a time-study man observed it and consulted the operator about it. The time-study man reported the matter to the engineering department, which installed a metal pipe to blow

2. For full details see my argument (Whyte, 1951, p. 269).

air on the underside of the punch press. Management claimed that this was a major improvement in machine and method justifying a revision in the piecework rate, and the price was thereby reduced by 9 cents a thousand pieces on one job and by 11 cents a thousand pieces on another. The worker in question and all the union people were incensed at this change. One of them said, 'They held us up on that just as if they had stuck a gun at us. That's what I thought then and I still think so.'

The union officers charged that management had cut the rate on a punch press job in violation of the contract. They seized upon this grievance as representing the most outrageous example of unprincipled and oppressive management action. The case was argued heatedly through the first three steps of the grievance procedure.

The union claimed that blowing the air from the bottom instead of from the top was simply an excuse for rate cutting and was therefore not justified. Furthermore, the original idea had come from a worker and not from management, and the job already had been run with an air hose for some time.

Management argued that the rubber air hose never worked properly and had been disconnected for some time before the metal air hose was put in the new position. Therefore, this constituted a major change, which justified a re-study of the job. Furthermore, management claimed that earnings on this job (which was run very seldom, anyway) had increased since the rate change. In the over-heated situation which then prevailed, no one on the union side would pay any serious attention to these management arguments.

It was perfectly clear by the time of the third step in the grievance procedure (the personnel manager's decision) that top management would stand by the new rate. The contract provided that rate grievances were not subject to arbitration. The workers took this to mean that management could cut rates anywhere in the plant at any time with no recourse open to the union. The executives recognized these fears but felt they were unjustified, since top management was firmly opposed to rate cutting. The union officers did not anticipate any wholesale cutting of rates, but it then seemed possible that management might take an inch here and an inch there until the whole rate structure was in jeopardy.

The fourth step of the grievance procedure called for a meeting of top management with the international representative and the grievance committee of the union. Since the union was reassigning its international representatives at the time this grievance was being processed, there was a delay of more than six months between the third and fourth steps of the procedure. Within this period, union and management met together to negotiate a new agreement. Both sides went in expecting a strike, and the negotiations teetered on the brink of collapse through eleven tense meetings over a period of three months. Finally they not only avoided the strike but worked their way through to establish the basis of a harmonious adjustment.

Following the signing of the new agreement, the parties met together to discuss certain common problems and to clear up a backlog of top-level grievances. At this point, 22 grievances were disposed of in less than an hour, with adjustments being made on both sides. Here the air-hose case which had been such a center of controversy reached its end in two minutes of discussion. The management representative simply cited figures to show that earnings on the job were higher following the rate change, and the international representative and his committee then immediately agreed to withdraw the grievance.

What had happened between the third and fourth steps in the procedure? In that interval the facts and figures of rate setting had not changed. But men's emotions are just as 'real' as facts and figures, and it was the emotions that had changed decisively.

We can understand this case only if we view it symbolically. Before the adjustment of relationships, the air hose had been one of the key symbols of the conflict. For the workers and union leaders the case had symbolized the hatred and distrust they bore toward management. It was evidence to them that management was unfair and ruthless. So long as they continued to believe that management was unfair and ruthless, the case could have no other meaning to them, no matter what logical arguments were presented to them. But as soon as relations were reorganized so that the hatred and distrust were beginning to be dissipated, there was no longer an emotional need to hold on to that symbol of conflict. It then became possible to treat the case in terms of facts and figures, and by that time it was hardly worth bothering about.

This statement brings us back to the observation made by one of the pioneers of scientific management, Frank Gilbreth (1913):

It should be stated here emphatically that there is nothing that can permanently bring about results from scientific management and the economics that it is possible to effect by it unless the organization is supported by the hearty cooperation of the men. Without this there is no scientific management.[3]

At that time the incentive engineers schooled in scientific management were implicitly assuming that the 'hearty cooperation of the men' existed and that the problem was to work out adequate systems of measuring effort and productivity. Experience has subsequently demonstrated the validity of Gilbreth's point, that a system of economic incentives will work badly or well according to whether it fits into a situation of worker–management cooperation or is injected into an atmosphere of conflict.

This suggests that no mere refinements in traditional incentive engineering techniques will cope with the problem of eliciting cooperation. We need first to determine the conditions under which cooperation can be stimulated before we can fit our incentive systems to those conditions.

Incentives and organizational structure

The harmonious relations upon which effective financial incentives depend are determined in part by the way in which the incentive engineering activities are fitted into the pattern of human relations within management and between management and the union. This may be illustrated by another aspect of labor–management experience at the Inland Steel Container Company's Chicago plant:

During the period of union–management conflict in this plant the industrial engineer had been free to move about the various departments and make any studies or observations that interested him. He set rates on new jobs without the approval of the departmental foreman and without any consultation with the union. When the industrial engineer judged that job content had been sufficiently changed, he made new studies and instituted a revised rate. Under this procedure, the rate-setting activity was the focus of much of the union–management conflict.

3. I am indebted to Georges Friedmann for drawing my attention to this.

As the over-all relations between union and management improved, certain important changes in the rate-setting activity were introduced. Under the new procedures the industrial engineer must have the written permission of the general production supervisor before he enters a production department for the purpose of making any studies or observations. When he enters the department, he must first show this authorization to the foreman and to the union steward and explain to them the purpose of his visit. Before the new rate or rate change becomes official, it must have the approval of the foreman and the general production supervisor. The rate is discussed informally with the steward before it is put into effect. If the steward feels that the rate is unfair, management has the opportunity to take this union point of view into consideration before making a final decision.

The union's approval is not required, but the management officers recognize that they have much less trouble with a rate when there is an opportunity for prior discussion than when the union can only be heard through the filing of a grievance. A grievance is, of course, an appeal against a management decision. Especially in the rate-setting field, it presents awkward problems for the executive who often faces the choice of standing by a rate that workers believe to be unfair or of reversing his industrial engineer and running the risk of discrediting the whole rate-setting activity. Management and union people alike believe that these new procedures on rate setting and revision are great improvements. The conflict over rates has virtually disappeared. Slowdowns to exert pressure on rates have ceased, and productivity has risen to record high levels. (Whyte, 1951, p. 269.)

What lesson can we draw from this case? The particular procedures involved here might not fit the needs of other situations, but the general conclusion is clear: only when the rate-setting activity is *effectively integrated* into the pattern of supervision and union–management relations will workers respond strongly to financial incentives.

Financial incentives and job evaluation

We see another aspect of the integration problem when we examine factories having both piece-rate and job-evaluation systems.

In recent years personnel men have been devoting untold man-hours of effort to setting up systems of job evaluation. This has involved a careful study of all the jobs in a given plant, an assessing of the degrees of responsibility, skill, difficulty, and importance of the jobs so that they may be rated and compared to each other. Great effort has gone into arranging an orderly scale of jobs and setting wage rates so that the jobs that are higher on the scale will pay the worker more money than those at lower points.

When the job-evaluation program upsets traditional relations among jobs, workers and union officers protest, of course. They may object to the methods used by management in job evaluation, they may object to certain of the conclusions drawn, and they may express a desire to participate in the evaluation process. However, all these are objections to the means and methods used, and not to the general objective. Workers and union officers would agree that it is important to have an orderly arrangement of jobs so that the individual can place himself in the social system of the plant. They also believe firmly that the jobs which are evaluated higher should pay more than the jobs which are evaluated lower.

It is important to recognize that workers, union officers, and management are not dealing here with a technical problem alone. The decisions made regarding the arrangement and relative values of the various jobs tend to place the jobs in terms of a prestige scale in the plant. We are talking about what the sociologists would refer to as a *status system.* All our work in sociology suggests that the status system of an organization is an exceedingly tough organism. It is tough in the sense that changes are not readily introduced into it, and also in the sense that when changes are introduced, serious repercussions may take place.

Passing over for now the many difficulties that may arise in developing and installing a job-evaluation program, let us look at our basic problem in terms of a simplified example:

Let us assume that management has developed a job-evaluation program involving labor grades I through X. Each job in the plant has been assigned to one of these labor grades, and wage rates have been set accordingly. Let us assume furthermore that, while there are minor disagreements regarding certain jobs, on the whole the system of job evaluation is in accord with the viewpoints of workers and union officers concerning the prestige or relative values of the jobs.

So far all is smooth sailing, but at this point management decides to introduce individual and group incentives on various jobs. According to the nature of the jobs, there are certain ones to which economic incentives can readily be applied, whereas there are others (for example, service and maintenance activities) where no measurement of production is possible by conventional methods, and therefore no incentive rates can be set.

Let us look then at Department X where there are men working on jobs in labor grade V and on jobs in labor grade VI – and the men are in close contact with each other. Now suppose the jobs in grade V are put on incentive, whereas the jobs in grade VI cannot be. Then suddenly we have a situation where men on job V are earning more, and perhaps substantially more, than men on the jobs in the higher classification.

Or suppose that jobs in both grade V and grade VI are placed on incentive, but the rate on job V proves much looser than the rate on job VI. Here again, the men in the lower classification are earning substantially more than their fellows at the higher level.

What happens in such circumstances? I have noted all of the following reactions in a variety of situations:

1. The men in labor grade VI become highly antagonistic toward management since they feel that it is not fair for them to receive less pay than the men who are below them on the job-evaluation scale and in status. This may also lead to political conflict within the union in which the grade V and grade VI men are arrayed against each other.

2. Men in labor grade V do not want to be promoted to jobs in grade VI. This may create difficulties for the company in manning the positions in grade VI.

3. If men in grade V are dependent upon the men in grade VI for cooperation in the work process, this cooperation is likely to deteriorate. In some cases, we find the men in grade VI having to do additional work because of the increased production of the incentive workers. If this additional work is to be done without extra compensation, the men in grade VI raise complaints with the union and with management.

4. Where the jobs in grade VI are not on incentive, the grade VI workers try to pressure management into some indirect sharing arrangement in the increased earnings of the incentive workers.

Where the men in grade VI are on incentive but have a much tighter rate than the men in grade V, the grade VI men will do their utmost to pressure management into loosening their rate. The pressure may take the form of slowdowns or perhaps even work stoppages.

Are the problems described in this hypothetical case exceptional? On the contrary, in the plants I have studied they seem to be everyday problems. Such problems inevitably arise when an individual or group incentive program is introduced into a complex industrial plant. Sophisticated management people learn to expect some of these difficulties and beyond that can only hope that the disturbances will be scattered about the plant and that the disaffected employees will not be in a strategic position to tie up the entire plant.

We have here, it seems to me, a remarkable paradox. Management brings to bear all the knowledge and techniques of modern personnel management in order to develop a system of job evaluation. On the other hand, management brings to bear all the knowledge and techniques of industrial engineering in order to develop an incentive program. The two systems then run head on into each other with all the attendant confusion and friction I have described.

The conflict between incentive rates and job evaluation seems to reflect, in part, a lack of co-ordination within the management structure. Job evaluation is often handled by the personnel or industrial relations department, whereas incentive rates are usually set by an industrial engineering group that fits into some other department. Thus we have not only competing systems but competing management groups applying the competing systems. The confusion and conflict arising from this condition are difficult to exaggerate. Many executives and personnel men are well aware of these difficulties, but solutions have been hard to find.

Conclusion

This conclusion takes us back to our starting point. Systems of financial incentives in industry today probably yield a net gain in productivity, but most of them fail to release more than a small fraction of the energy and intelligence workers have to give to their jobs. Even when the financial incentive yields higher productivity, it may also generate such conflicts within the organization that we must wonder whether the gains are worth the costs.

What can management do to meet this problem? Certainly I can offer no neat 'packaged' solution. I can only seek to point out a more effective way of approaching the problem.

The setting of incentive rates has been traditionally considered a *technical* engineering problem. When difficulties arise, it has been customary to blame them upon failure to do the job according to accepted, *technical* standards. Now at last perceptive managers, engineers, and personnel men are recognizing that the problem has important human relations aspects that cannot be resolved through the enforcement of any technical standards. But all too often the insights and analyses of human relations come in only to mop up the spilled milk of the incentive engineering activity. At this late stage even the most skillful applier of human relations knowledge will be hard pressed to make a constructive contribution.

Management should recognize that financial incentives are both a technical engineering and a human relations problem. The two aspects are so intimately intertwined that it is impossible to separate them in action. Therefore management should not be satisfied with a planned engineering program and a catch-as-catch-can human relations program. These activities should be planned together and integrated in action.

Management might also consider the desirability of adopting a more experimental approach to the incentive problem. American management has been noted for its daring innovations in technology and applied science, but in the field of incentives most managements have been content to refine and polish systems that were devised many years ago. Variations are introduced, to be sure, but only a few managements have struck out with experimental boldness to develop a more effective integration of financial incentives and human relations.[4]

4. For experiments toward developing new types of incentive programs, note particularly the work of Joseph Scanlon of the Massachusetts Institute of Technology. For a popular account, see Davenport (1950). The Scanlon plans should not be accepted as panaceas but should be considered important experiments deserving careful study. (See also Whyte, 1947 and 1951, p. 269.)

Finally, the management that attempts to re-examine its incentive program and develop a new approach needs to focus research on worker reactions to financial incentives. In-plant studies suggest that the field is full of confusion. When an incentive system works badly, management explanations are usually a combination of half-truths and folklore. Even when a system works well, the explanations are likely to be so misleading as to make it impossible to generalize from one case to the next. If we are to have generalizable knowledge in this field, we shall need more searching analysis of worker reactions to incentive systems.

If financial incentives are to be used in the future with full effectiveness, management decisions must be based upon research and experimentation designed to devise an integrated program of incentives and human relations. (See also Whyte, 1947 and 1951, p. 269.)

References

DAVENPORT, R. W. (1950), 'Enterprise for everyman', *Fortune*, vol. 41, no. 1, p. 55.

GILBRETH, F. (1913), 'Units, methods and devices of measurement under scientific management', *J. polit. Econ.*, no. 21, p. 623.

ROETHLISBERGER, F. J., and DICKSON, W. J. (1939), *Management and the Worker*, Harvard University Press.

WHYTE, W. F. (1947), 'Union-management cooperation: a Toronto case', *Appl. Anthrop.*, vol. 6, no. 3, p. 1.

WHYTE, W. F. (1951), 'The case of the Bundy Tubing Company', in Schuyler Dean Hoslett (ed.), *Human Factors in Management*, revised edn, Harper & Row, p. 269.

7 Tom Lupton

On the Shop Floor: Output and Earnings

Excerpt from Tom Lupton, *On the Shop Floor*, Pergamon Press, 1963, pp. 170–83.

The workers at Jay's described their systematic manipulation of the incentive scheme as the 'fiddle'. From my observations of their behaviour, and from many discussions of the fiddle which I overheard or participated in, I concluded that the following advantages were claimed by the workers for the 'fiddle':

1. It was regarded as a defence against rate cutting.
2. It was thought to stabilize earnings.
3. It was seen as a protection from the effects of management shortcomings.
4. It gave a measure of control over the relationship between effort and reward.

I have myself hinted that the 'fiddle' was also a source of psychological satisfaction. It gave the workers a sense of being in control of the situation in a battle of wits with the boss. However, no worker explicitly claimed this advantage for it.

The claims made for the 'fiddle' by the workers at Jay's resemble the explanations which the workers in the Bank Wiring Room gave to justify their adherence to a norm of output which fell below the 'reasonable' expectations of the management. But the workers in the Bank Wiring Room placed less emphasis on protection from management shortcomings, probably because the problems of work flow in the Bank Wiring Room were more tractable. As I pointed out in chapter 2 [not included here], the Bank Wiring Room investigators were not satisfied that the workers' explanations really showed that they were controlling the situation consciously in pursuit of economic interests. The investigators suggested that the norm was the outcome of a social process by which the group adjusted its internal relationships and its relationship to the social and technical environment. The explanations came afterwards to justify a situation which was satisfying, but which had not been consciously brought about. One reason why this interpretation was favoured as against the 'economic man' interpretation was the demonstrable lack of understanding of the incentive scheme on the part of the workers. Surely workers who did not understand the incentive scheme could not manipulate it to serve their own economic interests. It was also shown that in fact the behaviour of the workers was, in some instances, plainly detrimental to their stated economic interests.

I do not think that the behaviour of the workers at Jay's permits this kind of interpretation. It is true that not all the workers I met at Jay's were familiar with all the complexities of the incentive scheme. Most of them were unable to give an accurate description of the procedure followed by rate-fixers in calculating rates from 'raw' time-study data. Few could explain exactly how the productivity bonus was calculated, and only three workers in the small transformer section could give me an accurate and complete description of the scheme. But to say that most workers in the shop did not have what Shimmin (1960) has called 'formal' understanding of the scheme is not necessarily to mean that they were therefore incapable of turning it to what they considered their best advantage. Most workers had what Shimmin calls 'functional' understanding. That is to say, they knew from experience how their own efforts were related to the cash rewards the scheme offered, and they had learned a procedure for booking work which seemed to offer them advantages. In her own study, Shimmin tested functional understanding by comparing workers' predictions of the bonus due in the pay packet with the actual bonus found there. The workers at Jay's were not only able to predict their bonus earnings, in many cases they were able each week to decide, within certain limits, what they would be.

The three workers who fully understood the scheme, Syd Smales, Baldy, and Bill Madden, were always ready to give advice, but their advice was seldom sought since all the workers understood the procedure for booking in work, and knew what the results would be in terms of cash reward, even if, as was obvious in most instances, they were unable to trace in detail the process from action to final consequence. Every worker in Jay's kept a notebook in which he recorded the jobs which had been allocated to him, the time which he took to complete them, and the time which he booked to them. All the workers knew how much time they had 'in hand'. They also knew the formula for translating time saved into percentage bonus, and from percentage to cash. In fact, this information was provided by the rate-fixing department to assist workers to understand the scheme. But few workers could say how the formulae were arrived at, and some needed help with their calculations. Yet I think that the workers had enough understanding of the scheme to operate the 'fiddle' as a rational means to certain economic ends regarded as desirable. One does not need to have detailed knowledge of such a scheme to manipulate it. It is enough to be able to see that certain actions lead to certain consequences, and by experience to learn to act in such a way as to produce results desirable to oneself.

But if I am to show that the workers were behaving like economic men, it is not enough merely to indicate that they had a sufficient knowledge of the incentive scheme. Nor is it enough to demonstrate, as I shall attempt presently, that the advantages claimed for the 'fiddle' were actually gained. Neither of these are, in themselves, proofs that the fiddle was deliberately designed and practised to gain the advantages it gives. It is still possible to argue that the 'fiddle' was a customary pattern of group behaviour, which had arisen spontaneously from the process of adjustment of internal and external relationships. It could then be said that the advantages claimed were merely explanations to justify behaviour and relationships which were valued.

I do not wish to argue here that this explanation is entirely inappropriate for the situation at Jay's. One would imagine that some of the processes by which, in adapting itself to the environment, the group came to develop the 'fiddle', were not planned as means to economic ends, although it is now impossible to demonstrate this. But I think I can show that the fiddle is in practice a rational means to ends which are valued, and that it works. I would argue that, in social adjustment, a process of trial and error can be discerned in which alternative modes are tried as new situations emerge, always provided that there is 'social space' within the management control system to make this possible. Some alternatives are rejected because they offer disadvantages. That they do indeed offer such-and-such disadvantages is part of the heritage of the group, and this knowledge is passed on to new incumbents of roles within the group. The modes of behaviour which seem to offer advantages become customary and routine and their value is unquestioned so long as they give good results. It is not necessary to know why custom works to one's advantage, it is enough to know that it does. It is also useful if one can point to the deviant to show the consequences of not behaving thus, and it is usually possible to do this. And, as I have shown, there were in the Jay's situation workers who could explain the why, as well as the how of the 'fiddle', and in doing so, support its efficacy as a rational means to certain desired ends. I have already shown, in my discussion of the mechanisms of the 'fiddle', that the workers discussed its details as if they themselves saw it as a means to certain desired ends. I shall now go on to show that, in fact, it worked like this, and to show the consequences of deviation. This, taken together with the argument in previous chapters, is, I think, weighty support, for the view not only that the 'fiddle' is objectively speaking a rational and sensible adjustment to the situation, but also that it is regarded and operated as such by the workers. I shall show also that they were prepared to alter the method of manipulation to meet new conditions and that this was done in the light of the rationale of the 'fiddle'.

But before I go on to examine some figures of output and earnings, I point out that my approach to my material, although superficially similar, differs in many important ways from the approach of the Bank Wiring Room observers. It seems to me as if their reasoning is essentially deductive, at least at a crucial stage in the argument. It is as if they had started off with certain propositions, gleaned from sociology and social anthropology, about the way in which groups adapt their internal structure and their relationship with their external environment so as to achieve security, stability, and survival. From this it would seem that they proceeded to say: On the basis of these propositions one would expect to find in any group certain norms of conduct and sanctions to ensure conformity. This they found in the Bank

Wiring Room. It was then argued that this must be the outcome of social adjustment. The question then arose whether this was a conscious and rational process. And, since the workers did not understand the incentive scheme, since they evinced no open hostility to and suspicion of management, and since, as it appeared, they had no previous experience of rate-cutting it looked as if it was not. Thus the proposition that the adjustment of the small group to its environment is largely an unconscious process seems to be supported. I myself have started, not by accepting certain propositions about human groups, but with the human beings themselves. I have tried to see what seems to emerge if one examines behaviour in the light of internal relationships and external influences. And it seems to me that in both the Wye and the Jay case, the logic of the field data itself is that behaviour is the outcome of adjustment to the circumstances such that certain valued ends are achieved and that behaviour will be constantly adjusted and custom changed in response to changes in the environment or in the structure of the group. I shall elaborate this point in my general conclusion to the two studies. I make it briefly here because it seems to me that a too close preoccupation with general propositions may hinder understanding of particular situations. I would prefer to see, at this stage in the development of the subject, an emphasis on the collection of 'raw' detailed field material, within the roughest of frameworks. The attempt to discern the logic, or lack of it, in the material, is the path of development, as I see it. To build elaborate models or to state wide and general propositions may be a hindrance.

Having digressed somewhat I now go on to show, by reference to earnings figures, that the 'fiddle' seemed to work at Jay's. That is, it was a good way for workers to get what they said they valued – a stable relationship between effort and reward in terms of their conception of a 'fair day's work', stable earnings from week to week, defence against rate-cutting and against management shortcomings or the influence of factors outside the control of workers and managers.

Figure 1 illustrates the stabilizing effect of the 'fiddle'. The first graph shows the bonus percentages booked by Claude Bissett, the job spoiler, and by Simsey, a conformer. For all except seven of the 25 weeks, Simsey declared bonus of between 90 per cent and 100 per cent, and a maximum range of bonus variation between about 50 per cent and 120 per cent. Bissett's bonus figures fluctuated wildly and his range of variation was between zero and 254 per cent. The effect on average hourly earnings is clearly shown in the second graph. It is clear that conformity paid in stability of earnings. I must point out that this graph is *not* open to alternative interpretation that for the most part Simsey had jobs issued to him which were 'reasonably' rated and allowed savings of time equivalent to a consistent bonus rate of 90 per

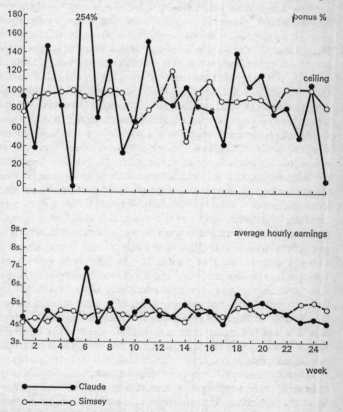

Figure 1 Comparison of 'job spoiler' and 'conformer'

cent to 100 per cent, or on the other hand, that Bissett was allocated an assorted bag of loosely and tightly rated jobs. I have already mentioned that, in fact, Simsey and his mate Tom Hendy, were at war with the foreman over his work allocation policy precisely because they claimed that the 'good' work went elsewhere, and they were given the 'shit' as they put it. Bissett, on the other hand, although he was not said to be unduly favoured, was known to have his share of 'good' work. I would say that the differences between the two graphs can be almost entirely explained by the fact that Bissett booked 'straight' and Simsey 'cross-booked'. There is no doubt, for example, that the most marked of the fluctuations in Bissett's earnings were due to incomplete work. In week 5, for example, I know that he worked for 47·8 hours on piecework (this was an overtime week). The fact that he did not earn bonus that week is entirely due to the fact that he did not finish the job that week. All the bonus he earned that week was therefore booked in the following week, and this helps to account for his inflated bonus earnings in the following week. Incomplete work was a difficulty which affected the medium-size erectors much more than their colleagues on the small transformers. Some of the medium transformers took over a week to erect so it was much more difficult to 'spread' bonus. It was easier on small transformers, and Simsey, faced with incomplete work, would no doubt have booked the work as complete and finished it the following week. But even for the small-transformer workers there were times of great difficulty. For example, a run of tight jobs would exhaust the 'kitty' and lead to an eventual slump in bonus. It was, therefore, not always possible for the conformer to keep his earnings completely stable. And sometimes, from choice, a conformer would book in high times saved from a run of loose jobs so as to compensate for a slump, and in doing so go above the customary bonus 'ceiling'. But this was not often done, as we shall see. I stress the point that if Simsey had 'booked straight' his earnings would have fluctuated very much more than they in fact did, possibly as much as Bissett's, and that because there were so many variables to control if perfect stability were to be achieved, all the workers' earnings showed some fluctuations and on occasions all of them exceeded the bonus ceiling. But not often. The general rule that to book over 100 per cent was to invite rate-cutting was generally observed.

I have already said that there were so many factors in addition to effort expended, which affected the workers' capacity to earn, that the attempt to control the effects of the operation of these factors – 'the fiddle' – fell short of complete success. I go on now to examine the earnings of a selected number of workers to try to show, where possible in detail, which particular factors were operating at any one time, and what steps were taken to offset their effects. But first I summarize the main factors affecting the capacity to earn.

1. *Waiting time*. Inevitably, there were interruptions in the flow of work. There was little the workers could do to control this directly. They could keep several jobs on hand in various stages of completion. But this was seldom practicable either for management or workers. It would probably have thrown the planned schedules out of phase. Certainly, the workers disliked having incomplete work around, for bonus payment was postponed thereby. Waiting time was paid for at the (lower) time rate and was therefore 'a dead loss'.

2. *Waiting for crane*. Time booked to 'waiting for crane' was paid for at 45 per cent bonus. It was quite common for workers to be waiting for crane because the crane served many sections of the shop. The incidence of 'waiting for crane' time was so unpredictable that no 'flat' allowance was incorporated into the allowed times. Instead, time was expected to be booked to 'waiting for crane' for each job, and to book it was the responsibility of the worker concerned. Often, on a loose rated job, the worker would book in for the whole job at (say) 90 per cent, as if no delay had been experienced. In effect, this was to use loose times to keep the shop bonus average high and so 'bump up' the productivity bonus, as well as using the loose times to compensate for 'waiting for crane' time.

3. *Bad design and faulty drawing*. When delays were experienced by bad design or drawing office errors it was sometimes possible to negotiate with the ratefixer 'on-the-spot' an allowance which offset the effect on earnings. For example Eddie the tanker once

Table 1 Average (Weekly) Hourly Earnings and Range of Variation. Jay's Transformer Assembly

No. of Weeks	*Syd Smales* (*a*) *Average hourly earnings*	(*Tanker*) (*b*) *Deviation from mean*	*Old Ches.* (*a*) *Average hourly earnings*	(*Tanker*) (*b*) *Deviation from mean*	*Eddie* (*a*) *Average hourly earnings*	(*Tanker*) (*b*) *Deviation from mean*
	s. d.	d.	s. d.	d.	s. d.	d.
1	4 6¾	+3	4 5½	+1¾	4 4	−½
2	4 2½	−1¼	4 2¼	−1½	4 4½	—
3	4 2½	−1¼	4 2½	−1¼	4 2½	−2
4	4 1½	−2¼	4 1¼	−2½	4 1½	−3
5	4 2	−1¾	4 2¾	−1	4 2¼	−2¼
6	4 3	−¾	4 2¾	−1	4 6½	+2
7	4 1¾	−2	4 1¾	−2	4 4¾	+¼
8	4 6½	+2¾	4 6	+2¼	4 6½	+2
9	3 11¾	−4	3 11¾	−4	4 3¼	−1¼
10	4 6½	+2¾	4 5¾	+2	4 5½	+1
11	4 5½	+1¾	4 3	−¾	4 2	−2½
12	4 4	+¼	4 4¼	+½	4 6	+1½
13	4 5¼	+1½	4 5½	+1	4 6¾	+2¼
14	4 5	+1¼	4 5	+1¼	4 3	−1½
15	4 3	−¾	4 3	−¾	4 3	−1½
16	4 3	−¾	4 3¼	−½	4 2¼	−2¼
17	4 0¾	−3	4 0½	−3¼	4 0	−4½
18	4 3	−¾	4 3½	−¼	4 3½	−1
19	4 3¼	−½	4 3	−¾	4 5¼	+¾
20	3 11¾	−4	4 5	+1¼	4 2	−½
21	4 2¼	−1½	4 2¼	−1½	4 3¾	−¾
22	4 10½	+6¾	4 10½	+6¾	5 0½	+8
23	3 11¾	−4	3 11½	−4¼	4 0	−4½
24	4 10¼	+6½	4 10	+6¼	4 10	+5½
25	4 6	+2¼	4 6	+2¼	4 8½	+4
Mean of (a)'s	4 3¾		4 3¾		4 4½	
Mean of (b)'s		2½		2		2¼
Max. (a)	4 10½		4 10½		5 0½	
Min. (a)	3 11¾		3 11½		4 0	
Range (a)	10¾		11		1 0½	

Bill Madden		*Lionel*		*Fatty*	
(*a*) *Average hourly earnings*	(*b*) *Deviation from mean*	(*a*) *Average hourly earnings*	(*b*) *Deviation from mean*	(*a*) *Average hourly earnings*	(*b*) *Deviation from mean*
s. d.	d.	s. d.	d.	s. d.	d.
4 6	+½	4 3¾	−1½	3 3	−8¼
4 2½	−3	4 3	−2¼	3 3¾	−7½
4 2	−3½	4 1	−4¼	3 4¼	−7
4 6¾	+1¼	4 8	+2¾	3 6½	−4¾
4 4½	−1	4 4½	−¾	3 5	−6¼
4 6½	+1	4 3¾	−1½	3 5	−6¼
4 2½	−3	4 5¼	—	3 6¾	−4½
4 2½	−3	4 5¼	—	3 4½	−6¾
4 4	−1½	4 6¾	+1½	3 6¾	−4½
4 5½	—	4 6	+¾	3 10	−1¼
4 5½	—	4 5½	+¼	4 1¾	+2½
4 1	−4½	4 3¾	−1½	4 1	+1¾
4 10¼	+4¾	4 8½	+3¼	4 1½	+2¼
4 7¾	+2¼	4 7½	+2¼	4 1¾	+2½
4 5¾	+¼	4 0¾	−4½	4 5¼	+6
4 5½	—	4 5½	+¼	3 10½	−¾
4 5	−½	4 4¾	−½	4 2¾	−3½
4 4¾	−¾	4 4¾	−½	4 1¾	+2½
4 6½	+1	4 4½	−¾	4 2	+2¾
4 3½	−2	4 2½	−2¾	4 2¼	+3
4 8¼	+2¾	4 2¼	−2¾	4 1½	+2¼
5 5½	+12	5 4	+10¾	4 11	+11¾
4 8	+2½	4 7¼	+2	4 6½	+7¼
4 8½	+3	4 3½	−1¾	4 2½	+3¼
4 7	+1½	4 8¼	+3	4 5¼	+6
4 5½		4 5¼		3 11¼	
	2¼		2		4¾
5 5½		5 4		4 11	
4 1		4 1		3 3	
1 4½		1 3		81	

Table 1 continued

No. of Weeks	Simsey (a) Average hourly earnings	Simsey (b) Deviation from mean	Tom Hendy (a) Average hourly earnings	Tom Hendy (b) Deviation from mean	Fred Cotton (a) Average hourly earnings	Fred Cotton (b) Deviation from mean
	s. d.	d.	s. d.	d.	s. d.	d.
1	4 0¼	−5¾	4 0	−4¾	3 3	−7¼
2	4 0½	−5½	4 4	−¾	3 3¾	−6½
3	4 0½	−5½	4 3	−1¾	3 4¼	−6
4	4 7¾	+1¾	4 7½	+2¾	3 6½	−4
5	4 6½	+½	4 6	+1¼	3 5	−5¼
6	4 4½	−1½	4 4¼	−½	3 4¼	−6
7	4 6¾	+¾	4 6¾	+2	3 6¾	−3½
8	4 8¼	+2¼	4 8	+3¼	3 6½	−3¾
9	4 5½	−½	4 4¾	—	3 6¾	−3½
10	4 3¼	−2¾	4 3½	−1¼	3 10	−¼
11	4 5½	−½			3 7¼	−3
12	4 6¾	+¾			4 2¾	+4½
13	4 4½	−1½			4 6	+7¾
14	4 0½	−5½			4 0	+1¾
15	4 10	+4			3 8¼	−2
16	4 6¼	+¾			3 11¼	+1½
17	4 3¾	−2¼			3 11	+¾
18	4 7½	+1½			4 3¼	+5
19	4 7¼	+1¼			4 6¼	+8
20	4 4¼	−1¾			3 7½	−2¾
21	4 6¾	+¾			3 9	−1¼
22	4 5¾	−¼			4 3¼	+5
23	4 11¼	+5¼			4 6¾	+8½
24	4 11¼	+5¼			4 7¾	+9½
25	4 8	+2			4 4¾	+6½
Mean of (a)'s	4 6		4 4¾		3 10¼	
Mean of (b)'s		2¼		2		4½
Max. (a)	4 11¼		4 8		4 7¾	
Min. (a)	4 0¼		4 0		3 3	
Range (a)	11		8		1 4¾	

Mac (*a*) *Average hourly earnings*	(*b*) *Deviation from mean*	*Tot* (*a*) *Average hourly earnings*	(*b*) *Deviation from from*	*Harry Birtwhistle* (*a*) *Average hourly earnings*	(*b*) *Deviation from mean*
s. d.	d.	s. d.	d.	s. d.	d.
4 4½	−¾	4 4¾	−¼	3 3	−9¾
4 4	−1¼	4 4¼	−¾	3 2	−10¾
3 11¾	−5½	3 11¼	−5¾	3 2	−10¾
4 8¼	+3	4 8	+3	3 2¼	−10½
4 7½	+2¼	4 7¾	+2¾	4 1¼	+½
4 6¾	+1½	4 6¾	+1¾	3 9¼	−3½
4 0	−5¼	4 5¼	+¼	3 6¼	−6½
4 5½	+¼	4 5¼	+¼	4 0¾	—
4 4	−1¼	4 3	−2	3 5½	−7¼
4 3¾	−1½	4 3¼	−1¾	3 7½	−5¼
4 4¾	−½	4 3¼	−1¾	7 8	−43¼
4 5¾	+½	4 5¾	+¾	4 4	+3¼
4 4	−1¼	4 4	−1	4 1	+¼
4 2¾	−2½	4 2¾	−2¼	4 4	+3¼
4 8¾	+3½	4 8¾	+3¾	4 2¼	+1½
4 3	−2¼	4 3½	−1½	4 0	−¾
4 1½	−3¼	4 1½	−3½	4 3¼	+2½
5 0	−6¾	4 6½	+1½	4 3	+2¼
4 2	−3¼	4 1½	−3½	4 4¾	+4
4 10¼	+5	4 9¾	+4¾	4 1¼	+½
4 1	−4¼	4 1	−4	4 2¼	+1½
4 2½	−2¾	4 2	−3	4 6	+5¼
4 6	+¾	4 7¼	+2¼	3 8¾	−4
5 5¾	+12½	5 4¾	+11¾	4 10¾	+10
4 5¾	+½	4 1	−4	4 3	+2¼
4 5¼		4 5		4 0¾	
	3		2¼		6
5 5¾		5 4¾		7 8	
3 11¾		3 11¼		3 2	
1 6		1 5½		4 6	

Table 1 continued

No. of Weeks	Lofty (a) Average hourly earnings	Lofty (b) Deviation from mean	George Panton (a) Average hourly earnings	George Panton (b) Deviation from mean	Claude (a) Average hourly earnings	Claude (b) Deviation from mean
	s. d.	d.	s. d.	d.	s. d.	d.
1	3 7	−8¾	4 1½	−1¾	4 3¼	−3½
2	4 5½	+1¾	3 7¾	−7½	3 6½	−12¼
3	3 4	−11¾	4 3¾	+½	4 7¼	+½
4	4 1¼	−2½	4 2	−1¼	4 0¾	−6
5	4 5½	+1¾	4 6¼	+3	3 2	−16¾
6	4 1¼	−2½	4 4¾	+1½	6 10¼	+27½
7	4 2	−1¾	3 10¾	−4½	4 0	−6¾
8	3 6¾	−9	3 6½	−8¾	4 11	+4¼
9	4 4½	+¾	4 10	−6¾	3 7¼	−11½
10	—	—	4 11¾	+8½	4 6½	−¼
11	—	—	3 11¾	−3½	5 3	+8¼
12	4 5	+1¼	4 4¼	+1	4 5¼	−1½
13	4 0¾	−3	4 2¾	−½	4 4½	−2¼
14	4 4½	+¾	4 10	+6¾	4 11½	+4¾
15	4 5¼	+1½	4 0	−3¼	4 5½	−1¼
16	4 4¾	+1	4 2	−1	3 10½	−8½
17	5 10	+18¼	4 2½	−¾	5 5½	+10¾
18	4 6¾	+3	4 9½	+6¼	4 8¼	+1½
19	4 3¼	−½	4 3¼	—	5 0½	+5¾
20	4 0¾	−3	3 9¾	−5½	4 6	−¾
21	4 3¼	−½	4 2¼	−1	4 5	−1¾
22	4 10½	+6¾	5 0¾	+9½	4 1¼	−5½
23	4 9¾	+6	4 5	+1¾	4 11½	+4¾
24	4 2	−1¾	4 8	+4¾	3 10	−8¾
25						
Mean of of (a)'s	4 3¾		4 3¼		4 6¾	
Mean of (b)'s		3½		3½		6¼
Max. (a)	5 10		5 0¾		6 10¼	
Min. (a)	3 4		3 6½		3 2	
Range (a)	2 6		1 6¼		3 8¼	

Garvey (*a*) *Average hourly earnings*	(*b*) *Deviation from mean*	*Marmaduke* (*a*) *Average hourly earnings*	(*b*) *Deviation from mean*	*45% Wilf* (*a*) *Average hourly earnings*	(*b*) *Deviation from mean*
s. d.	**d.**	**s. d.**	**d.**	**s. d.**	**d.**
4 5¼	−1¼	3 4½	−1	4 2½	−1¼
4 8	+1¾	3 3¾	−1¾	3 9¾	−6
4 0	−6½	3 3¾	−1¾	4 1¾	−2
4 4½	−2	3 6¼	+¾	4 5	+1¼
4 0¾	−5¾	3 6¾	+1¼	4 2½	−1¼
3 11	−7½	3 6¼	+¾	4 4½	+¾
4 6	−½	3 6½	+1	4 5½	+1¾
4 4	−2½	3 3½	−2	4 2½	−1¼
4 4¼	−2¼	3 6½	+1	4 8	+4¼
4 11¼	+4¾	3 9¼	+3¾	4 0¼	−3½
3 9	−9½			4 8¼	+4½
5 2	+7½			4 2	−1¾
5 6½	+12			4 7¾	+4
4 3	−3½			4 0	−3¾
4 8½	+2			4 0	−3¾
4 5½	−1			4 7¾	+4
4 0	−6½			3 6¾	−9
4 8½	+2			4 7¼	+3½
5 0	+5½			4 4	+¼
4 7¾	+1¼			4 5	+1¼
4 5¾	−1¼			4 9	+5¼
4 10½	+4			4 4¾	+1
5 0	+5½			4 6¾	+3
5 2	+7½			4 7	+3¼
4 2	−4½			3 6	−9¾
4 6½		3 5½		4 3¾	
	4½		1½		3¼
5 6½		3 9¼		4 8¼	
3 9		3 3½		3 6¾	
1 9½		5¾		1 1½	

complained when, due to faulty design, he took hours to connect up some terminals. He was unable to get an 'on-the-spot' allowance sufficient to compensate for his losses and his earnings suffered.

4. *Faulty material*. Sometimes the components delivered to the worker were faulty and had to be returned to the 'feeder' departments for rectification. Delays of this kind were compensated for as follows. All time booked in while waiting until faulty materials were rectified was counted as piecework time, and a bonus of 45 per cent was paid. But a worker could ignore the delays if the time were a loose one and book in a time which would pay 90 per cent (say). Of course, to do this was to reduce potential 'time up the cuff', and thus to limit opportunities for the future off-setting of the effects of waiting time and 'tight' times.

5. *Allocation of work*. As we have already seen, the allocation of work in the shop was in the hands of the foreman. Complaints were often heard that work was not evenly distributed amongst the workers, as I have shown. Nor did work flow evenly through the shop. Since there were 'tight' and 'loose' rates the effect was to create unequal opportunities to earn bonus. The capacity of all to stabilize earnings was also affected. But pressure was brought to bear on the foreman to reform his method of allocating work, and sometimes he would yield. To the extent that he did so the workers controlled the allocation of work within the shop, but neither they nor the foreman had any control over the flow of components into the section.

I have already mentioned in general terms how the 'fiddle' operated to offset the effects of some of the above factors. I now go straight on to consider the earnings of workers in the shop to show in a little more detail how this worked out.

Table 1 shows the average hourly earnings $\left(\dfrac{\text{Weekly earnings}}{\text{hours worked}} \right)$ for each of twenty-five weeks together with mean average hourly earnings, mean deviation, maxima, minima and range of variation. It is clear from the table that, despite the 'fiddle', there were considerable fluctuations in average hourly earnings, in some cases. The job-spoilers Garvey and Claude Bissett show a mean deviation of $4\frac{1}{2}$ and $6\frac{1}{4}$ respectively, which is, as one might expect, much higher than the general run. But there are others with high mean deviations: Cotton, Birtwhistle, and Fatty. Birtwhistle's mean is distorted by the 'freak' figure of 7/8 due to his windfall, otherwise his mean would be like that of most of the others, perhaps a little larger, since during the period he progressed to piecework. His average jumped by 11d in week 5 when this change took place. With the exception of the first 4 weeks and the 'freak' week there were very few weeks when deviation from the mean was large. This only helps confirm the general impression which I have conveyed of Harry, as wanting to do the right thing – cross-booking and the like. Cotton and Fatty both changed to piecework during the period. Fatty's earnings show a marked tendency to increase steadily throughout the period, thus reflecting his improvement during his period as a trainee, and this partly explains his relatively high mean deviation. And the same goes for Fred Cotton. Again, as we might have expected from our previous discussion, Simsey and Syd Smales have low mean deviations, as have their mates Tom Hendy and Old Ches. And Bill Madden and Lionel are at about the same level as these four.

In Figure 2 there are graphs showing the average hourly earnings, the bonus percentages, and the daywork hours for four workers for each of the twenty-five weeks of the period. In a moment I shall examine these in some detail so as to show how cross-booking was used, but first there are one or two general points to be noted. It is clear from the graphs that high daywork hours, when these are associated with low bonus earnings, produce low average hourly earnings. This follows logically from the structure of the incentive scheme. I have set the 'ceiling' at 100 per cent, although I do not think the figure was ever so sharply defined in the shop. 'Not too far above the 90 level' was 'alright'. This was the generally expressed idea about the proper booking-in policy, and this general prescription allowed a good deal of personal discretion in the operation of the 'fiddle'.

I now examine the graphs in Figure 2 in detail. Graph no. 1, shows the movement of hours, bonus, and earnings, for Syd Smales. With the exception of the two 'boom' weeks 22 and 24, Syd's earnings were remarkably steady throughout the period. I say 'remarkably' because the amount of daywork experienced by Syd, and the fluctuations in the daywork graph, were quite large.

Daywork reduced the opportunity to earn bonus, and given straight booking would be exactly represented in the average hourly earnings so long as bonus remained steady. Syd, despite the burden of daywork, seems to have ironed out his earnings fluctuations while at the same time keeping his bonus at a level

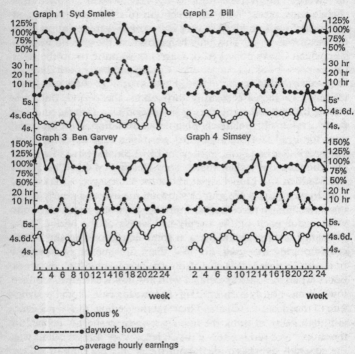

Figure 2 Bonus per cent, daywork hours and overall hourly earnings: 4 workers

below the ceiling. This shows his great skill in the art of cross-booking.

Week 17 is a good example of the way the technique was used. There was a sharp rise in daywork hours. This was compensated for by booking in high bonus, well above the ceiling, and a drastic slump in earnings was avoided. It was possible to book in high bonus percentages: (a) if rates were loose, (b) if rates were reasonable and tremendous effort were exerted, or (c) if there was time 'up the cuff' for an emergency such as this. My field-notes do not indicate that Syd worked extra hard during this week. I conclude either that Syd exploited 'loose' rates to the full, or used time from 'up the cuff'. In weeks 9 and 23 it seems as if Syd was unable to avoid a slump in earnings occasioned by sharp rises in the amount of daywork. Although I have no record of this I infer from the figures that in these weeks there was a run of 'tight' work or an absence of 'time up the cuff'. My knowledge of Syd, and of the general custom of the shop, justifies such an inference.

There are two features of graph 2 which merit special mention. The bonus percentages are low in comparison with those on the other graphs, and there is much less waiting time. These features are explained by the fact that Bill Madden, whose graph this is, was often given exhibition or prototype work. This work was not paid according to the incentive scheme. A percentage bonus was paid regardless of time taken – this was known as 'covered time'. This percentage was usually somewhat lower than the ceiling. No cross-booking was possible, of course, in a week occupied wholly by special jobs, but when Bill combined work on 'specials' with ordinary piecework jobs, it was possible to make 'tight' jobs pay by declaring time to have been saved which was actually saved on the special jobs. The fact that Bill worked so much on special work explains his low daywork hours.

I often had long talks with Bill. He told me that he thought it unwise to book above the ceiling. He said that during the war he had worked for a large firm in the Manchester area on war work. The workers were on piecework and they were asked by the management to step up production to the limit in the interests of the war effort. A solemn undertaking was made by the management that the 'sky was the limit for earnings' and that no rates would be cut if they were found to be loose. According to Bill, things went well until the war ended and then the management went back on its promise. All the loose rates which had been exposed during the war years were cut, and the workers' capacity to earn, and their scope for control, were reduced. The lesson of all this for Bill was never to expose loose rates however good the management happened to be (and he thought very highly of Jay's management). For all his status as a 'Blue Eye', he operated the 'fiddle' with the rest.

He himself said that he kept his earnings steadier than they would otherwise have been, and protected himself from rate-cutting, by cross-booking. The reason that he was so much envied by Simsey and 'the youngsters' was that the covered-time jobs offered him more scope for this kind of manœuvre. But Bill pointed out that a long run of prototype work at covered time brings the bonus average down. His high bonus earnings in week 22, well above his own average, were probably due to the booking in of incomplete work, from the previous week.

Graph 3 shows Simsey's earnings, bonus, and daywork hours. I have already mentioned how infrequently he exceeded the ceiling. He did so, as the graph shows, only twice in the period, that is in weeks 9 and 16. On both occasions high bonus compensated for high daywork hours. Week 10 shows a drop in average hourly earnings associated with low bonus percentage and high daywork indicating perhaps a run of 'tight' jobs and a shortage of time in hand. Simsey had much less daywork than Syd Smales, therefore his problem of ensuring stable earnings was much less difficult to solve.

Graph no. 4 is the graph of a 'job spoiler', Garvey, who seemed to care little about the consequences for himself and for others of exposing 'loose rates' and booking in high bonus percentages. An examination of the graph shows that happened when the bonus ceiling was disregarded, and when cross-booking was little used. Take week 11, for example. In this week, for Garvey, there was a marked slump in bonus earnings combined with a sharp rise in the amount of waiting time. This had a catastrophic effect on earnings. In the absence of detailed evidence, I think it reasonable to presume that in this week Garvey had a run of tight work during the time he was on piecework, or that he had incomplete work at the week-end. It is likely that Garvey faced a similar situation in week 17, another week of low bonus and high daywork hours. But when daywork was low and bonus high, there was obviously no thought in Garvey's mind of saving for a time of high daywork and no bonus. He booked in 'straight' and earnings soared.

There is one more piece of evidence to refer to before the advantages of straight and cross-booking can be assessed. It seems to me that the evidence referred to so far shows a balance of advantages for the 'fiddle', at least in so far as it does what it claims to do. The conformers to the 'fiddle' have reasonably stable earnings, they protect the 'loose' rates, they compensate for the effects of management shortcomings, i.e., waiting time, faulty design, and so on. But if we look again at Table 1 where the mean of average hourly earnings is shown for each worker, it will be seen that the two workers scoring the highest are Garvey and Bissett, the rate busters. So on the face of it, it seems that if one is ready to regard stories of ratecutting as myths one is slightly better off by booking straight. But there is a difference of only $\frac{3}{4}$d. between Simsey, a strict conformer, and Bissett, a job-spoiler. This amounts to about 2s. 9d. a week. Even if we forget all the other imputed advantages of the 'fiddle' and argue that the 'job-spoilers' do best financially, we must remember that the measure of advantage rests not merely in the comparison of cash received but in the relationship between effort and reward. When this measure is used it is clear that the 'job-spoilers' are at a disadvantage. Simsey bought a lot of leisure at work for his 2s. 9d. per week, if one may put it thus crudely. Garvey and Bissett were not only 'job-spoilers', they were 'teararsers' as well.

It was pointed out to me many times by Syd Smales and others that a shop could tolerate a couple of job-spoilers. If they were known to be speedy workers, then their behaviour would not lead to a 'blitz' on the job times. There was little pressure on the two job-spoilers in Jay's to conform. Bissett was something of a social isolate, but he was not unhappy to be so. Garvey was regarded as a somewhat special case, a man of great strength and, in many ways, 'one of the lads'.

I conclude that the 'fiddle' worked. I also conclude that it was seen by the men as a logical means to desired ends. I can say something, but not a lot, about the reasons why these particular ends were regarded as desirable. Stability was desired because of the advantages it afforded in family budgeting. Many men told me that they liked to give the same amount each week to their wives. This meant that fluctuations in earnings were fluctuations in the pocket money of the breadwinner. Secondly the 'fiddle' was regarded as important as a protection against ratecutting. In view of the difference in the conceptions of a reasonable rate between the shop floor and the rate-fixing office, which I discussed earlier, it seemed a necessary protection. Thirdly there were obvious advantages in having some sort of compensation for dislocation of the planned work flow.

I was not able to ascertain accurately whether the 'fiddle' did, in fact, result in restriction of output. This was because management made no estimate of the daily or weekly output of the shop against which I could measure actual output.[1] The reason why management made no such plan was due to the great variety of transformers of different sizes and designs which went through the assembly shops each week. And, as I was told in the Planning Office, the time schedules for the completion of a transformer were based upon past experience and not on some calculation from raw time-study data. So there was no hypothetical maximum against which to measure actual production. This did not mean, of course, that the firm were unable to calculate estimates for delivery. Such a calculation would be based upon the usual time taken to complete such a transformer and the work load already on the departments. It did mean that any charge of restriction of output was a general one stating that the workers could work harder than they were doing. And, as I have shown, such charges *were* made by management. But they had a hollow ring in the ears of the workers, who could show that most of the time wasted in the shop was the consequence of stoppages in work flow, for which management was responsible. As was the case at Wye, it was dislocation of management planning which gave rise to difficulties. But at Jay's the attempt was made to cushion these effects by the 'fiddle' or the control over time booked which the 'fiddle' afforded. I think that it is, in general, unhelpful to describe behaviour such as I observed at Jay's as 'restriction of output'. To do so is to make a judgement which in most cases will rest on shaky foundations. To support a judgement that a given group of workers was restricting output, one would have to have a neutral measure of a proper day's work. Even if one had such a measure, which is unlikely, one would also require

1. Nor, because of the 'fiddle', was there any accurate record of time spent on various items of output.

techniques to assess actual against potential output so that those differences entirely due to a deliberate withholding of effort by workers might be isolated. I submit that in most situations there will be neither neutral measures nor effective means of assessment. To speak of restriction of output in such circumstances is merely to express an opinion that workers ought to do more. I have therefore discussed the 'fiddle' not as part of a policy of restriction of output but as a form of social adjustment to a given job environment.

In Jay's, I would also say that the 'fiddle' was an effective form of worker control over the job environment. The strength and solidarity of the workers, and the flexibility of the management system of control, made a form of adjustment possible in which different values about a fair day's work, and about 'proper' worker behaviour, could exist side by side. I have no doubt that, if management controls had been made less flexible, and management planning more effective, the 'fiddle' would have been made more difficult to operate and probably output could have been slightly increased. But this might have destroyed the balance of the social adjustment between management and the workers, and the outcome might have been loss in work satisfaction. The shop would no longer have been a 'comfortable', may be not even a 'happy', shop. And in turn, this might have produced higher labour turnover, absenteeism and the like. One can only guess about these things, since there are so many other considerations involved: the existence of alternative employment, the ability of existing management–worker relationships to withstand the impact of radical change, for example, but it seems to me that when relationships are adjusted in a way similar to that I have described, which resembles the indulgency pattern noted by Gouldner, then any attempt to 'tighten up' might lead to resentment and resistance. In the circumstances, management might prefer to live with the 'fiddle' at the cost of what they believe to be some slight loss of output, and regard this as the price they pay for a good relationship with their workers.

Reference

SHIMMIN, S. (1960), *Payment by Results*, Staples.

Part Two
Measured Daywork and Similar Schemes

In recent years, for reasons that the researches reported in Part One make fairly obvious, disillusion with payment-by-results schemes has become widespread. Various alternatives have been proposed, all aiming at a high pay–high performance situation but eschewing the offer of *increments* of reward for increments of effort. Measured day work is the term used to describe some of these; stepped daywork and controlled daywork are examples of other names. In the readings by Anne Shaw and Tom Lupton some of the problems of installing and running such total task/total reward schemes are discussed. The paper by David Sirota proposes to offer rewards for innovation in method as well as for performance using present methods, a novel suggestion of which little experience has so far been gained.

8 Anne Shaw

Measured Daywork: One Step Towards a Salaried Workforce

Anne Shaw, 'Measured daywork: one step towards a salaried work force', *Manager*, vol. 32, no. 1, 1962.

In industry today there is an increasing tendency for work-people to want a steady wage to enable them to meet the commitments of an affluent society. This coincides with the modern trend of management to require controlled production, that is to say controlled output from both operators and machines. 'Measured daywork' is a system of payment which meets both these requirements. Moreover in a climate of opinion in which the unions are tentatively moving towards salaries for work-people as for office staff it can be effectively used as a step towards this end, for it guarantees to workers the same amount of money all the year round – provided that they maintain a certain level of output.

Roughly a third of all wage earners in Britain are paid by piecework or output bonus schemes, so that two-thirds are not yet under any incentive scheme. In many cases managements do not know what kind of incentive scheme to apply and although they would like to raise the level of effort, they doubt whether payment-by-results would meet the case. They could well find, in suitable circumstances, that with measured daywork effort could be raised to a payment-by-results level without many of the disadvantages inherent in payment-by-results schemes.

Measured daywork is a system of payment in which an additional fixed award is paid on top of the basic rate for a job. This fixed 'bonus' is in return for extra effort and it is paid regularly as long as a required standard of output is maintained. If this standard cannot be achieved for reasons for which the management is responsible, for instance, if there is not enough work to do, or if there is failure of machines or in the flow of material, the bonus is still paid. But if the standard is not met because of some fault of the worker, such as carelessness, then the bonus can be withheld.

The bonus is a fixed sum added to the basic or minimum rate, and although different operators may be on different basic rates the bonus for each is the same. For each operator the standard of work for which this bonus is paid is calculated by normal work measurement techniques, and is set to require the same level of effort from each. This is, generally speaking, the equivalent of the effort normally regarded as average under a payment-by-results scheme.

The bonus is therefore a reward for a fixed amount of extra effort above 'daywork' level, and it is a guaranteed payment provided that the worker consistently meets the standard required of him. Management, however, retains a sanction because if the operator fails to meet the required target for any reason for which he is responsible the bonus can be withheld.

It is important at the outset to distinguish between measured daywork and high day rates. With a system of enhanced day rates workers are, in fact, paid hourly rates which are higher than the agreed minimum rates. Any previous bonus element has been consolidated into one payment. High day rates are used as an incentive to attract and to retain labour, particularly in certain industries, like parts of the motor-car industry, where above minimum earnings are expected because of a history of payment by results, and where there is a high proportion of machine control of output. It should be said that if high day rates can be used successfully they have the advantage of being the simplest of all incentive schemes to operate.

The fundamental difficulty of the high day rate system is that consolidated rates are paid automatically according to the number of hours worked. Therefore unless the management has absolute control of production, as on a machine controlled operation or line, it may find it difficult to control effort or output. Under this system there is a tendency for the workpeople rather than the management to be able to control the amount of work which has to be done in overtime. Measured daywork, on the other hand, is a disincentive to operators to work unnecessary overtime and one of the chief advantages of this type of scheme is that management rather than the workers are in control of overtime.

High day rate systems have another feature differing from measured daywork. Since all payment is usually consolidated into a single hourly sum, overtime rates of pay ('time and a quarter', 'time and a third', 'double time') is calculated on this enhanced rate. Under measured daywork the basic rate remains the basis of overtime calculation. This can be a considerable advantage to management where much seasonal overtime is worked.

I have for many years been an advocate of measured daywork in the right circumstances, but I think it important to be clear in which situations it can be expected to operate successfully and in which circumstances it cannot. It is by no means a suitable incentive for everybody all the time, in other words it is not a universal panacea but a useful incentive in certain cases.

The object of measured daywork is to maintain a steady, high level of output, and it can be used either as a means of increasing output, where previously there has been no incentive scheme, or where an existing payment-by-results scheme has been working badly. Where the objective is not a steady high level but the maximum possible output from individuals, measured daywork is not the right type of incentive scheme to install. For instance, where there is an opportunity for operators with exceptional skill to excel in individual work it would not be the best choice. In certain types of carpet weaving, for example, there are wide variations of competence among weavers, and no difficulty in allowing the best people to do the most work. Here payment-by-results, properly applied, is more appropriate since the management wants not a steady general effort but the highest possible results from each weaver.

There are certain essential conditions for measured daywork. In the first place, work must be fairly steadily available. If there is a shortage of work the obligation to pay bonus is on the management, as opposed to payment-by-results schemes where bonus is not paid if there is not enough work available.

Secondly, management must be able to control man hours paid for. This is important particularly in conditions of fluctuating trade. It applies also where there are very considerable seasonal variations in work, though these can often be controlled by the intake of temporary staff at peak periods and by the postponement of replacements until the season of heavy work.

This indicates that the fundamental requirement for the installation of measured daywork is that management must be strong, and must be both able and prepared to control labour.

In what circumstances, then, could measured daywork be the answer? Given the right conditions, as outlined above, we might well recommend it in cases where management want to achieve a certain level of output and no more – a steady output up to and maintaining, but not exceeding, a given target. Where it is wished to achieve a certain pace or a prescribed quality of work with no inducement to skimp or go too fast, measured daywork may well be suitable.

Again we might recommend this system where it is necessary to control inter-related operations where one failure affects all subsequent operations, or where management need a financial incentive to obtain a satisfactory level of effort on such work as maintenance or transport. Here payment-by-results may depress effort in the long run, because of the special difficulty of measuring the work. On this type of work so many contingencies and irregularities have to be allowed for that to be fair under a payment-by-results scheme standards must be set over-generously. This then tends to cause restrictive practices. When a repair or a journey is, on occasion, easier than the standard allows for, there will be an inducement to spin out the work to fill the time allowed, to avoid showing up a loose rate.

Under measured daywork standards can be set disregarding the minority of extreme contingencies, since when they occur they will merely serve as an acceptable reason for falling behind target without losing bonus. In this way time standards can be much more accurately assessed and are much more realistic when used for planning and control.

Where measured daywork can be applied successfully it has positive advantages for management. It allows control of output – of how much is done and when it is done both by men and by machines. It also provides control of overtime. Measured daywork is a disincentive to unnecessary overtime except when production demands it.

Measured daywork gives a strong sanction, for bonus is paid

for above average effort and it is not paid if the worker fails in his obligations. This is a very useful point in bargaining and wage negotiations. Under this system negotiation of standards can be carried out with less friction than under payment-by-results schemes because the workpeople are sure of their earnings. Arguments are, in the main, about effort and not about money, and therefore a more dispassionate view can be taken of problems which arise.

With measured daywork there is less resistance to change of method than with payment-by-results schemes because earnings will not be affected by them. This is very important in industries where new developments are constantly taking place. Similarly measured daywork encourages flexibility – there is less tendency for workers to refuse to help each other or to do jobs other than their own. Their bonus is the same on any job.

Low running costs

A major advantage so far as management is concerned is that measured daywork is cheap to administer. The bonus is set at a flat rate and only the exceptions have to be calculated, which simplifies administration and substantially reduces cost.

The advantages of measured daywork for the workpeople are, if anything, even greater than the advantages for management. In the first place they are guaranteed even earnings. A fixed bonus is paid for a steady effort and the operator can be certain that if that effort is put in his money will be the same each week. This means that he has much greater security, for his earnings, will be steady over the year provided standards are maintained when work is available.

Apart from its financial advantages for workpeople, this form of incentive secures improved working conditions. It develops better relations with fellow workers, since they are not competing against each other and may in fact help each other to achieve targets.

There are certain general points to be considered in relation to the organization of such a scheme. The basis of measured daywork is a fixed bonus in return for a specified amount of effort. This bonus can be applied individually, but in this case there is a tendency for the weaker workers to have difficulty and for it to be necessary to transfer them to non-bonus work. If, on the other hand, bonus is related to small groups the better workers tend to help the weaker ones and to work together as a team to achieve a joint target.

As under any other financial incentive scheme it is always necessary to have some people on a basic rate, and whenever measured daywork is applied some jobs should always be kept out of the scheme. This is because the bonus is in return for above minimum effort, and some people cannot or should not be asked to make this effort. Certain jobs can usually be set aside for these people (who are usually a very small minority) and very occasionally transfers can be made from bonus work to non-bonus work.

At the other end of the scale it may be desirable to give an extra award to particularly valuable workers who have special skills or who are capable of being used on a number of different operations. To such people an additional payment can be given, that is to say a sum based on merit rating assessment and paid in addition to the standard bonus fixed for the scheme as a whole.

The movement towards salaries for workpeople is a social development which will no doubt gather strength as the years go by. But today, generally speaking, people are not yet used to doing a good day's work without incentives. I see in measured daywork a half-way house between payment-by-results schemes and a salary system. It retains almost all the advantages of payment-by-results schemes, particularly of group payment-by-results schemes, without many of the disadvantages. It looks forward to a system of salaries for workpeople in as much as it guarantees steady and regular earnings throughout the year, but at the same time management retains such control as is necessary.

A case in point

An example of the application of measured daywork is provided by the tea factories of the English & Scottish Joint CWS. This group of four factories in London, Manchester and Glasgow, produces packet tea for sale to co-operative societies. Original tea from overseas plantations, bought in chests, is blended to the required quality. Up to forty different original teas make a blend. Chests are opened, the tea hopper-fed to mills, passed into mixing drums, and fed as required to quarter-pound packing machines running at a pre-determined rate per minute. Packets are placed in cardboard cartons which are sealed and held for despatch. These operations are interdependent but not entirely continuous.

The requirement in this case was for an incentive scheme which would:

1. Raise effort to an 'incentive' level in return for increased earnings.
2. Maintain a steady level of effort throughout each working day, rather than individual maximum effort.
3. Maintain a balance between operations, avoiding too much work-in-progress between processes.
4. Provide a disincentive to overtime working.
5. Encourage team working and reasonable interchange of jobs.
6. Use machinery and equipment to full capacity.
7. Avoid setting up an expensive clerical department to administer the scheme.
8. Give no inducement to restrictive practices or resistance to necessary changes.

Production requirements did not fluctuate very greatly, and any slight seasonal variations could be evened out by packing for stock. It was possible to make satisfactory arrangements for planning work and training operators. The supervisory structure was sound.

These are ideal conditions for measured daywork. Since effort had to be raised from a lower level, this system was more suitable than a high day rate system which would have lacked the sanctions of the measured daywork bonus. It was also advisable to have earnings divided between basic rate and bonus to avoid interference with the existing arrangements for absence and sickness payment, and to avoid increasing the cost of overtime work.

Measured daywork was acceptable to both employers and operators. The former could determine the amount of work to be done for any period of time, and control the balance between processes without restricting operators' earning capacity. The latter would receive a regular wage at a higher level than normal weekly rates, and security of weekly bonus, so long as they were available and willing to meet their work allocation.

All sections in the factories were studied, existing methods were analysed, and where improvements could be made new methods were developed. Experiments and trials confirmed the changes and, where necessary, operators were trained in the new methods. Time standards were set to require a degree of effort equal to that achieved as a shop average where a payment-by-results scheme is in operation.

As soon as each section had met and maintained the required standard of output for a full fortnight a fixed sum was paid weekly to each individual on bonus work in return for maintaining a target output of work. Targets are expressed in weekly, daily and hourly terms to help both operators and foremen to check on progress throughout the week. They are treated as weekly targets when calculating success or failure.

If there is failure to meet target the circumstances are examined and where the failure is outside the operators' control (such as shortage of tea, or packing materials, or machine breakdown), bonus continues to be paid. If the failure is held to be due to lack of effort on operators' part, bonus may be withdrawn for that week and only resumed when the target has been achieved again in another week. Absence is covered by holding a small 'pool' of trained operators to whom bonus is paid regularly in return for the ability and willingness to fill any vacancy.

The result of the scheme has been a substantially increased capacity in each factory and the attainment of a very satisfactory level of individual effort at a substantially reduced cost per pound of tea packed.

9 Tom Lupton

Methods of Wage Payment, Organizational Change and Motivation

Tom Lupton, 'Methods of wage payment, organisational change and motivation', *Work Study and Management*, vol. 18, no. 12, 1964.

Managers have always divided into opposing camps on the issue of piecework or time rates. The 'pro-pieceworkers' strike a posture of hard-headed realism. Everyone, they say, except a starry-eyed idealist, knows that people want more money and will work to get it. We allow, of course, they go on, that a system of piecework payment must be technically well-devised to suit the particular situation, and well administered. Given these things efficiency and job-satisfaction will follow. The 'pro-timeworkers' claim to be realists of a different kind. They argue that it is obvious to commonsense and proved by research, that men are interested in more things than money and that if they are to be efficient and satisfied all these interests must be met. Also, they say, men want stability of earnings, security of job and pay and continuously satisfying relationships with their fellow men. Piecework only breeds competition and insecurity. Therefore, time rates plus other kinds of non-monetary incentives are the answer.

It is not my purpose in this paper to contribute to one side of the argument or the other, but it occurs to me that a discussion of theories of motivation might have more meaning for the practical manager if it is related to the debate. I am convinced, moreover, that the debate is often conducted in terms of conflicting psychological theories and neglects organizational factors in motivation. Therefore, I want to discuss what some firms are contemplating; namely, a change from some form of payment by results to some form of time rate system of wage payment. In doing so I will examine the arguments which might be adduced to justify such a move – and these will be arguments about organization and motivation – and some of the problems which might attend the actual change. My paper is an exercise in the socio-psychological analysis of a particular kind of organizational change.

Some definitions

Piecework, as I use the term in this paper, refers to any method of wage payment which offers increments of cash as an inducement to higher output and threatens to reduce earnings if output should fall below an acceptable standard. Into this category come all methods which offer straight payment per piece and all the numerous fancy schemes for paying bonuses for output. Also into this category would fall what is sometimes called *measured daywork*. *Measured daywork* rests upon standards of work set by time study and agreed between the management, and the worker and his representatives. If the worker, through no fault of his own, falls short of standard, he still continues to draw his regular weekly wage. If his shortfall is his own fault, then this will be reflected in his pay packet, depending on how much he falls short. Because measured daywork has been accepted by many people as involving a monetary sanction I have used the term controlled daywork to describe the alternative to piecework which is discussed here. *Controlled daywork* is based upon standards set by time study and agreed between the worker and his representative(s) and the management and its representative(s). Once it has been agreed that a standard is fair and reasonable then there is an obligation placed on both worker and management. The worker undertakes to work consistently and conscientiously to that standard, and the management sees to it that he is provided with the tools and services to make it possible for him to do so; in short, this is a *contract*, binding on both parties. At this stage it is worth mentioning a point which will be dealt with more fully later; controlled daywork emphasises the respective *functions* of managers, supervisors, and workers, and plays down the boss-subordinate aspect of the relationship.

So far in the definition of controlled daywork, money has not been mentioned. All that has been said is that a man, or a group of men will agree with the management that such-and-such a stint of work is a reasonable one to ask of them, and that the management will agree to provide the conditions under which that stint can be efficiently done. However, money must be paid each week which is appropriate to the work being done; and this is also a subject for argument and agreement. This argument can, however, take place at fairly long intervals, at an annual review, for example. There is no need to start negotiations over again about the weekly wage every time there is a new layout or methods change. So long as the working force is sensibly graded for pay purposes according to skill, the arduousness of the work, and so on, then the level of wages may remain until the annual review. All that is needed with a new layout is to get agreement about new standards.

The emphasis in controlled daywork, as it is here defined, is on the separation of arguments and agreements about standards, i.e. how much can one reasonably expect a man to do in an hour or a day? from agreements about his weekly pay, i.e. how much should a man doing a job within a certain range of skill, etc. get each week as a regular income from the company? The first set of arguments must naturally take place on the shop floor, where the workers and the work study men and the supervisors know in detail what they are talking about when they speak of a reasonable stint. The second set of arguments take place more naturally between managers and trade union officials, where the relevant comparisons can be made and a broader view taken about gradings and differentials.

Although these two sets of arguments and agreements are separate in the ways described, they are also related closely to one another. At an annual review, for example, it might well be argued by the trade union side that, as a result of the standards agreed on the shop floor having been met or exceeded, or as a result of improvements made by management to machinery and layouts, labour productivity has increased and there is a case for an increase in the weekly wage of the workers.

It is reasonable to ask where the sanctions lie in controlled daywork. What happens if a worker does not produce to the standards agreed? Before dealing with this question it is essential again to emphasize the contractual nature of controlled daywork. If the record shows that the worker or group of workers has not produced to standard for a period of, say, one week, then the question must first be asked whether any responsibility lies with management for this state of affairs. Have the men been kept supplied with the materials and the tools to make possible the achievement of standards? This question must first be asked and answered satisfactorily before anything else is done, and the reason why this must be so is that implicit in the contract is the notion that in the last resort management must have the right of dismissal for breach of the contract. From the point of view of the man on the shop floor this makes the contract uneven for he has no rights under the contract to exercise similar sanctions on management. However, he can act through his trade union to obtain redress of grievance and this, of course, constitutes a strong latent sanction in his contract. Therefore, it is, in equity, incumbent on management to demonstrate that a breach of the controlled daywork contract has been committed and that the responsibility does not lie with management. Even if it can be shown that the fault lies with the operator there is another step to be taken before breach of contract can be established, and that is to ask whether the operator(s) were physically or otherwise up to the task, or whether the standards agreed to were for some reason too difficult. Unless all these things are done, then operators may well have no confidence in the method . . .

Controlled daywork demands that the system of record keeping by management be efficient and that the workers have confidence in it. Accurate information on performance must be readily available not merely as a matter of record but as a tool for diagnosis, and as the basis upon which discussion can take place, and agreement reached. These matters will be taken up again presently.

Viewed theoretically, controlled daywork is a method of arriving at, and securing adherence to, a set of rules to govern the performance of work. The main interlinked motives which are supposed to be at work are a sense of obligation and a conviction that the reward for work has been justly determined. The cash motive is at work, of course, during the argument about the relationship of effort and reward which precedes agreement. Under piecework by contrast the financial motive receives greater and more continuous emphasis, and this is adduced as a strong argument in its favour.

From piecework to controlled daywork

The arguments in favour of piecework are well known. It is said that men come to work to make money and that the more they can make while they are at work the better they like it. Therefore, so the argument goes, they will look for opportunities to make more. Management wants high output from its workers. If a man is offered rewards for higher output, he will strive after them, and so both sides are satisfied. Some men are more skilled than others, some more conscientious, some more greedy. Individual piecework allows each man to work out his own pecuniary salvation. The hard worker earns more money, the layabout less. The man who is ingenious enough to find efficient ways to high outputs will do well, the less ingenious less well. If a man finds, under piecework, that management inefficiencies are preventing him from making money then he will put pressure on supervision and management to do something about it. Underlying all these arguments is the assumption that the operator has, under piecework, the power to control the amount of effort he puts into the job, and that he relates effort solely or mainly to monetary return.

The arguments levelled against piecework point to its practical inappropriateness and its theoretical naivety. It is said that increasing mechanization, where it has happened, has removed from the worker some of the control over his pace of work. In such circumstances piecework seems illogical and anachronistic, unless of course the rewards are offered not for quantity but for, say, machine utilization or quality; and there has been a proliferation of schemes in which factors other than quantity have been introduced as the basis for monetary increments. The tendency has also been noted under piecework for earnings to get out of control and to gallop ahead of labour productivity. The adherents of piecework can see no reason why this should have happened other than sheer bad practice, because on the face of it piecework seems ideally suited to balance earnings and productivity. If, the argument goes, a man gets paid increments of cash for increments of output, this must help keep productivity and earnings in line. This argument ignores the scope that piecework gives both to the management and to the workers and the unions for exploiting the labour market. Because piecework, by its nature, gives workers some control over the effort-reward relationship they may resort to limitation of output on the job, while using their bargaining strength to raise the bases on which their piecework earnings are calculated. The engineering wages structure, for example, lends itself very easily to this kind of manoeuvre. The incidence of layout changes and retooling give occasions when these manoeuvres can be carried out. Management, on the other hand, in order to attract and retain labour in conditions of full employment, may slacken rates to make higher piecework earnings possible with the same effort. There are all manner of ways in which this can be done while maintaining the fiction of adherence to negotiated terms for the industry. In short the 'pro-time-workers' say, under all the pressures of a technologically changing, full-employment economy, piecework is a fine way of promoting 'wage-drift', because of the scope it affords to move earnings up without corresponding increases in productivity. It also has the disadvantage that because it leaves too much control in the hands of the worker to establish the effort-reward relationship, there is no pressure upon management and supervision continually to seek improvement; not from the operators anyway.[1] Attempts to improve performance as a result of pressures from other quarters may well find that control by operators is an obstacle to change. It is tempting to elaborate here upon the group processes which, under piecework, make for resistance to change, but these are fairly well understood, and will be touched upon presently anyway.

Arguments such as are advanced by R. M. Currie (1963) in his book on incentives that piecework systems will work effectively provided that proper procedures for the settling of standards are employed and that the systems are effectively administered by management, are persuasive. It *is* possible that they might give good results under these circumstances without leading to discrepancy between earnings and productivity. However, this argument leaves out of account the pressures in the market for labour, both upon management and workers, to relax standards,

1. In my experience, they grumble about management inefficiency, but see no reason why they should do anything about it. In fact, they are more likely to exploit it if this appears to be in their interest.

and it underestimates the effect of the informal organization of workers and managers on the effort-reward relationship. Even so, if a company were starting with a clean sheet, and could install effective procedures for control, piecework might well give good results. The fact is, however, that in firms where piecework has been in operation for many years, it would need a major upheaval to place the system on a new basis. It is in these cases that there exist strong arguments for controlled daywork.

The problem of changeover

It is one thing to argue the social and economic superiority of controlled daywork, it is another to introduce and administer it. Theoretically, a company with a piecework system in an advanced stage of 'drift' might be wise to move to controlled daywork. Practically, this is a move fraught with difficulties, largely because the pattern of obligation and expectation has to be changed and different motives relied upon.

It might well be disastrous were the introduction of controlled daywork to be seen merely as the continuation of present standards of work except that the piecework scheme would be replaced by a high day rate. The aim should rather be to put the relation between managers and workers on a new footing. The actual mechanisms of standard setting are ancillary to that. The new relationship has to be based on a recognition of function, and on a contract which, while recognizing the ultimate sanction of management to dismiss, sets out the mutual expectations of managers and workers of the behaviour of each other, and allows *each* to sanction the other for breach of contract. This is, as was noted earlier, a system of establishing the rules by which work in the organization is to be carried on – a legislative process. Such a process requires that deviation from rules when these are proved shall merit punishment, and this implies a carefully worked out procedure for establishing the facts and a well-understood code of punishment. The ultimate objective in introducing controlled daywork is to establish a structure of management and administration which allows a contractual relationship based upon agreed rules and a code of discipline to emerge and to persist. When a code of discipline is mentioned in the industrial context some managers have difficulty in envisaging anything other than men being suspended or sacked for having disobeyed rules made by management. They find it difficult to imagine that some rules may be agreed by everybody and that everybody might well accept the punishments which attend upon deviance with a much better grace were it so. This is a commonplace in political democracy, but some people find it difficult to see it working in industry. Yet why cannot men agree what is a reasonable performance on a job, what wages should be paid to men doing certain kinds of jobs, what procedures are needed to make sure that management can continually diagnose the organization of production so as to reveal shortcomings and to take action? And if men are found, in the course of such investigation, to be wilfully in breach of a contract freely entered into, then they will expect to be punished for it, and will know what is to be the extent of their punishment for it. Yet, there is likely to be little need to invoke a code of discipline if the process of establishing the rules or standards is done in such a way that agreement is seen to be just and obligation is felt.

It seems clear therefore, that if controlled daywork is to be accepted the aim must be:

1. To establish a procedure through which individual workers and groups workers will be involved, together with management, in agreement about what is a 'reasonable stint'. The services of competent work study engineers are essential to provide some of the objective data for the discussion. Work study must be seen as a service to both parties and not as a management gimmick to squeeze out more work from the workers.

2. To establish a procedure for keeping up-to-date records of the performance of each production section, so that the efficiency of managers, supervisors, and functional specialists such as production controllers and maintenance men may also be watched as well as that of the workers.

3. To establish a managerial structure so that the information on performance of all kinds goes quickly to those who have the responsibility to act. For example, the managing director does not wish to know that Smithson 298043 has fallen two points short of standard for two weeks running. He will, however, wish to be shown where the factory is off programme so that he can act.

It might eventually turn out that Smithson's foreman, who ought to know about his performance, will have to do something about Smithson, if his section is falling behind. It might equally well turn out that Smithson has been getting faulty sub-assemblies and action can be taken to get that remedied. To manage controlled daywork needs teams of specialists clustered under the line manager in each section of a works, responsible for collecting and processing diagnostic data and, as a team together with line management and supervisors, to act appropriately upon it, and comprising a work study man, a cost accountant, a production control man, a maintenance man, and so on. This team would work together with the supervisors to control the production processes in each section.

The management structure appropriate to controlled daywork is, in outline, as in Figure 1.

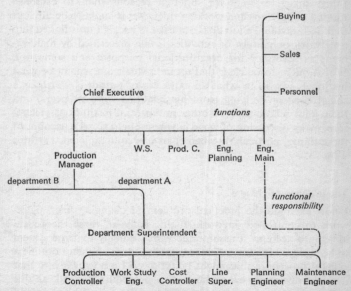

Figure 1 Note that the functional men in the department are responsible to their departmental superintendent for *what* they do and to their functional chief for *how* they do it

This kind of structure facilitates the establishment and main tenance of the working rules at shop floor level, while allowing for uniformity of procedure to be established from the top, and the necessary coordination of activity, and collation of relevant control information. Under piecework this kind of organization is not thought to be necessary because the cash motive is seen as adequate to control behaviour.

I pause here to give reasons why I have devoted so much attention to the organizational prerequisites of controlled daywork. The theoretical notions considered to be relevant to controlled daywork are job, job organization, job expectations, and motives. These are also relevant to piecework but the theoretical basis of piecework is usually expressed as a simple relation between individual or group output and money. Organization and control tend to be neglected in practice, and to be treated as things apart, existing for different reasons than to establish mutual obligations and working rules. Yet it ought to be obvious that an individual's job does not exist *in vacuo*, but is linked into a network or pattern of activities, some prescribed by management as necessary for organizational purposes and some not. It also ought to be clear that an individuals assessment of what his job is worth, or what an extra erg of output is worth, is a social concept deriving from his relations with his peers, and their joint relationship to other groups and institutions. Therefore, every discussion of wage payment ought to take account of these things, particularly when change is contemplated. I wish it were so.

The problem of change

I now examine the practical problem of changing from piece-work to controlled daywork, taking some of these theoretical ideas into account. I assume the worst, namely that the system to be replaced is in an advanced state of 'drift'. When I outline a general procedure that might be followed I am fully aware that it might not apply everywhere. Any procedure derived, as this is, from inadequately tested general principles must be examined closely and modified to meet a specific situation.

One would guess that under piecework a stable pattern of

expectations and beliefs has been built up which are appropriate to it, amongst which will be:

1. The expectation that on every occasion of modification of a process or a method, an argument will take place in which it will be customary for each side to strive to gain an advantage, and for management to give a little in order to get, or to keep, production going.

2. The acceptance by work study men as normal a customary rate of working which has been set by groups of operators.

3. The expectation that special allowances shall be built-in to job rates for all manner of contingencies and that arguments will continually take place about these on an *ad hoc* basis.

4. The shared belief, which arises from the establishment of these expectations, that almost everyone is interested in money and only money, whatever else they may in reality be interested in.

5. The belief that individual piecework is right because it rewards individual effort and sorts out the sheep from the goats.

6. The expectation that workers will set their own limits on output, and the belief that this is due not at all to the piecework system but to the shortcomings of supervision.

7. The expectation that management will always be pushing for extra output and that this can be cleverly exploited in bargaining for extra allowances, slack rates and so on.

It is not claimed that all these hang together as a logically consistent system of expectations and beliefs but that under piecework they tend to exist alongside each other, and tend to persist even when the objective conditions (e.g. mechanization) have made some of them inappropriate. They persist because people are used to living with them and get satisfaction from them. Therefore any change will have its difficulties and particularly one which attempts to change the pattern of obligation, belief and expectation.

However, there is reason to believe that workers try to manipulate piecework systems so as to give themselves regular weekly earnings, and that they expect those to increase from time to time. They also get the satisfaction which arises from control of their situation by the act of manipulation itself (which explains a lot of the argument about contingencies, methods changes, etc.). So to introduce a system which gives regular weekly earnings might be welcomed provided that it did not threaten the control which operators already have and which they value under piece-work.

Under controlled daywork the operator can still have control but this must be exercised in a different way. He and his colleagues, and their representatives, must be involved deeply in the process of deciding what a 'reasonable stint' is. If they are satisfied that they have been fully involved in the arguments about the rates for the grade of job they are doing, this can also be satisfying. They must also be involved fully in the investigations about shortfall of accepted standards. One can thus envisage a high degree of involvement and control which interferes less with production than the interminable wrangling over prices and allowances. But when control has been exercised in one way people take time to get used to exercising it in another way. Therefore, any attempt at the introduction of controlled day-work must proceed as follows:

1. It must start with a pilot experiment on a chosen section of a firm.

2. The section must be chosen after a study of the factory which will reveal:
(a) which section will find a change of this kind reasonably acceptable.
(b) which section has the managers and supervisors most capable of understanding the nature of the changes and the difficulties involved.
(c) which section is isolated sufficiently to minimise the effects of being 'got at' by the 'antis'.
(d) which section has managers and supervisers sufficiently flexible to modify the details of application without sacrificing the principles, in response to the demands of the situation.
(e) which section is not likely to have major engineering and methods changes for six months.

When the section which most nearly meets all these criteria has been chosen, a pilot experiment may be started. In a sense, one is building a prototype. Engineers will understand this, and they will know that you don't go 'into production' until you have gone through all the processes of design, testing, re-resting, trial runs, and so on. Therefore, they will see that long before discussion starts on the section, and long before the new system 'goes in' for trial, the following things must be done.

1. All procedures for the setting of standards must be worked out specifying who is to be involved at each stage, what documents will be used, who will use them, etc.

2. All the procedures for documenting performance and cost data, and the routing of the documents must be planned.

3. The managerial and supervisory structure has to be charted, the jobs in it described in detail, and the persons chosen carefully to fill them.

4. A skeleton programme and timetable must be prepared showing the sequence of sections to go over to controlled day-work if the prototype is successful, the managerial and supervisory personnel to be involved, and the phased introduction of the new managerial structure.

Once all this has been done preliminary discussions can take place with the people who are going to be involved in the pilot scheme; managers, supervisors, work study men, cost men, production controllers, maintenance men, shop stewards, and union officials. The principles underlying the whole exercise will have to be carefully explained, and the nature of a pilot scheme, i.e. that if a successful prototype cannot be built then the idea will have to be dropped and something else done. The 'Hawthorne effect' ought to work, that is to say, people will feel bucked at being singled out to take part in an important experiment and will be anxious to see it succeed.

As a next step the men on the section should be told what is going to happen, in the presence of their steward and union official and the managers. At this meeting it should be announced that two of the men in the section are to be elected by their fellows to attend, together with the management, the supervisors, the stewards, the work study men, and so on, a conference to go over in detail all the procedures for running the scheme into the section. It ought to be possible at each conference to get people involved in exercises which simulate the actual procedures to be followed in setting standards, in handling documents, and adjudicating cases of breach of contract.

The point I am emphasising here is that one must do more than 'put the chaps in the picture' by telling them what is in mind. They have to become aware of the role they have to play and this cannot be done by talking. It *can* be done by simulation and the careful development of successful prototypes; successful in the sense that they will lead to the establishment of a controlled process of earnings progression, which should satisfy management. The workers, for their part, will gain a large degree of control over their circumstances and stable but improving earnings which ought to satisfy them. Importantly, if the organizational concomitants of controlled daywork are also taken seriously management will be in possession of the information it needs, when it needs it, about the various factors affecting efficiency; and can take action.

It will be argued, no doubt, that the same could be said about systems of payment by results, i.e. that if questions of organization and documentation are properly handled, many of the same advantages accrue. One can only agree. Yet there is at least one important difference – most schemes of payment by results, at any rate where changes in product and productive method are prone to short term changes, are subject to a multitude of arguments and agreements about prices, special allowances, etc. which take place each day on the job. It is these in the context of labour market pressures under full employment, which contribute to 'drift'. And it is these which defy administrative control. The consequence is that control comes to be exercised unofficially by the working group and not by management. The system gets out of control not because of ill-will on the part of anyone, or even inefficiency, but because piecework in conditions of full employment usually creates too many problems which are only susceptible of solution at great cost. The advantage of controlled day work is that it makes the administration of the wages system simpler and brings 'drift' under control. Whether it will be adopted or not must surely depend on the confidence which managers have that the sense of obligation to adhere to rules of work jointly defined and administered is as powerful as the cash motive; or to put it another way, that working men would be willing to argue about the effort-reward bargain within the framework of joint rules. It will also depend upon the confidence which managers themselves have of their own capacity to work efficiently in terms of such a framework, and on an appropriate relationship of Trade Union officials at various levels.

I hope I have said enough to show that when one looks at the sociology as well as the psychology of motives, the nature of the piecework-timework debate becomes clearer, and some of the practical problems of deciding what system to adopt and how to introduce it emerge more sharply defined.

Reference

CURRIE, R. M. (1963), *Work Study*, Pitman.

10 David Sirota

Productivity Management

David Sirota, 'Productivity management', *Harvard Business Review*,
vol. 44, no. 5, 1966, pp. 111–16.

There are few issues in industrial organizations which have
aroused as much controversy as that of engineered work standards. The debate takes place not only between management and
employees, but also within the ranks of management itself. It is
difficult to find anyone in industry taking a neutral position on
work standards. At best, people are ambivalent. They have often
witnessed large productivity improvements accompanying the
introduction of standards in plants, but they are uneasy about
the costs of the system. The latter include the obvious expenses of
maintaining large industrial engineering staffs and the less obvious, but no less real, costs of the time consumed managing the
conflicts between employees and management so frequently engendered by standards. The most prominent of these hidden costs
is the time spent dealing with the large number of worker grievances about standards.

I, too, am uneasy about standards. Some of my uneasiness is
due to the discomfort I share with managers about a system that
generates such costly conflict. But part of it stems from my
observation that standards have a self-defeating quality: *in the
long run, they act to discourage precisely what they are designed to
encourage – namely, high worker productivity.* While this is a disadvantage not often considered, it is one which I am going to
examine in detail in this article. It has received little attention, I
believe, because of the impressive productivity gains realized by
many plants – often run previously in a loose, slipshod manner –
when work standards are introduced. Employees in these plants
are pressured to increase their productivity to the levels demanded
by the standards. Not surprisingly, output rises. My point, however, is that the benefits to the company so derived fall far short
of the productivity levels that are, in fact, possible.

I shall first discuss why I believe standards act as barriers to truly high productivity, and then proceed to describe an alternative approach to the management of production workers. I will contend that this other approach not only overcomes the productivity-inhibiting properties of work standards, but also is devoid of many of their human and financial costs.

First, a few words of definition are required. I shall limit the discussion to standards as traditionally developed and used. I define the traditional approach as having these three major components:

1. The development of standards is the responsibility of staff specialists – usually industrial engineers.

2. The engineers rely on time study or some form of predetermined ('synthetic') data for standards development.

3. The evaluation of worker productivity is based on output relative to the standards.

It is true that there are a number of variations in standards techniques, some of which are designed to overcome the recognized disadvantages of the traditional approach. But my observation has been that most companies which employ standards do so in a way closely approximating traditional usage.

The article has one further limitation. For the sake of brevity, it will be confined to a consideration of standards within a piecework setting. While there are important differences between piecework and the other major system of measurement and remuneration (measured daywork), much of what will be discussed can, with some modifications, be applied to both. I am concerned here with engineered standards, and both systems, by and large, use standards for determining productivity expectations.

Piecework problems

The theory underlying piecework is attractive in a number of respects. For example:

1. It predicts a straight-line relationship between the wages a worker can earn and the effort he is willing to expend on the job.

2. It assumes that industrial engineers, through the use of objective, scientific techniques, can determine with a high degree of accuracy the number of pieces that should be produced.

3. It expects that these techniques – because of their precision and objectivity – will be acceptable to all parties.

We know, however, that the reality is quite a bit different from the theory. In general, workers do not seem to view piece rates as products of a highly objective and scientific methodology. This view is evidenced by the enormous number of grievances about them that are generated each year in industry.

We are familiar, too, with the widespread phenomenon of productivity restriction whereby work groups set their own production norms and expect their members to adhere to them. This, too, is contrary to the piecework theory, which avers that employees will make an all-out response to financial incentives unhindered by the attitudes of their co-workers.

Numerous other difficulties beset the system – for example, cheating on claiming, hiding methods changes, the inequities of 'tough' as opposed to 'soft' jobs (despite the claim that standards equalize effort requirements), slowing down when being time-studied, fears of rate cutting, and poor-quality work. No doubt the reader could add many more problems to this list of difficulties.

My contention is that many of the problems in piecework proceed from the engineered standards approach to judging employee performance. Many would dispute this, claiming that the problems derive from maladministration of standards programs rather than from inherent liabilities. Certainly, standards programs vary in the competence with which they are administered, and there are corresponding differences in the financial and human costs they incur.

Over the years, many companies and their industrial engineering staffs have modified their practices considerably. They have come to accept the importance of providing adequate grievance channels for employees, preventing arbitrary changes in standards, systematically auditing standards for accuracy, and so forth. But while these changes have been useful, they tend to be undertaken within the context of an unquestioning acceptance of the fundamental objectives and methods of traditional engineered standards. It is these fundamentals of the system – 'what' is being done, not 'how' – which are at issue in this article.

Productivity determinants

Let us examine what the term *piecework* means when applied to a system employing engineered standards. I would argue that, in this context, piecework is a rather inaccurate label. It is true that employees are paid a certain amount for each piece produced. But it is also true that, by and large, only one determinant of worker productivity – *physical effort* – is considered. Under this system, the major way a trained and experienced worker can increase his output, and hence his earnings, is by applying greater physical effort on his job.

We know, however, that there is another, and usually much more important, determinant of productivity. This is the *method* by which the job is done. But it is inherent in this approach – indeed, in the very process of 'standardization' – that variations in methods are eliminated from the standards and pay calculations. If someone were to improve significantly a method for doing a job – increasing output say, by 25 per cent – the standard would be changed to take this improvement into account. This is what I mean when I say that the term *piecework* is, in part, a misnomer. The employee is not paid for pieces produced *per se*; he is paid for pieces produced *within the context of a given method*.

The foregoing has two major consequences.

1. There is little or no motivation for production employees to make methods improvements which will increase the overall output on their jobs.

It is true that employees will frequently improve methods, but, typically, these improvements will be kept to themselves. In my opinion, this situation represents an enormous waste of an extremely important resource: the talent, the initiative, the creativity of the blue-collar work force. Of course there are those who would contend that I exaggerate the importance of the contribution which workers can make to methods improvements.

Many believe that, with few exceptions, a good methods engineer and competent management are all that is needed to develop the 'best' method for doing a job. They are dead wrong. The fact is that workers make methods improvements frequently, but they realize that it is to their advantage not to tell anybody about these changes. Moreover, there is considerable evidence that when management deliberately structures the situation so as to encourage methods improvements on the part of employees – through training, rewards, and so on – a remarkable number of significant innovations can be produced.

The traditional approach to engineered standards helps to account for the paucity of worker methods improvements currently observed in industry. The cycle of events generated by this approach has all the properties of a 'self-fulfilling prophecy'. We say that employees, by and large, cannot contribute significantly to methods improvements. Consequently, a system is set up in which employees are measured and rewarded solely on the basis of physical effort. It is a system which effectively discourages the reporting of methods changes. We can then say: 'We told you so. They have nothing to contribute.' Let me ask the reader: Would you tell the company about a method change if the major consequence for you would be a tightening of the standard under which you work?

In addition to resulting losses in productivity due to holding back methods improvements, this approach often discourages the output of high degrees of physical effort on the part of workers. It is rare that an employee will intentionally expend effort that will cause him to exceed the standard by a large amount. He is concerned about rates being cut by management, and he is also concerned about the reactions to him of his fellow workers. This is not a severe problem when the standards are accurate or tight because exceeding them to any significant degree through sheer effort is difficult. But it is a very important problem when a rate is loose. In this situation everything possible is done to make sure that management does not learn about its error. Workers will either perform below their capacity, or if they find it profitable and feasible, they will exceed the standard and 'bank' the surplus rather than report it.

My major point then – whether concerned with methods changes or physical effort – is that the atmosphere which develops under engineered work standards is, in a key respect, antithetical to *improvement* goals. While the system is designed to get workers *up to* the standards, it tends to discourage them from *beating* the standards. I maintain that the losses in productivity thus engendered are very large indeed.

2. *By placing a heavy emphasis on sheer physical effort for performance evaluation, the company is, in effect, depriving its work force of important sources of self-esteem.*

I ask you to think of yourself and the kinds of things that make a job satisfying for you. Are these not the activities which contribute to your sense of self-worth, to your conception of yourself as someone who has certain unique and significant skills? By treating employees as if the only thing that mattered was their physical exertion, we remove from them a major source of self-esteem – namely, the opportunity to demonstrate their ability to think, to innovate, to create. We set up systems in which we have specialists in creativity: the method engineers. It is the job of these people to develop 'best methods' by which workers should do their jobs. All we ask of workers is that they follow orders and work hard.

Workers rebel against this approach. They do so by attempting to sabotage the system in any number of ways – fooling the time-study man, submitting formal grievances whenever possible, hiding new methods, and so on. We often attribute such behavior to simple laziness. This is nonsense. There are economic motives involved (a worker can usually 'make out' better if he does these things); there also are psychological reasons. Since management is not judging the competence of the worker in terms of the skills he values, such as creativity, he then demonstrates these skills in other ways. And he can be mighty creative as he goes about the job of making life difficult for line management and its staff representatives.

I know that I am painting an extreme picture, and that there are many deviations from it. For example, there are various techniques, such as suggestion plans, which companies use in an attempt to tap the creative potential of their work forces. But I believe that these, while usually introduced with great sincerity, are in practice little more than facades tacked onto a fundamental system which, in fact, discourages creativity.

Alternative approach

What, then, would I propose? Rather than try to concoct some theoretical and Utopian scheme for your consideration, I will instead describe a system currently in operation in a plant with which I am familiar. In my view, this system represents a highly attractive alternative to traditional engineered standards. (I make no claim that it is the only alternative. Management's discomfort with traditional methods has resulted in the development of a number of novel approaches. Some of these resemble, if not in the specifics of their procedures, at least in their basic philosophy, the system to be discussed. There are, for example, some fundamental similarities between this plant's approach and that of the Scanlon Plan; see Lesieur, 1958).

The plant, which produces office equipment, is part of a large corporation with many manufacturing facilities. It is generally agreed in the corporation that this plant is a highly efficient enterprise with outstanding records on numerous performance and cost dimensions. Moreover, employee morale in the plant, as revealed by systematic surveys of employee attitudes, is among the highest of all of the company plants.

There are no doubt many factors which account for the achievements of this plant. For example, it has a relatively young work force, a successful and fairly stable product line, and a favorable industrial environment. But research performed in this plant clearly indicates that there is an additional factor: the plant's approach to managing production workers.

The plant has neither piecework nor measured daywork. Its method of compensation lies somewhere between these two extremes. The approach differs from daywork in that individual productivity *is* an important determinant of an employee's pay. However, productivity is defined as *sustained* output over a number of months. Supervisors evaluate their employees' performance periodically, and pay increases are then based on these evaluations. It is rare that pay will be reduced. Rather than reduce earnings, management generally handles declines in performance by eliminating or markedly decreasing pay increases.

The system is therefore similar to daywork, and different from piecework, in that it produces a large degree of pay stability and predictability – short-term fluctuations in production will not affect pay. But in its emphasis on tying pay to performance – albeit performance on a sustained basis – the system does strongly resemble piecework. In the plant there are clear, well-defined ground rules stipulating the relationship between the output of workers and the wages they receive.

Output measurement

We come now to a key question: How is productivity measured? Many plants in this corporation have formal engineering standards. This plant does not. It is true that all of the jobs in the plant have estimates which do provide rough guidelines as to the amount of work that should be expected. These estimates are developed in a variety of ways, ranging from quick-and-dirty 'guesstimates' to occasional use of MTM data. The estimators tend to rely heavily on historical experience – that is, the estimate on a new job is very likely to be some approximation of the times recorded for similar jobs in the past. Estimates on these new jobs will be revised as experience is gained in actual production runs. Flexibility is therefore a key characteristic of the approach used. The estimators use whatever techniques and inputs seem most appropriate for particular situations. And these inputs include the advice and opinions of the line managers.

The approach is also relatively inexpensive. The industrial engineering staff setting estimates is a small one, probably about half the size of the staff that would be required for an equivalent amount of coverage with standards.

Purely from an industrial engineering point of view, the measurement system in this plant no doubt appears sloppy. For most estimates, nobody in the plant would claim the ±5 per cent accuracy commonly claimed for the more traditional methods. You might well ask: How can the management of this plant tie pay to productivity so closely with this relatively imprecise form of performance measurement? The answer is that the estimates themselves are not used for this function.

The purpose of the estimates is to give management an idea as to whether production is 'in the ball park'. In general, employees' production is considered satisfactory if it is at about 90 per cent of the estimate. But once having attained this level, an employee is evaluated on his ability to *improve* over it. Maintaining satisfactory performance is a condition of employment on that job; improving over it is a condition for receiving more than just minimal pay increases. *In essence, the standard shifts from one developed by an industrial engineer to one based on past output.* This latter standard is commonly referred to as a 'past actual'. The plant provides its supervisors with a set of guidelines specifying quite clearly the amounts of productivity improvement required for different pay increases.

Methods improvement

The system is truly *output*-oriented, because within broad limits management does not really care *how* output is improved. It may be by increased effort, but it can also be – and often is – through better methods. This plant has rejected the thesis that there is one best method for doing a job and that managers and industrial engineers are the only ones who can determine what this method is. Instead, the philosophy is that employees on the job know that job best, and thus major improvements can be achieved by encouraging and training the work force in methods improvement activities.

Every employee in this plant receives intensive work simplification training. The goal of this program is to instill in employees a dissatisfied, questioning attitude towards all aspects of existing methods and procedures. They are also taught specific techniques to aid them in developing improvements. The plant also has a suggestion plan; but, unlike so many other companies, this is not a facade overlaying a philosophy and system basically antithetical to worker creativity. In this instance the suggestion plan is not an exception to management's basic orientation; it is part and parcel of it.

Thus, when an employee comes up with an idea for a methods improvement – perhaps as a result of his work simplification training – he submits it to the suggestion plan. If it is accepted, and the criterion for acceptance is very simple – does it increase output? – he gets an award. *And*, because of the productivity improvement, he also soon gets a pay increase. The reward to the individual worker for his methods innovation is therefore substantial indeed. Furthermore, when others doing the same kind of work in the department use the new method, and thus increase *their* own productivity, they too soon receive commensurate pay increases.

Perhaps some would view this plant's approach as consisting of little more than a series of 'give-away' programs. Let me therefore repeat that the plant has an extremely good cost-reduction record. In part, at least, this record has been achieved because of management's willingness to pay – and pay well – for what it gets from its employees. When rewards are closely correlated with contribution, nobody is giving away anything.

In essence, what this plant had been able to do is markedly reduce individual and social impediments to productivity improvement. The approach is dynamic rather than static: it provides incentives and training for exceeding – not just meeting–past records; and for bettering–not just acquiescing to–predesigned methods. This, of course, is in distinct contrast to the 'fair pace', 'one best method' vocabulary of traditional engineered standards.

Basing employees' pay primarily on improving over past achievement has one further advantage over a system in which pay is geared to performance relative to engineered standards. There is considerably less hostility on the part of workers to productivity expectations. Employees under engineered standards frequently complain: 'The time-study man doesn't know what he is talking about. Nobody can meet that standard.'

Workers in the plant under discussion tend to be less antagonistic in this respect for a number of reasons. First, once the 90 per cent figure is reached, *the standard becomes what the worker has already produced.* That is, it is clear that the standard can be met because it has been met. Second, the estimates themselves are credible because they are to so large an extent based on past production records, rather than on synthetic data or stopwatch time study. And, finally, the supervisors have a considerable amount of say in the process of setting estimates for work in their departments. There is a great deal of interaction between them and the estimators, and this results in estimates which both parties usually agree are fair.

Conclusion

It is not my contention that the method of productivity management which I have described is, in all its specifics, the only one which can overcome the disadvantages of the traditional engineered work standards approach. It would be ludicrous to attempt wholesale transplantations of this particular system to existing organizations. Companies, and even plants within the same company, differ from each other in the nature of their production operations (man-paced versus machine-paced, stability of product line, and so forth), their labor relations atmospheres (including union contract obligations), their current levels of worker compensation, and their size. A system must be tailored to the individual characteristics of organizations, and there are numerous alternatives. Some of these possibilities may even involve the continuation of formal engineered standards, but with fundamental modifications in the way they are applied.

I also do not contend that the described plant's approach is necessarily the best one even for its particular conditions. Many readers will no doubt take issue with one or more aspects of the specific procedures employed. Such dissents are inevitable and, in fact, are present within the plant itself and in other parts of the corporation of which the plant is a part.

The variable I stress, therefore, is not the particulars of this or any other procedure; there is not, and cannot be, a cookbook recipe for this. Rather, it is the basic philosophy which people bring to the task of productivity management. I believe that this philosophy, as evidenced in the plant under discussion, involves four major components:

1. A high emphasis on output improvement as the criterion for the evaluation of worker performance. (This means that past performance becomes, in effect, the standard.)

2. A willingness to reward workers for output improvement.

3. A recognition of the importance of methods changes as key contributors to output improvement.

4. A conviction that blue-collar workers can – and want to – make significant methods improvements.

In the case of the plant described, management's belief in these principles led to its explicit rejection of the traditional engineered standards approach. In addition to the host of grievances which it could foresee generated against standards, this management was convinced that the standards system would stimulate behavior detrimental to the plant's output improvement goals. It was convinced the system would result in the ingenuity and effort of workers being used against rather than for the company. Managements of all plants need to ask themselves whether they are indeed interested in improvement and, if so, whether improvement is promoted or retarded by their current approaches.

Reference

LESIEUR, F. G. (1958) (ed.), *The Scanlon Plan*, MIT Press.

Part Three
The Scanlon Plan, Profit Sharing, etc.

Joe Scanlon's enthusiasm for his plan to involve everyone in
a business in the fortunes of that business was infectious; and
this is reflected in Russell Davenport's paper. The only balanced
and objective examination of the claims made for the plan that
I have been able to find is the one by Industrial Relations
Counsellors, which is reproduced here. The study by Flanders
and others of the John Lewis Partnership is, as far as I know,
the only detailed and systematic attempt to study the outcome
of an experiment to achieve economic success and human
satisfaction through profit sharing and democratic management.

11 Russell W. Davenport

Enterprise for Everyman

Russell W. Davenport, 'Enterprise for everyman,' *Fortune*, vol. 1, 1950.

There is nothing about the Lapointe Machine Tool Company that would lead the visitor to suspect that it houses the makings of a far-reaching management-labor revolution. It is a small, neat factory in Hudson, Massachusetts, where the executives walk up three flights to get to their varnished offices and most of the 350 employees eat lunch at home because they live nearby. Founded in 1903 by a French-Canadian named La Pointe, it was later purchased by John J. Prindiville, whose son, big, six-foot-six John Jr, is now President and owner of the equity stock. It is a modest enterprise with a reputation for high quality; there is even a trace of modesty in its boast that it is 'the world's oldest and largest manufacturer of broaches and broaching machines.' Yet the social achievement at Lapointe is something to make one pause and consider, for the discoveries that its management and union have made concerning the enterprise system could have repercussions around the civilized world.

Labor relations at Lapointe were never 'bad' – yet they were not 'good' either. They were just about like labor relations anywhere else, which is to say that there was mistrust on both sides leading on occasion to ill will. There was constant trouble, for example, over the piecework incentive system. Some rates were so easy that the men earned big bonuses and had to hold back production lest the rates be cut. Others were so hard that only the most skillful could earn any bonus at all. The indirect workers had no incentive rate and resented those of the others. Grievances abounded – the union was processing fifteen or twenty a month. There were numerous production delays, spoilage was too high, and deliveries were bad. In short, the picture was a typical one as industrial relations go – worse than some, not so bad as others.

In 1945 the plant was organized by the United Steelworkers, and about a year thereafter the Steelworkers called a national strike for a postwar wage increase. The Lapointe contract still had six months to run, and many of the men didn't want to go out anyway. However, the decision was to strike. Management thereupon sought an injunction, on the ground that the contract had been violated, and won a favorable decision from Judge Charles C. Cabot of the Massachusetts Superior Court. The union was enjoined from picketing the plant or otherwise interfering with operations. Early in April the strike at Lapointe ended. But there was bitterness in the air, and the situation was not improved by the realization that the machine-tool industry, after its war boom, had fallen on lean times. The unsettling possibility of a layoff hovered constantly over the shop.

It so happened about this time that Jack Ali, then president of the union, picked up a copy of *Life* and his eye fell on an article by Chamberlain (1946) with the intriguing title of 'Every Man a Capitalist'. Mr Ali read it. It told about a small maker of steel tanks called the Adamson Company, where union and management had come together to install an amazing productivity plan, with the result that the company's profitability had increased two and a half times and the men had taken home bonuses ranging up to 54 per cent of a high basic wage. The author of the plan was one Joseph Scanlon, of whom Mr Ali had never heard. However, he took the article to the union executive committee and together they became tremendously excited. After two evenings' discussion, the committee got in touch with Executive Vice President Edward M. Dowd, second-in-command to Mr Prindiville – a big man, up from the ranks, whose intimate knowledge of the broaching business is matched only by his sure-footed understanding of the men in his shop: Mr Dowd turned a willing ear to what the committee had to say and on reading the article was deeply stirred.

There then followed some very active weeks. Messrs Dowd and Ali journeyed out to East Palestine, Ohio, where they went over the Adamson plan in detail. They discovered that Mr Scanlon was now teaching at MIT, scarcely forty miles from Hudson, and they presently made their appearance in his office. Mr Scanlon, in turn, sent them to Roy Stevens, the regional field representative of the United Steelworkers. When they had obtained this gentleman's blessing they returned to the Scanlon office and began to dig down to bedrock. In the meantime Mr Dowd had had frequent conferences with Mr Prindiville, who was at once interested, and after some deliberation gave them the green light. Negotiations with the union were begun. And by 1 December, 1947, the Scanlon Plan was installed at Lapointe.

The Scanlon development

Now the Adamson experiment that started this chain of events was no mere accident in labor-management relations. It had its roots in the painful Thirties, when a group of labor leaders in the steel country evolved certain principles that have within them the power to revolutionize labor's relationship to enterprise, and vice versa. One of these leaders was Joseph Scanlon, whose versatile career included cost accounting, a spell as a professional boxer, a return to cost accounting (his basic profession), and then a shift over to the production side as an open-hearth worker. In 1936, during the formation of the SWOC, Mr Scanlon was on the open hearth of a marginal steel company, where he took a leading part in the organizing drive and was elected president of the new local.

Like many other steel manufacturers, this company was close to the rocks in 1938. Costs were high, the ink was red, liquidation seemed inevitable. Mr Scanlon and his fellow union officers felt that something had to be done. They persuaded the president of the company to join with them in a visit to Pittsburgh to see Clinton Golden, then vice president of the Steelworkers and Phil Murray's good right arm. Mr Golden had long been preaching a gospel of cooperation between management and labor for the good of both; nevertheless, he received this contingent with some degree of astonishment. Said he afterward, 'The union headquarters in those days was about as popular a place for industrial excutives to visit as a pesthouse. I was immediately impressed by the fact there was something extraordinary happening here'.

Mr Golden advised them to go back and try to work out a plan by which union and management could join together to save the enterprise. And the upshot was a pioneer union–management productivity plan, which provided that the workers would get a bonus for tangible savings in labor costs. Despite the fact that the primary aim of this plan was merely *survival*, it worked almost like magic and became the seed of all of Mr Scanlon's future work. Costs were cut so much that the company actually began to make a profit, and the workers got a bonus to boot. One suggestion by the union production committee, for example, cost less than $8000 in new equipment but saved about $150,000 in one year.

Scores of other companies doing business with the union found themselves in this same tough position in the late Thirties. Primarily to save the jobs of union members, Messrs Murray and Golden brought Mr Scanlon into the national headquarters to work on these cases. Sometimes at the request of the company, often at that of the union, productivity plans based upon union–management cooperation were installed in forty to fifty companies. The largest of these early-period plans was at a basic steel company employing about 4000 people; the smallest was at a water-heater company with 150 employees. According to Mr Scanlon, 'The successes were just as marked in the larger companies as in the small ones.'

Out of this work came a book – *The Dynamics of Industrial Democracy*, by Clinton S. Golden and Harold J. Ruttenberg – and a proposition. The proposition was that collective bargaining, as thus far developed, was a primitive affair and that the future task of labor and management would be to evolve a more mature relationship. In this new relationship collective bargaining would include, not merely wages, hours, working conditions, etc., but intelligent cooperation between the bargaining parties. Such cooperation could not be expected if the workers were shoved to one side, kept ignorant of the business, and treated as pawns in a game going on over their heads. A new principle must be introduced, which has since come to be called the principle of *participation*.

Last October [1949], in the first article of the present series, 'The Greatest Opportunity on Earth,' this principle was referred to as the most important area in which to implement the economic rights that the article set forth. But, unfortunately, when he uses the word participation, the average executive usually has something rather superficial in mind. He seeks to develop in the worker a *feeling* of participation, a *sense* of belonging. But is this quite honest? To make the worker feel that he is participating without giving him a real participation is, after all, to fool him; and deception is a flimsy, not to say an inflammable, foundation for industrial relations. Real participation consists in finding a means by which to reward labor for any increase in productivity and *then in building around this formula a working relationship between management and labor that enables them to become a team*. Once a team has been established, it is found that labor's prime interest, just like that of management, becomes *productivity*.

Such, at any rate, was the fruitful vein that Messrs Dowd and Ali had come upon at the Adamson Company, the most spectacular of the Scanlon developments. The performance of Adamson, indeed, had attracted the attention of Douglas McGregor, then head of the industrial-relations section at MIT, now president of Antioch College; and Mr McGregor had persuaded Mr Scanlon to come to MIT. There, with the help of economists, engineers, statisticians, and other experts on the MIT faculty, Mr Scanlon's work has entered a new phase, in which he can draw upon his vast experience in the labor-management field to give advice in the installation of real participation plans to those companies that seek him out.

The formula

The first task in the application of the Scanlon plan is to find a 'normal' labor cost for the plant under consideration and then to devise a means for giving labor the benefit of anything it can save under that 'norm'. In every case, therefore, some kind of link must be found between the worker and over-all shop productivity. Because every company is different, the nature of this link differs in almost every case; and because labor usually objects to having its costs accurately measured, some of the accounting handles that Mr Scanlon has used are rather weird. At a manufacturer of silverware it is ounces of silver processed; at a wholesale warehouse it is tons warehoused; at a steel foundry and machine shop in the Deep South it is pounds of castings produced. At the Market Forge Company, a versatile steel-fabricating shop in Everett, Massachusetts, it is a calculated percentage of operating profits per month.

This last method, linking labor saving to the profit and loss statement, is of course the basis of many profit-sharing plans. But Mr Scanlon feels, and Market Forge itself agrees, that it is the least desirable of any of the links, because the connection between the worker's productive efficiency and the final profit is too remote for many to grasp. It was adopted at Market Forge because the types of jobs coming into that shop are so variable that a labor-cost figure was impossible to determine. Notwithstanding this seeming weakness, a high level of participation has been developed at Market Forge, where more than 300 recorded suggestions for improved productivity have been put into effect in the past two years.

At Lapointe, where measurement was relatively easy, Mr Scanlon decided on the most direct and understandable accounting handle – the ratio of labor cost to total production value, the latter figure being equal to monthly sales plus or minus the change in inventory. Since this labor ratio is a highly competitive figure, Lapointe will not make it public. However, the principle can be illustrated, and all the Lapointe moves intelligently followed, by taking the average for the whole machine-tool industry. According to the Department of Commerce the ratio of wages and salaries to the value of shipments for the entire industry for 1947 was 40·7 per cent – which, to speak in round figures, we may call 41 per cent. In actuality, the company felt that the 'norm' derived from its war records was too high, and the union consequently agreed to a reduction of three points. If this were applied to the industry-wide average, the norm would be 38 per cent, and the plan would work as follows. If total shipments for a given month were 70,000, and inventory change was plus $30,000, total production value would be $100,000 for that month. The 'normal' pay-roll would then be calculated at 38 per cent, or $38,000. If the actual payroll were only $35,000, the difference of $3000 would go to the workers as their bonus.

Several important points are to be noted regarding this approach. First, labor gets *all* of the laborsaving; management's profit from the plan is derived from increased sales with no corresponding increase in total 'burden' (i.e., overhead and labor costs). Second – and absolutely basic to the Scanlon system – the bonus is given to all the workers and not just to those individuals who made productivity suggestions. At Market Forge it goes to every person in the business, including Leo M. Beckwith, the owner – and Mr Scanlon prefers this setup. At Lapointe, however, it goes to all except the fourteen top executives, who have a bonus system of their own, based on sales. Lapointe distributes the Scanlon bonus to every individual every month, as a calculated percentage of his basic rate – that is, his hourly, weekly, or monthly pay.

Mr Scanlon believes that the broadest and most meaningful participation requires a union – in the two or three instances where he has proceeded without one there have been delays and difficulties that a union would have helped to untangle. A firm distinction is made, however, between ordinary union affairs and the productivity affairs; grievances, for example, are handled through the grievance committee and are never discussed in the union–management productivity committees. Preferably, the original suggestion to try the plan should come from the union (as at Lapointe); but if it comes from management, the consent of the union must certainly be obtained, together with the approval of the regional representative. In many instances the plan rests on a simple 'memorandum of agreement'; at Lapointe it is actually part of the collective-bargaining contract.

Thus the basic theory is that labor should profit from labor-savings, while the company profits from a better use of its assets (for example, lower unit costs). And in order to maintain this dynamic balance at the original point agreed upon, it is provided that changes can be made in the formula to compensate for changed conditions on either side. Thus, some weeks after the plan actually went into effect, management decided to cut prices by 10 per cent on about half the products. Since this would result in a decrease in production value from a nonlabor source, about three points had to be *added* to labor's norm. This would bring our average norm for the industry back to 41 per cent. If management were to raise prices, the opposite adjustment would have to be made.

If a further general rise in wages were to occur, the union at Lapointe would insist that the workers get it in their wage rates;

one of Mr Scanlon's cardinal principles is that a productivity
bonus must not be used as a substitute for a wage increase. But
again, in order to maintain the dynamic balance, such a change
in the wage level, since it would be an additional labor cost,
would require a revision of the norm, here, too, upward. The
change can be avoided in only two ways: management may pass
the increase along in the form of increased prices, in which event
the labor ratio to sales will remain the same; or consideration
for the company's competitive position may induce labor to absorb
part or all of the increase by agreeing to let the ratio stand as it
was. Thus at Lapointe the union and the company undertook to
eliminate basic wage inequities, and this resulted in a sizable
increase in payroll. Since, however, this cost could not be passed
along in prices and still keep the business at a good volume,
labor consented to the maintenance of the original norm (41 per
cent by our hypothetical figure), instead of insisting on a larger
share of the sales dollar. In effect, therefore, the increase in payroll cost came out of increased productivity; and since prices did
not go up, the customers of Lapointe were the chief beneficiaries
of the difference. This benefit to the customers comes back, in
turn, to the company in the form of more secure jobs and
profits.

On the other hand, there is built into the agreement a provision
that where management makes an investment that will raise labor
productivity, without any increased work on the part of the labor
force, such investment may entail a recalculation of labor's
norm, this time downward. Lapointe has, in fact, invested in
about forty major pieces of equipment in the past year. It is impossible to tell how much of this is actually new investment and
how much is in reality replacement, though the total would run
to six figures. Nevertheless, management feels that this investment is to some extent a fair exchange for labor's extra rise in
productivity and has not therefore exercised this provision of the
agreement.

All this is collective bargaining of a high order, brought about
by the participation principle. The entire factory competes, from
the ground up. Because management sees its best hope in the
cooperation of the workers, it decides to forgo claims that it
would otherwise exact. And because the workers know the com-

pany's competitive problem in detail, their bargaining for labor's share is oriented to that problem.

One more provision was needed at Lapointe to put the plan in balance. Three times in the first two years the productivity curve has dipped below the norm – that is, labor costs were *greater* than our hypothetical average of 41 per cent. The company had paid out bonuses for the gains; who was to reimburse it for the losses? Owing to the extraordinary understanding that is developed by participation, the men were quick to see the injustice that was being worked on the company, and even though the contract contained no such provision, the union voluntarily agreed to an adjustment. The final arrangement was that the company should hold back half of the first 15 per cent of each month's bonus to take care of possible months when the payroll was greater than labor's norm. This amount is kept in a reserve fund, and whatever is left is distributed at the end of each year.

The reserve has had a salutary effect. It gives management a reasonable protection against temporary but unforeseeable slumps. On the other hand, it gives the workers a better perspective on the business. The desire to protect the reserve gives them the same dread of red ink that management has.

Implementation of the formula

The increased productivity of the shop under the Scanlon system is not achieved by a 'speed-up' in the ordinary sense of the word. Possibly the men work harder, and certainly they work more steadily, but the rise in efficiency is brought about chiefly by suggestions as to how time and effort can be saved. These suggestions are handled by shop committees, called 'production committees', whose members are always on the job and easily accessible. They are empowered to put any suggestion into effect that does not involve some other department or a substantial outlay of money. Over the production committees there sits the screening committee, composed of representatives of management and labor from the various departments, which rules on suggestions of wider scope. Each suggestion is carefully tagged with the name of the person making it; if it is accepted, some member of the committee is specifically assigned the job of following it up; if rejected someone is instructed to make a thorough explanation to the worker. At Lapointe the screening committee has received 513 suggestions in twenty-four months. Of these, 380 have been accepted, 28 started, 32 are pending, and 65 have been rejected.

Employers who have installed a casual 'suggestion box' system in their plants can have little idea of the kind of thing that goes on in a Scanlon Plan committee. For that matter, the average employer has little conception of the wealth of imagination and ingenuity lying untapped in the heads of the workmen. Under conventional management such ideas are blocked by a number of factors. A worker who has an idea may be given no incentive to suggest it. But even if there is an incentive, he may decide to withhold it, rather than incur the enmity or jealousy of his fellow workers, and especially of his foreman, who may construe the idea as a criticism of his own management. The individual is frustrated; and, moreover, since he can see how a saving could be made, and since management obviously does not see it, his respect for management declines. Add to this the fact that his communications with management are virtually nil. He has no idea of company problems, and hence no idea of why some moves are made that seem to him (and may in fact be) very stupid.

All this is fertile ground for the kind of animosity that has grown up in some labor circles against what the managers advocate as 'free enterprise'. Indeed, a number of workers at Lapointe, who feel that they can now talk with freedom, admit that in the old pre-Plan days they never associated themselves or their jobs with the profits of the company and maybe even got a little kick when they heard that the top floor was using red ink.

If one steps from that kind of shop, which often exists even under what is ordinarily called 'good' management, and takes one's seat as an observer at a Scanlon Plan screening committee, one passes, with Alice, through the looking glass and into an entirely different world. Like a crack out of a gun the meeting opens with an announcement of the figures for the past month. There follows a roundup by management of the current situation of the company. Then the suggestions are read out, one by one, and debated. A lot of criticism is generated and is of necessity accepted, since it is all directed to the same end – a better profit. Sometimes the workers throw the book at management, sometimes management points out where the shop has fallen down.

Engineers argue against machine-tool operators, foremen attack the engineers for unrealistic blueprints, someone demands better maintenance, management points out that more maintenance means bigger labor costs. In the process of this debate, almost every aspect of the business comes up for discussion – sales problems, competitors, orders, bids, spoilage, the business outlook, quality of materials, customers' foibles, management difficulties, etc. The result is a dynamic, working unity, which grows out of the bargaining table and yet wholly transcends it. The sudden realization dawns that here at Lapointe *collective bargaining has come of age*.

The meetings are not recorded verbatim. But minutes are distributed to everyone in the plant, and the important points in the debate are carried by the committeemen back into the shop, where they become the subject of further discussion – at the lunch hour, in the evening, or even at the union meeting. The result is that everyone at Lapointe knows the business and takes pride in his particular contribution.

Company benefits

The extraordinary results of this formula, implemented by the intimate labor-management committees, could make a long and fascinating tale. For our present purposes it will be necessary to concentrate on the most important.

First of all, the Plan has resulted in a good return to the owners. Since Lapointe does not publish its profit figures it is impossible to be precise about this.[1] The profits at Lapointe have not been so spectacular as those at Adamson – indeed it is probable that during the first year of the Plan the company made hardly any profit at all. This goes back to the nature of the machine-tool industry, which has been in something of a slump ever since the war. It is commonly accepted in the industry that Lapointe has been gaining an increasingly large percentage of the business ever since the Plan was inaugurated. During 1948 great strides were made at Lapointe in its ability to compete, which may not have shown up immediately in the profit and loss statement. In 1949 the results have been much more tangible; in

1. The Kiplinger magazine recently published figures on Lapointe, but many were inaccurate and were denied by the company.

contrast to much of the industry the company is now operating at a good profit.

All of this improvement cannot be attributed to the productivity plan. Lapointe has a sharp-eyed management that has been quick to follow up new leads in the hitherto obscure broaching business. It has been rewarded by the fact that modern engineering is finding new uses for broaching – for instance, machine-gun barrels, which were formerly rifled at the rate of one an hour, can now be broached at the rate of sixty an hour. Moreover, an entirely new business is opening up through the fact that certain parts of jet engines cannot be efficiently manufactured except by broaching. These are long-range gains attributable to factors other than labor.

However, management and labor are now cooperating so effectively at Lapointe that it is impossible to tell where the contributions of one ends and that of the other begins. Certain intangible benefits have accrued from this teamwork that affect the company's whole operation. For example, there has been a vast improvement in deliveries. Formerly delivery on ordinary broaches had been from three to five weeks and was often late. Now delivery can be made in from one to three weeks and is usually on time. This has become a great selling point for the company.

A second advantage is the reduction in complaints from spoilage and imperfect workmanship. Lapointe's policy is to take back any unsatisfactory product and fix it without extra cost. Under the Scanlon Plan this means *a loss to the workers as well as to the company*, and as a result great care is taken all along the line. The workers, indeed, get very excited about the big jobs. In one instance, when a new machine for a big automobile manufacturer was being tried out in the Lapointe plant, several of the union committee left their own jobs and gathered around to see whether the automotive manufacturer's engineers were duly impressed. While losses from customer complaints probably never amounted to as much as 1 per cent of the business, the intangible result of satisfied customers willing to reorder is a real one, for which management can thank its own foresight in installing a plan that gives the workers an interest in their product.

Moreover, the problem of instructing younger workers has

been greatly advanced. Formerly, under the piecework incentive system, a highly skilled workman was reluctant to show a younger man the tricks of his trade. But today the older workers are eager to teach their skills, in order to raise shop productivity. The most dramatic example at Lapointe was that of Robert Juliani, the best and most experienced form grinder, who made $3.57 an hour under the old piecework system. Formerly Mr Juliani was given no incentive to share his knowledge and skill, but after the plan he reorganized his work, took on two helpers, and taught them many of his ways of doing things. It is estimated that his increased efficiency is in the neighborhood of 300 per cent.

The plan, indeed, has completely solved the problem of 'controlled production' – that is, the policy, common to almost all labor, of holding back so that management will never know how fast a man really can work. The very first day it was installed a toolmaker, who had been producing twenty units in eight hours, produced sixty-two units. A surface grinder, whose average weekly earnings had been $76 on piecework, turned out $184 worth of work in four days. And so forth, through innumerable examples.

Labor benefits

On labor's side the benefits have been equally great. The average pay at Lapointe is in line with basic steel for the region, and for two years the workers have taken home an average bonus of 18 per cent over and above this. The bonus has, naturally, varied widely, ranging from zero to 39 per cent in June, 1949. Even better results are expected in 1950.

But the workers, like management, have derived many intangible benefits that cannot be measured in dollars and cents. They seem to enjoy working together and sharing the good and bad times. As one of them said, 'Formerly everyone was on his own. Now we all work for each other.' Innumerable versions of this observation can be picked up around the plant. One can spend little time here without reflecting that one of the weaknesses of conventional management is its almost exclusive emphasis on the money incentive. For the money incentive cannot satisfy the many demands of human nature – and this goes for management as well as for labor. Other incentives are needed if a man is to lead a healthy and happy life. Among these, two are of the utmost importance. One has to do with one's self – a feeling of accomplishment, a recognition of one's own abilities. This is provided for in the Scanlon Plan through the suggestion system, because a man who makes a good suggestion gets a profound satisfaction out of it; he carries the story home to his wife; he is admired and thanked by his associates. But the Scanlon Plan goes further, in that the reward for such suggestions does not go to the individual alone but to the entire shop. On the one hand, this eliminates jealousy; on the other, it opens up for the ordinary worker a kind of social or community incentive to which he eagerly responds. Cynics to the contrary, men do get a kick out of helping their fellow men; and this is demonstrated at Lapointe, where an atmosphere prevails in the shop that cannot possibly be duplicated under the selfish piecework system.

Yet another intangible advantage that the workers have derived is a strengthening of the union. If any employer becomes interested in this plan as a means of undermining the union, he had better skip it. Mature collective bargaining that has reached the evolutionary stage here described has precisely the opposite result. When the Plan was installed, union membership at Lapointe was about 70 per cent of the working force, exclusive of the office workers, who were not organized. Today all but three or four employees are union members, and the office workers have joined in a body. Interest in the union is keen. The advantage of this from the employer's point of view is that union meetings, instead of being dominated by a few malcontents, are heavily attended; and often enough most of the discussion is devoted to company affairs and how productivity can be increased. The union president, energetic and imaginative Fred Lesieur, who has succeeded Mr Ali, is enthusiastic about the Plan. The result of all this is that grievances have almost disappeared – only three have been processed in twenty-four months, and none of them has had to go to arbitration.

One of the greatest advantages of this kind of collective bargaining, from the worker's point of view, is the knowledge that it gives him of the business. When a slump is coming, he knows it. He is even given a chance to combat it, in the sense that if he can devise a cheaper way of turning out his product, perhaps the company will be able to take business away from somebody else. In a number of instances the Lapointe workers have actually done this, the most spectacular example being that of an order from a big automotive concern in December, 1948. The workers had been pressing management to accept orders even at the break-even point so as to tide over a bad period. Mr Prindiville, who sometimes sits in on the screening-committee meetings, had given in to the pressure some months previously to the extent of taking an order from this firm for 100 broaches at $83 per broach. But Lapointe had lost 10 per cent on the deal, and Mr Prindiville now put his foot down. If this business was to be taken again the price would have to be raised. In view of new competition, it meant that Lapointe almost certainly would not get the business – and at a time when work was scarce.

The gloomy gathering that listened to Mr Prindiville's pronouncement was then electrified by a question from Jimmie McQuade, skilled grinder and one of the most outspoken members of the screening committee. Who says we can't make those broaches at that price for a profit? Mr McQuade wanted to know. If you'd give the men in the shop a chance to go over the blueprints before production starts and to help plan the job, there are lots of ways of cutting costs without cutting quality. The idea grew, and the next day the suggestion ran around the shop like wildfire. The order was taken at the old price, this time with a *profit* of 10 per cent – a total gain in efficiency of 20 per cent.

The truth is that the Scanlon Plan has generated a competitive spirit throughout the factory: one hears as much about competition from the workers as from management itself. If there is a question of struggling for existence the whole company struggles collectively, and all the brains available are focused on the fight. The worker is no longer a pawn in a game he does not understand. He is a player. He enjoys it. And his contribution is worth money to all concerned.

The team at work

The effectiveness of such teamwork becomes especially apparent in the crises. Lapointe has been through three critical periods since the Plan was installed, and it has lifted itself out of them principally because the Plan creates an overwhelming incentive to cooperate.

The first crisis occurred in the fourth month. Mr Scanlon had warned management that output would greatly increase and that they had better begin hustling up some new orders. But management had a normal backlog, and inasmuch as it was having trouble with deliveries it did not dare put on any extra sales pressure. The very first month, however, productivity shot up to 133 per cent (100 equals the predetermined 'norm' already defined); the second month registered 128 per cent and the third 121 per cent. The result was that the company's backlog melted away. Management, of course, sprang to action as soon as the danger was realized. Telegrams and telephone calls poured out of Hudson. The salesmen were lashed to activity. Though himself a production man, Vice President Dowd – and even several engineers – took to the road. But broaches and broaching machines are technical tools that sometimes require weeks of designing before production can begin. Consequently the new orders did not give much immediate help, and the next three months were bad; the company ran a loss and the workers got no bonus.

Yet, as it turned out, the strength of the Plan was best demonstrated when things went bad. The workers had had three months of participation; they looked forward to bonuses in the future; and they liked the Plan because it gave them a *chance* – a chance to fight, a chance to pit their skills against other enterprises. Consequently, despite the setback, sentiment among them was overwhelming to continue the Plan, and suggestions kept pouring in for improvements. By June, 1948, a small bonus (4·7 per cent) was earned.

But then there was new trouble. The usual practice of the plant was to shut down for vacations for two weeks in July. Big new orders had come in, but these had to pass through the engineering department for designing, and when the engineers were on vacation no designing would be done. Would anybody dare to ask the engineers to give up their vacations? – especially in view of the fact that, as is usual in machine shops, there was continuous bickering between the engineers and the machine operators, who were inclined to criticize the drawings as unrealistic. A delegation from the union approached Vice President Dowd, who said that he would put it up to the men themselves. When he went to the men, however, he found that agreement had already been reached at the workers' level – the engineers had sacrificed their vacations. They worked hard during July in an otherwise empty plant, and by August drawings were pouring out of the drafting room. Productivity soared again, yielding a bonus of 25 per cent for September and 19 per cent for October. A better example of community incentive could hardly be found.

Still another difficulty then arose. The problem was to devise a machine capable of broaching certain parts of a jet airplane engine. Everybody had said the parts in question could not be broached, but the Lapointe engineers insisted they could be, providing a new machine was developed. The problem centered around a very hard steel, close to the limit for cutting tools, and the company's efforts to solve it resulted in many a setback. Labor watches every job at Lapointe, and the men became impatient when they saw so much work being done on which there would be no shipping dollars. But management went back to the screening committee again and again and said in effect, 'Bear with us. This is experimental stuff. If we can get it right, we're in.' So the screening committee went along. Then at last the bugs were out, production began, and everybody went to town. The monthly productivity curve shot up, from a dismal low of 71 per cent in December, 1948 (in the middle of the experimental work), to 119, 138, 140, 145, 150, and finally, in the twentieth month of the plan, to 161 per cent.

These three incidents provide three dramatic examples of teamwork. In the first, the workers held on despite an unexpected discouragement. In the second, the engineers came to the rescue of all concerned. In the third, management exercised its proper function with great intelligence, by insisting that temporary losses be sustained in order to grasp a future profit. If this experimental work had failed, a certain field of sales would have been closed to Lapointe. As it is, the firm got in on the ground floor of a new and growing business, and all concerned will profit from that achievement.

Will it work for you?

Many objections will be raised to the Scanlon Plan by those who have never seen it in operation. But perhaps the least fruitful objection of all is the one most commonly encountered: 'This plan may work at Lapointe – or wherever – but that is because of special, perhaps accidental, circumstances. *My* plant is different.'

Of course, everybody's plant *is* different. Every union is different also. For this very reason Mr Scanlon refuses to crystallize his work into a formula. He relies on certain principles fundamental to human nature; and he adapts these in almost infinite ways to the particular problems of each particular company. He has now met with success, in varying degrees, in more than fifty enterprises in several different industries, of many different sizes, under many different circumstances; where the original labor relations were good and where they were bad; where profits were good and where they were non-existent; where labor productivity was easy to measure and where it was virtually impossible; among skilled workers and unskilled workers. There are, of course, shops where this plan would not work. But the burden of the evidence is accumulating that those in which it will not work are the *exceptions*.

Yet there are two prerequisites to the Scanlon Plan, and where they do not exist time would be wasted in trying to install it. One is that the union leadership must be intelligent. This does not mean that the union should be acquiescent: on the contrary, it may be quite aggressive. But real intelligence is needed to bargain at a participation level, which involves an understanding of such things as competition, competitive pricing, profitability, and many other factors that never enter into collective bargaining at the lower level. This prerequisite to Scanlon Plan success is provided at Lapointe by Fred Lesieur, the new union president, who, as a good union man, considers it his *responsibility* to have an intelligent grasp of the productivity side of the business. The other union officers share this responsibility.

Second, and even more important, there must be someone in top management who is vitally interested and *who is able to stand the gaff*. A management that wants to stand off and look down its nose at the workers cannot operate a Scanlon Plan. Nor is it possible to turn this vital area of the business over to a vice president in charge of industrial relations. Someone who actually runs the company or the plant – the president or his executive representative – must be a regular member of the screening committee (he need not be chairman); and this person must be willing to enter into any kind of debate and to accept in a fair and impartial manner any criticism hurled at his own management. He need not worry about his dignity. The men will invest him with the dignity he deserves – no more, but no less.

It is precisely in this respect that Lapointe has been so fortunate. Lapointe has in John Prindiville a man of open mind, who believes that the incentives of enterprise should reach down, through management, to the shop floor. And it has in Ed Dowd a man who became the Plan's prime mover, utterly dedicated to its goals. Mr Dowd is not afraid of criticism – and is not afraid to give it. The men know he is sincere in his efforts to make the Plan work, and they consequently trust him. Besides, he sets quite a pace. When the argument gets hot, he takes off his coat, and everyone interprets this as permission to do likewise. Comfortably in his shirt sleeves, Ed Dowd pitches into the suggestions, throws upon each of them the light of his enormous knowledge of the business, tosses them back to the committee, and finally designates some individual to 'follow it through'. When there is a tough one involving important company policy, Ed Dowd takes it himself.

If such men can be found – an intelligent union leader and a forthright management leader – the Scanlon principles can be applied virtually anywhere. And the way is then opened up to a new and creative area of industrial relations – the area of mutual interests. In the process of entering upon this area, and of consolidating it, *everyone* in the shop, high or low, joins the enterprise system.

Reference

CHAMBERLAIN, J. (1946), 'Every man a capitalist,' *Life*.

12 Industrial Relations Counsellors Inc.

Excerpt from 'Group wage incentives: experience with the Scanlon Plan', *New York Magazine*, 1962, pp. 18–40.

Analysis of company experience

There seem to be two major reasons why a company would want to adopt a Scanlon Plan. Firstly, in many cases, financial difficulty has been at the root of a company decision to look around for a panacea for existing ills. This was the major reason for adoption in one, and a contributory reason in two other companies in the IRC case studies. In such circumstances, the concept of a group wage incentive plan, developed in an atmosphere of cooperation, with its attempt to tap resources neglected in the past, has a distinct appeal. Workers facing job loss are also frequently ready to grasp at any straw of hope and to work with management to save the company. Secondly, a Scanlon-type plan may be adopted because of dissatisfaction with an existing incentive system. This was the case in four of the firms surveyed by IRC, though in two companies, it was combined with a weak financial situation. In each of these cases, an individual incentive system had become, over a period of time, loose and difficult to administer, with pressure from the employees to further emasculate it.

Companies having had a successful experience operating the Scanlon Plan have received widespread publicity, and the advantages flowing from it to management and the workers have been detailed. A study of most wage incentive programs, however, will reveal both strengths and weaknesses. Since the operation of an industrial plant in today's world of advanced technology is most complex, it is natural that a plan, whose foundation rests upon cooperation of the workforce with the management, can be expected to also develop complications. This section, therefore, will attempt to analyse company experience in terms of the Scanlon Plan's major components, already discussed, and the factors both promoting and inhibiting the adoption or success of this type of incentive plan.

Appraisal of the plan as a suggestion and incentive system
Suggestion system

The major advantage attributed to the plan has been a rise in the efficiency of a company, brought about chiefly by employee suggestions as to how time and effort can be saved. This was confirmed by the four companies in the IRC sample still operating under the plan. Two of them disclosed that slightly more than half of the employee suggestions had been accepted and put into practice. In one of the plants, a regular suggestion system with an individual payoff had been in effect before installation of the plan, but since adoption of the Scanlon approach, the rate of suggestion submission had more than doubled. This probably can be attributed to the increased management interest in suggestions that the plan had brought about.

Both sample companies that had abandoned use of the plan, however, reported that the suggestions offered were not very effective, that in some cases they only represented the wild dreams of employees unfamiliar with running a plant, and that time was consumed in reviewing ideas that experience had taught management to discard because of impracticality or costliness.

To a large degree, this difference of experience with respect to the value of employee suggestions stems from a difference in the basic attitude of the companies. If management *believes* that suggestions will be worthwhile, then it probably will interpret them as such, but if it has little confidence in the ability of employees to contribute meaningful ideas, then even those suggestions that are accepted may be regarded as trivial.

Even where employees have much to contribute in the initial stages of the plan, experience shows that the value of employee ideas falls off very precipitously over time. There was some confirmation of this phenomenon in the companies studied by IRC, even in the four successful applications of the plan.

Incentive system

Individual incentive plans are not applicable to all businesses. A company whose work is of a job-lot character with variations in quality would find that an incentive system, based on individual jobs, would be costly and difficult to administer with any degree of accuracy. If labor costs were still a high proportion of total costs, then a group incentive system such as the Scanlon Plan might help to improve productivity.

As a group incentive system, the effectiveness of the Scanlon Plan has varied. The experience of some companies indicates that it tends to inject teamwork into company operations by contributing to good morale and employee attitudes favorable to the company. Active joint participation in working toward a common goal has strengthened team spirit, and the plant-wide incentive has seemed to increase cooperation between departments and various organization levels and to decrease bickering. Since each individual's earnings are dependent upon the efforts of every other individual, the plan tends to reduce the normal rivalries between groups that are so characteristic of most industrial plants.

On the other hand, such results have not occurred in other companies, where the plan has developed all the drawbacks of any group incentive system. Since an employee sees no direct quid pro quo for his ideas or intensified efforts, he finds the group bonus an insufficient incentive. Furthermore, factionalism has arisen among departments, as one group blames another for the failure of the plant to achieve a bonus.

A necessary condition for the success of a group incentive program would seem to be low labor turnover and high worker attachment to the plant. A study of an unsuccessful use of a group incentive plan in a small New Jersey ceramics plant, for instance, indicated that the workers' loose ties to the factory and to each other tended 'to fragment the work group' and to make the plan unworkable. In this case, the main orientation of the female labor force of secondary wage earners was to the outside and not to the factory for any personal satisfaction beyond the pay check. For such workers an individual incentive system would probably have been more effective.

The Scanlon Plan would also seem to be more successful where workers are tied closely together by the flow of work, but in the New Jersey pottery, the workers lacked an integrated perception of the work process and solidarity within their own group. Being unable to perceive the consequences of their actions in terms of the whole, they developed the attitude 'Why should I work my fingers to the bone, no one else does?'

It has been hypothesized that where a plant is technologically a single unit (for example, assembly-line production and certain chemical processes), the plan is difficult to operate, because the efficiency of individual departments is hard to measure. The IRC sample included a continuous process operation of the sort referred to, but the hypothesis could not be fully tested because this plant's modified Scanlon Plan did not include a financial payoff, and, indeed, management has not been able to devise a yardstick by which to evaluate savings and efficiency.

The plan's drawback in a technologically single-unit operation is that frequently rivalry arises among plant groups. This had developed in the sample company, but not seriously enough to prevent the plan from working. The ability to overcome interdepartmental rivalry requires a high degree of cohesion and identification with the plant as a whole, as well as with the individual department. Since the attainment of this depends on a number of factors, including the size, homogeneity and history of the workforce, it is possible that the plan may be most successful within a narrow range of technologies.

Most important of all, no incentive system can work unless it pays off, and the difference between success and failure in applying the Scanlon Plan lies primarily in the ability to pay the bonus. The two companies in the IRC samples which had abandoned the plan had done so after operating for periods of eight or nine months during which no bonuses were earned. The consequence was employee disillusionment and a worsening of labor–management relations. Even in the two cases studied by IRC in which the plan had been successfully operated for a number of years and where bonuses were paid quite regularly, when a period of nonbonus payment cropped up, the value of the plan to management, as well as to workers, dropped and relations deteriorated. In the one case, where no financial payoff has been included in the plan, the union has made it clear, after less than one year of successful operation, that its members want some share of the money savings due to the operation of the plan, though it is not seeking the normal Scanlon Plan type of bonus arrangement.

Bonus formula

An important advantage claimed for the Scanlon Plan is that the bonus calculation provides 'a sense of direction: an over-all target by means of which individuals can assess the effectiveness of their contribution to the over-all effort.' The inability of employees to understand the bonus formula, however, is a major drawback. Despite the fact that Scanlon Plan proponents emphasize that the spirit which the plan engenders – not its formula – is the key to its success, workers want to understand the basis of the payoff in their incentive system. The Scanlon formula, however, is complicated (in one company, the formula for determining the employee's share is $I = 0.55 \{\Sigma \ [(W + S + Md + Mi)P] + CS - [Wa + Ma]\})$. It is no wonder that very few employees, if any, are able to understand the basis on which their incentives are paid, or to evaluate an increase in productivity of the total group. This is in decided contrast to an individual incentive system, in which a worker usually knows exactly how much he will earn for producing a given number of units of output.

In companies that have abandoned the plan, including the two studied by IRC as well as those reported in other studies, employees had never really understood the complicated formula, and this had contributed to the plan's failure. In the successful cases, also, a lack of understanding was reported, but since bonuses had been paid on a regular basis, this had not mattered materially.

The lack of precision inherent in the formula for determining incentive pay can be another serious flaw. When a firm manufactures a variety of products, a labor-cost ratio cannot easily be computed, and so some rather arbitrary figure is likely to be agreed upon, which does not always work out in practice.

Furthermore, over long periods of time, the actual labor-cost ratio is likely to change, but company experience indicates that it is difficult to revise the formula downward when that becomes necessary. The union is most reluctant to see it moved downward, and since the payroll and sales ramifications of the formula are complicated, it is not easy to make the employees understand the need for downward revision. Political overtones, lack of understanding, and a general feeling against hurting or taking anything away from employees can influence the company to leave the formula alone, even when this operates to the detriment of the business. This had occurred in one of the successful cases studied by IRC, and the company management was bitter because the present formula for sharing the fruits of efficiency was eating up all the increased profits, which were needed for future growth of the business.

Company problems under the plan
The plan may limit company flexibility

While the plan is centered on reducing labor costs, company experience has also included such side effects as improvements in deliveries, reduction in waste, and more efficient training of new employees. Cost reduction, of course, improves a company's competitive position – a result of particular importance to those companies that have adopted the plan to overcome their basic inefficiencies.

In practice, however, the results may not always be what is expected. For one thing, some companies have found that, since the bonus payments are computed on a monthly basis, a sudden, temporary decrease in labor costs can put extra money in their employees' pockets even though the business is losing money over the year.

Second, there exists the distinct possibility that short-run competitiveness may be purchased at the price of longer-run non-competitiveness. To remain competitive, a company must retain its flexibility, for it is impossible to anticipate all new events. Yet, companies have, on occasion, found their flexibility limited in many ways by the Scanlon Plan. Despite the fact that expansion of engineering, research and development, or sales operations might be in the long-run interests of the company, since both direct and indirect labor costs are included in the calculation of the bonus formula, production workers often protest increases in salaried payroll and put pressure on management to hold it down. This was the exact experience of one of the companies studied by IRC.

Flexibility is necessary also because the nature of a company's business does not remain static over time, and a company might find it necessary to diversify business and include operations not particularly suited for the Scanlon Plan. Yet the plan may not be easily dropped, for once it has achieved some measure of success, company officials find themselves proponents of it in the eyes of their employees, the union, and the community; thus, the impact of a business decision to discontinue operation of the plan could create serious public relations problems. Such was the dilemma facing the company just cited that had found the sharing formula eating up its increased profits.

Finally, when an outside consultant is used to service the plan, flexibility may be hampered, because it can prove difficult in some cases to convince him of the need for changes before even attempting to convince employees. Moreover, use of an outside consultant under the Scanlon Plan introduces a new element into labor-management relations, which may be good, but there is also evidence that a third-party can serve to disrupt established relationships.

It may be unwieldy to administer in large operations

Companies operating with the Scanlon Plan have reported many administrative advantages. For example, the need for a time-study or other rate-setting group is eliminated. Thus, not only is there a cost saving, but the normal conflicts that surround the work of a time-study department are not present either. On the other hand, however, it is quite obvious that establishment of the Scanlon Plan means that time, both of workers and management personnel, must be spent in committee meetings reviewing and evaluating the suggestions submitted. One of the survey companies that had abandoned the plan offered as a contributory reason for doing so the fact that administering the plan simply consumed a disproportionate amount of management time in comparison to the reductions in labor costs stemming from its operation.

Administration can prove particularly difficult for the larger scale establishment. In the smaller plant, only a two-step procedure is required to process employee suggestions: production committees plus a screening committee. At Stromberg-Carlson, the largest factory operating under the plan, a third level of administration, the Planning and Review Committee, has been added. In still larger establishments, additional levels might be needed, but as they multiply, much of the ease of two-way communication, and thus the benefits of plan, would be lost. At the same time, it has been seriously questioned whether support for a plant-wide goal can be maintained in larger plants. Even Professor McGregor has admitted that there would be obvious difficulties in applying the plan in a big organization, but he has suggested the possibility of 'utilizing the Scanlon approach in the context of divisional "profit centers" which are popular among decentralized big companies today'.

The formula is not suitable to some operations

The nature of the Scanlon Plan formula, with its calculation of labor costs as a percentage of value produced, makes it most difficult to apply in those companies whose product line is constantly changing. Both of the companies that had discontinued the plan emphasized the problem of product mix as an important factor in its abandonment. One of them called particular attention to the bookkeeping problem involved – since the product was constantly changing, there was sometimes a lag of two or three months in calculating savings, to the utter displeasure of the employees. In this company, everybody, particularly the accounting department, breathed a sigh of relief when the plan was discontinued.

Management reorientation is needed

Experience has shown that institution of the Scanlon Plan forces management to rationalize its policies in the area of production planning and to pay more attention to accurate cost determination. The whole suggestion and committee meeting procedure, even if it produces no startlingly new ideas, forces top management to review its operations, and this reappraisal tends to make management improve the performance of its own functions.

The role of supervision, however, can be an important deterrent to adoption or success of the plan. The plan puts supervisors in a particularly vulnerable position, and without proper psychological preparation, foremen and department heads can develop deep resentment toward suggestions emanating from their subordinates as reflecting upon their own competence. The change in role and attitude of management from one of direction to one of participation and partnership is not easily obtained, and the initial loss of prestige and power on the part of supervision is bound to develop conflicts and tension.

In one of the companies studied by IRC, the tendency in the early stages of the plan was for the workers to entirely ignore first-line supervision and take all suggestions directly to the production committees. This served to overload the agendas of the committees and, at the same time, breed resentment against the plan among the foremen. Management had to take steps, using the plan's production and screening committees as the channel of communication, to correct this situation. Workers were encouraged to first bring their ideas to their foremen, who were, in turn, encouraged to act upon them themselves, sending on to the production committees only those suggestions that they disapproved or that required higher approval.

Those who have closely observed the Scanlon Plan in operation point out that the most difficult adjustment called for by the cooperative approach is that which must be made by management. A management fearful of surrendering any of its prerogatives should not consider the Scanlon Plan, for it clearly involves union participation in production matters, the acceptance of critical comments and suggestions about managerial deficiencies from employees, and joint decision making on many important problems of the business.

Similarly, a company that has not clearly delegated decision-making authority down the line should avoid the Scanlon Plan, because it would only lead to further confusion. Workers make suggestions which go up the line to somebody who finally must accept and implement them, or reject them and explain why. If suggestions 'kick around' and die because of indecision, employees will be discouraged from taking the plan seriously. This difficulty of 'finding the boss' has been cited as being of special significance in multiplant operations, where all or most authority may lie beyond the bounds of the particular plant.

A universal experience is that top management devotion to the plan is essential for its adoption and success. Most often the head of a small firm becomes a 'convert to Scanlonism'. It is his enthusiasm and faith which dominates and carries the rest of management and the employees along through thick and thin, when otherwise it would founder on some snag.

Not only must there be a follower of the 'new religion' within the company, but there also must be an 'evangelist' on the outside. One observer linked successful application of the plan to 'the impact of Joe Scanlon's personality and moral influence on the thinking and reactions of the people participating in the situation', but warned that 'the principal danger of the Scanlon Plan is the host of second-class imitators who lack Joe Scanlon's insight.' The success of new installations of the plan since Scanlon's death, however, might serve to dispel such fears.

Management relations with employees and unions
Labor–management relations

Much of the value of the Scanlon Plan is derived from a decided improvement in in-plant labor–management relations. Firms have reported that resistance to change on the part of the workers is reduced because, through the suggestion system and production committee meetings, they participate in the formulation of policies of change, and because they feel that the incentive system insures their sharing the benefits of increased efficiency resulting from the change.

The plan also provides a good two-way communications system between management and employees on a regular basis, especially in small plants. The plan develops better employee understanding of the functioning of the organization, and through the suggestion and production committee system enables management to find out what employees are thinking, and, at the same time, to inform them of company problems and to educate them as to sales, accounting, production, engineering, and research activities.

Grievances are reduced and a general improvement in labor relations takes place. In the two companies surveyed by I R C that had had long experience with the plan, there had been almost no written grievances in several years. This does not mean that everything always proceeded harmoniously, but probably indicates that the suggestion–production committee procedure provided a more informal channel for settling grievances, and that energies that would normally go into battling on grievances were being channeled into joint efforts to reduce cost and improve efficiency. The plan, moreover, has apparently fostered cooperation rather than conflict in management–union relations. It is only fair to point out, however, that the companies successfully applying the plan had had good labor–management relations before they adopted the Scanlon approach, thus confirming one conclusion that in many cases 'union–management cooperation stems from the pre-existence of relatively harmonious relationships'.

In the view of some observers, the success or failure of the plan rests upon the functioning of the production committees, and upon the ability of each department representative, in cooperation with the departmental supervisor, to stimulate active participation of employees in the solution of production problems. There is always the inherent danger, however, that the production committee meetings will degenerate into mere gripe sessions, and this had been the unfortunate experience of the two companies in the IRC sample that had abandoned use of the plan.

Too much of an improvement in the relationship between management and the union can boomerang, and both the union as an institution and the company can suffer if union officers become so enamored of the Scanlon Plan that they pay more attention to its operation than to their job of representing employees. Identification of union officers with management could lead to worker frustration, a drop in morale, and possibly even direct action outside of established grievance channels.

Benefits to employees

The benefits flowing from the Scanlon Plan cannot, obviously, be solely for management, for cooperation would not take place unless employees also got something out of it. Since it is a group wage incentive system, its chief advantage to employees is the opportunity for increasing their earnings. The formula guarantees them that they will share in the benefits of increased efficiency, and in the two survey companies that had successfully applied the plan for many years, the employees had enjoyed over the period bonuses above normal earnings that averaged 5 per cent in one case, and $6\frac{1}{2}$ per cent in the other.

Bonuses, however, do not always accrue, and this was the experience of the two companies that had abandoned the plan. Furthermore, the nature of the formula, which can work to the disadvantage of the company under certain circumstances, can do the same with respect to employees under other conditions. Increased effort on the part of employees may not lead to bonus payments because of the role of indirect costs, and this is particularly true during any downswings in production.

The industrial revolution, from the earliest division of labor to the assembly line, has continually structured and simplified the job of the operative to the point where he may feel that he is a mere appendage to the machine and his work is unpleasant. The plan tries, with mixed results, to increase job satisfaction and, through the suggestion and group incentive systems, to make work meaningful by relating the individual's job to every other operation of the plant.

The thinking of some industrial sociologists and human relations advocates has been directed toward giving workers 'a sense of participation in the enterprise'. The Scanlon Plan, by encouraging actual participation, raises the worker's status and importance, making him more than a mere 'hired hand.' Workers, however, do not always respond positively to the opportunity to participate, and many of them do not care to share the burdens of decision making with management, being content to do their jobs and draw their pay. In fact, even among the academicians engaged in advanced research in the behavioral sciences, there are those who believe that a sense of participation and happiness at the work place are not actually desirable end products.

Benefits to the union

Union as well as management thinking must undergo reorientation for the successful application of the plan, and the union must cease to think of the employer solely as an antagonist. In return for its help in trying to improve the company's economic situation, the union will expect greater security for itself, and the Scanlon Plan, like any other form of union–management cooperation, depends upon management's wholehearted acceptance of unionism.

Indeed, the Scanlon Plan tends to strengthen unionism within the plant. Where the group incentive system is established jointly with the union, the resulting bonuses are a feather in the union's cap, particularly where it could not otherwise have negotiated higher earnings for employees. The union, moreover, usually plays an important role under the plan. In some instances, the plan had originally been proposed by the union, and union officials took an active part in its operation, but in others, the union's role was subordinated by having employee representatives to the production and screening committees elected in the plant independently of union participation. It is interesting to note that in one of the two companies that had abandoned use of the Scanlon Plan, management had introduced it unilaterally, even before the union had been on the scene, and the lack of union involvement in its operation contributed to its demise.

Since the plan usually covers all the employees of the establishment, white-collar as well as blue-collar, unionism may be extended to the nonproduction employees, too. This occurred at Lapointe, where office employees, who had no thought of joining the Steelworkers when the plant was organized, did so after the plan went into effect. They were in the Scanlon Plan and felt that they should belong to the union as well.

But officials of certain national unions have criticized the Scanlon Plan on the ground that the local union may become identified more with management than with the national union. Antagonism between local and national unions can flow from the fact that the aim of the plan is to improve the earnings of employees in the particular establishment, while the goal of the national union is to get better conditions for all workers in that particular industry or occupation. This antagonism does not arise in inefficient companies, since the plan merely enables them to meet union scales.

Basic obstacles to acceptance of the Scanlon Plan

Probably the greatest deterrent to acceptance of the Scanlon Plan, as with other proposals for union–management cooperation, has been that it runs counter to prevailing management philosophy, which looks upon union participation as an encroachment upon management's prerogatives. The present ideological framework of industrial society places upon the management of each enterprise the responsibility for production, and this philosophy is also accepted by American labor. Solomon

Barkin, Research Director of the Textile Workers Union, has written as follows:

In our country, responsibility for enterprise rests primarily on management. Most executives of expanding and prosperous companies are reluctant to share these rights to consider innovations or determine their application. Moreover, unions usually find that companies with aggressive programs present them with enough problems and changes and disturb the existing job relationships and patterns so frequently that there is little reason for them to accelerate the process.

Moreover, most members of management would disagree with the assumption of the plan that the single greatest source of ideas for improving efficiency is the employee on the job. They would contend that the employee is not competent to suggest and solve deeply complex changes in operations, and that experience indicates that employee suggestions are not a substitute for an industral engineering department. For the company that has been operating inefficiently, employee suggestions may point up many cost-saving devices, but for the efficient firm they may only be of peripheral value and possibly not worth the cost of the entire plan.

The value of any incentive plan, individual or group, in increasing productivity has been questioned, and according to one observer, 'most of the cost reductions (effected in plants with wage incentive plans) can be traced to management's efforts to make the incentive workable, not to the incentive itself.'

The Scanlon Plan also runs against the dominant union philosophy. Unions fear that participation in management may undermine the union by lessening the militancy of employees. They have also been unsympathetic because, as noted by Mr Barkin, one of their fundamental beliefs is 'that improvements in working conditions and income must be worked out for all groups within a union's jurisdiction rather than in a single company or plant.'

Furthermore, the underlying concept of the Scanlon Plan – that there is a fundamental harmony of interests between labor and management – is an exaggeration. While it is true that both depend upon the successful functioning of the enterprise for their livelihood, there are also areas of conflict between them, and it is impossible to eliminate all discord from the industrial relations field.

Finally, the very need for devices such as the Scanlon Plan is highly questionable from the points of view of both management and labor. The pressure of market forces keeps most firms efficient without their having to rely upon employee suggestions; American unions have proved quite proficient in wringing wage increases out of employers and in getting for the employees their portion of the gains in productivity without having to resort to formal sharing plans; and experience has shown that there are a variety of ways of approaching the goal of better labor–management relations, and that the sharing of authority over the production process need not be one of them.

13 Allan Flanders, Ruth Pomeranz and Joan Woodward

Experiment in Industrial Democracy

Excerpt from *Experiment in Industrial Democracy*, Faber, 1968, pp. 180–93.

The John Lewis Partnership is a thriving commercial enterprise deliberately founded on an ideology. This is the master key to an understanding of the effects as well as the working of its special institutions; those institutions which together constitute its claim to be an experiment in partnership. By an ideology is meant, not a body of vague sentiments and aspirations, but a logically consistent set of beliefs which serve as a guide to action. It is not suggested that all, or even a majority of, the Partners share those beliefs. Their acceptance is not a condition of employment, and most of its employees join the Partnership with little or no knowledge of its ideas and institutions. They enter its employment for much the same reasons that would lead them to seek work in any other firm. They want to gain a livelihood in return for their services and to enjoy the rights and benefits that go with the obligations and responsibilities of their job. The Partnership as such, rather than any individual partner, expresses the ideology, although this implies that the work behaviour of its members, especially those in authority, is strongly influenced by it. This ideology has moreover a missionary quality. The Partnership believes that it is setting an example that other firms would do well to follow and actively propagates its principles as an answer to many of the contemporary ills of industrial society.

The ideological basis of the Partnership might appear to be the most obvious of all its features. The very language used to describe its objectives has this ring. What is less immediately apparent is the actual content of its system of beliefs and consequently whether they are in fact systematically related to each other. Anyone reading the writings of Spedan Lewis, who was responsible for the creation of the Partnership's ideology, could easily be misled by his discursive and anecdotal style into thinking that he is presenting nothing more than a discordant patchwork of ideas. The complex character of the special institutions also masks the comparative simplicity and rigour of their underlying principles. Yet the truth, as we came to see it, is that the strengths and weaknesses of the Partnership system derive from its having a clear and coherent system of normative principles which govern its conduct as an employer.[1] What are the more important of those principles?

Their starting-point is the premise of common ownership. All who work permanently for the business are its owners and share the rewards of enterprise. Because of the nature of the arrangements for profit sharing, they also supply the business with capital on which it is possible to pay a fixed rate of interest. These things being so, it is believed – and here we come to the first normative principle – that the usual division in industry between 'we' and 'they' has been abolished: in the Partnership everyone is working for the good of the whole. It follows that the pressing of sectional claims by means of power is incompatible with the ideology. Such action can only result in privilege, in some groups gaining unfair advantages at the expense of the rest. But as the Partnership is broadly committed to the values of democracy, it cannot logically prevent its members from joining trade unions; freedom of association is their democratic right. Collective bargaining may therefore have to be accepted where there is a demand for it, but it should not be encouraged. The principles of the Partnership are held to have deprived it of its *raison d'être* within the organization.

The second normative principle settles and justifies the general distribution of rewards in the Partnership. It is not intended to be an egalitarian society in the literal sense that every Partner receives the same income. Partners should be remunerated, the Partnership believes, according to the worth of their services to the success of the enterprise. This is decided partly on what must be paid to secure their particular services and partly on how they

1. The ideology also includes principles which govern its commercial practices such as 'never knowingly undersold', but these were not so relevant to our research.

actually perform in their jobs. As the Rules state: 'the Partnership will pay the full, local, commercial rate and as much above that as can be justified by performance.'[2] The second principle leads in practice to a pay system of personal rates with great care being taken to fix them impartially and on merit. His rate of pay in turn determines the individual's share of distributed profits. Thus the ultimate rationale of income distribution by remuneration and bonus is to be found in the notion of 'to each according to his contribution to the common good' on the assumption that everyone's contribution can be fairly assessed on the basis of his work and the market rate for the job.

The Partnership does not, however, distribute its income solely according to such economic criteria. The further benefits of working for the Partnership – pensions related to the cost of living, minimum income supplements, children's allowances, grants and loans to employees – are seen principally as meeting social criteria of need. These fringe benefits, as they might be called elsewhere, are the expression of another ideological principle. The Partnership looks upon itself as a community as well as a business, and like any other community believes it should be concerned with caring for its less fortunate members. Assistance of this sort would carry the stigma of charity if it depended on power or personal favour. By granting aid according to impersonal criteria and by making its administration the subject of representative self-government the Partnership seeks to avoid this objection. Its democratic institutions with executive functions are, as we have seen, occupied with the control of internal (and to some extent external) welfare activities.

Democracy should also, in the Partnership's view, influence business decisions but not at the cost of efficient management. This brings us to the fourth main strand in its neatly woven pattern of beliefs: managers should be accountable for their decisions to the managed. The idea 'that industrial democracy must consist in giving the workers the right to appoint their bosses' is rejected as prejudicing the economic viability of the enterprise and thus the interests of all its members. In the present Chairman's words 'industrial history has shown that where attempts are made to put it into practice the results are

2. Rule 55.

unfortunate and often disastrous'. This leaves the alternative of accountability.

The requirements of the democratic ideal may be equally well and more efficiently met by ensuring that bosses are completely accountable to the workers. This is the principle which is observed within the Partnership. Its management can be and frequently is called upon to account to the Partners for its actions. This adds to the managerial burden. But it does not lead to inefficiency. The manager who knows he may have to account, by chapter and verse, for all he does thinks very hard before he acts – and he thinks even harder before he fails to act.[3]

Having stated the leading principles influencing the design of the Partnership's special institutions and, no less important, the behaviour of its management within this institutional framework, we may turn to the results of our enquiry. These can be considered under two headings: the effects of the system (in so far as we were able to discover them) first on management and second on the rank and file. With regard to its on effects management several important conclusions stood out quite clearly from our interviews.

First, it was apparent that the ideology inculcates a strong sense of responsibility among managers at all levels. This could be observed in both a high degree of commitment to the organization and a concern for the welfare of its members. The obligations of accountability are taken seriously and, though the personality of individuals and the earlier traditions of some branches affect the actual styles of management, a general awareness exists that decisions have to be defended on rational grounds. Intelligence and application are rated highly, and promotion is normally on merit as measured by Partnership standards. Above all, freedom of criticism pervades the organization, and the general ethos is such as to encourage managers to be constantly and genuinely concerned with the interests of those who are subject to their authority.

Another major effect of the system on management is paradoxically to reinforce its authority so that it is stronger and commands greater power than is usual, and often possible, in the normal run of private and public enterprise today. One can hardly speak of there being a problem of 'managerial prerogatives' in the Partnership. As long as management respects

3. In a letter to *The Times*, 20 July 1966.

the Partnership's ideology the moral justification for its decisions is unequivocal and complete. It has no cause to suffer any qualms of conscience that in talking about the welfare of the rank and file it may really be thinking about increasing dividends for shareholders. When it acts resolutely within the limits set by the Rules and Regulations it has little to fear. It is unlikely to be faced with concerted, let alone organized, resistance from its subordinates.[4] Nor is it greatly subject to those pressures and divisions within its own ranks which are often caused by political manoeuvres for personal power and prestige in large companies. The security felt by its management is a notable feature of the Partnership and one of its several sources of attraction in recruiting talent.

Apart from its influence on the quality, attitudes and authority of management, the further effects of the ideology are especially important for the Partnership's system of managerial control. We have shown how the ideology contributes to two features of the system: its consistency and its coherence. One would expect consistent and predictable managerial behaviour to result from a system with well-defined rules and principles and, what is more, a widespread acceptance by managers of the validity of their rationale. The very existence of these guidelines, almost regardless of their actual content, makes control far more acceptable to those who are being controlled; they know where they stand and are not left in uncertainty or bewilderment. Besides, consistency makes control less personal and arbitrary. The Partnership's formal structure of managerial organization,

4. Gray (1966, p. 9) suggests that three elements are important in the legitimization of managerial authority:
1. Does the manager have superior, reliable, usable knowledge about important aspects of the business which enable others to work more effectively?
2. Does the manager come to his authority with clean hands, or is he selectively righteous?
3. Does the manager work hard, in the sense of taxing himself, enlarging his potential and pressing the limits of his capacity?

If the answers are negative, the manager may have title, status and ambition but he will not have authority. Know-how, clean hands and hard work earn the *consent* without which managerial power today is hollow.
We formed a strong impression that in the John Lewis Partnership these conditions are substantially fulfilled.

Allan Flanders, Ruth Pomeranz and Joan Woodward 219

however, appears from some points of view loose and slack and from others excessively complex and confusing. Here again ideology is the factor which not only compensates for these apparent deficiencies but, by giving the system the cohesion it would otherwise lack, turns them to positive advantage. The looseness facilitates decentralization and allows branches to enjoy considerable autonomy, while the complexity in the organization of top management, associated with the division between the Executive and Clerical Sides, permits the interplay of an unusually wide range of experience and ability at this level in deciding issues of policy. A structure whose benefits might easily be dissipated by dissension and schisms appears to work quite successfully because the ideology acts as cement.

Granted that the commercial success of any large business enterprise depends first and foremost on its management, the reasons for the commercial success of the John Lewis Partnership are not hard to find, although to many people it may come as a surprise that basing a business on an ideology could have the results we have described. But what of the effects of the ideology and the Partnership's special institutions on its non-managerial employees? These after all are the great majority of the Partners and their response is the crux of the answer to the question: is this really an experiment in partnership? Before we return to the main results of our attitude survey some of the conclusions which we reached on the character and working of the special institutions must be summarized.

Of the Partnership's three leading aspirations, the arrangements for sharing gain call for least comment. The profit-sharing system is radical and complete in the sense that any outside shareholding interest in or control over the behaviour of the organization has been eliminated, and all distributed profits, after payment of the fixed interest on capital, are fully shared by those who sustain it by their work. On the other hand by distributing bonus according to pay, the system accentuates the prevailing hierarchical structure of remuneration accepted by society at large, with which the Partnership does not quarrel. The much more closely interwoven arrangements made for sharing knowledge and power are decidedly less radical. They also present greater difficulties of analysis and assessment.

One condition essential for the realization of both these aspirations, free speech, is certainly cultivated and protected within the Partnership to a degree that is not customary in most business organizations. Its internal press, particularly the device of anonymous letters, is one important safeguard, but so are the constitutional powers of its representative bodies and, not least, the general ethos of its management. Furthermore the Partnership fully respects those other basic freedoms we associate with political democracy, such as freedom of association including the right to join a trade union, but in this respect it is no different from any other progressive firm today. And the absence of a published structure of negotiated rates of pay, although common in retail distribution, means that its employees are deprived of knowledge which is of considerable interest to them. The publication of the trading results of individual sales-people, on the other hand, would often be resented as an infringement of personal liberty because of the anxiety it was liable to cause.

Nevertheless the Partnership undoubtedly lays great stress on giving everyone the maximum amount of knowledge about the business and about their own affairs, and its system of communication is highly developed and comparatively successful by any standards. Any system of communication, however, is always auxiliary to some system of control. The arrangements made for sharing knowledge in the Partnership have also to be judged in the context of the arrangements made for sharing power – and for using it. The representative institutions set up with this aim in view cannot be said to contribute very much towards its realization. Rather do they constitute a means of reinforcing the power of management over the managed. For what are their practical limits as an expression of democracy in business administration?

In the first place the activities of the elected bodies with powers of decision, the Central Council and the various Branch Councils, are concerned in their executive capacity with the administration of expenditure on welfare and amenities inside the Partnership and on gifts to 'good causes' outside. True, they also serve as forums of internal public opinion and may initiate proposals on anything they choose to discuss, but in this respect they are no more than the equivalent of the machinery for formal consultation which has become a prominent, if now somewhat discredited, feature of Britain's post-war industrial scene. Secondly, even in the exercise of these modest functions, the Councils in fact – though it need not be so in theory – are more representative of management than of the rank and file. Although the proportion has been growing, only twelve per cent on average of the Central Council's membership has come from the rank and file over the past eight years; and only 1·7 per cent of the membership of the committees where most of the work is done. Even in the Branch Councils, which are in any case wholly subordinate to the Central Council, no more than about half of elected councillors are rank and file Partners.

In contrast, the Committees for Communication, apart from their full-time chairmen, are entirely rank and file in composition but they exist only to 'enquire, discuss and suggest'. We have seen that their main functions are the settling of grievances and the securing of improvements in the local work situation, although they also play an important role in forming opinion and transmitting it to central management. Taken together with the powers of the Partners' Counsellor and some of the activities of Registrars and the Chief Registrar, this feature of the Partnership system undoubtedly provides an effective means of prompting management not to neglect the human side of its problems and enabling the rank and file to raise their complaints. Even so it is not, and was not intended to be, a democratic control over management. It depends for its effectiveness on a division of authority and on checks and balances within management itself.

Finally, there is the control of management by accountability which Partnership ideology holds to be the crucial one. That this is a real and all-pervading control is not in doubt. But equally it is not a control based on a sharing of power; nor a control which the managed can exercise over management to further their interests *as they see them*. One can only be accountable for one's actions in terms of certain aims and principles, or the values they embody. What this implies in the Partnership we have shown. Its management has to justify its decisions and behaviour not to shareholders but to the Partnership as a whole, not simply in terms of business efficiency but according to the tenets of the Partnership's ideology. So control by accountability is in effect control by ideology. This, to be sure, is a most impersonal and binding control. No individual, whatever his standing, can afford to disregard it: not even the Chairman – perhaps he least of all. It is upheld by the most powerful sanctions any business enterprise can command, the possibility of loss of advancement and perhaps loss of employment.

One can readily agree that, because of the nature of principles in the Partnership's ideology, accountability functions as a humane control over management. It is another question whether it can truly be called democratic. The emphasis in the ideology is decidedly on 'government for the people', rather than on 'government by the people'. If industrial democracy is envisaged as a system which enables the managed to share in the decision-making processes of business management, and so exercise some control over it to secure respect for their own group interests and values, then control by accountability does not fulfil that condition because it rests on an ideology which may be alien to the rank and file. As far as they are concerned this is something that goes with the job; perhaps to be welcomed, perhaps to be ignored or endured, perhaps to be disliked and rejected. In any event it lies beyond their influence. While all the sanctions of the organization safeguard the ideology, they have no effective sanctions to revise it, or to challenge managerial decisions which are in keeping with its principles.

Our attitude survey was intended to find out what rank and file Partners thought about their relations with the Partnership. We did not, of course, ask direct questions on the ideology which would have been far too abstract to have any precise meaning for most of them. In our pilot enquiry their knowledge of the Partnership's constitution was tested and this on the whole proved to be slight and imperfect. No reliable conclusions could be drawn from a knowledge test in isolation, however, apart from the expected ones that managerial employees had a much better knowledge of the constitution than non-managerial, and that among the latter knowledge increased with permanent employment and length of service. As we had to rely for any exact results on internal comparisons, we decided in the main survey to measure

Allan Flanders, Ruth Pomeranz and Joan Woodward 223

interest in Partnership institutions[5] (interest being the only suitably universal measure of involvement) and to explore the differences in attitude displayed between rank and file Partners divided into two groups with relatively high and low interest. We found that these groups showed appreciable differences in job satisfaction and in their general attitudes to the Partnership as an employer and to its representative institutions; the higher interest group having more favourable attitudes than the lower interest group. On the other hand, they showed no consistent and significant differences in their attitudes to the separate personnel policies discussed with them, such as relations with supervisors, pay, profit sharing and security of employment.

We have set out earlier what appear to us to be the broad implications of these findings. It could be anticipated that rank and file Partners who showed more interest in the Partnership system would also attach greater value to its representative institutions and to its social and welfare facilities, whose administration lies in the hands of those institutions. But the survey also showed that they were more satisfied with their jobs and more favourably disposed to the firm as an employer. The system in other words elicits a measurable response, if only from a minority of rank and file Partners, who because of it feel more identified with their work and with the Partnership. But even this minority continue to view their immediate job interests in much the same fashion as the majority of rank and file Partners; in this respect involvement in the Partnership system has no particular influence on their attitudes. Hence our conclusion that the ethos of the employment relationship for the non-managerial employees of the Partnership closely resembles that to be found in employing organizations of the usual kind. Although they may regard the Partnership as a 'good' employer, their relationship with it remains a 'calculative' rather than a 'normative' one; except for a small minority it does not entail any firm commitment to the Partnership's ideology.

Other results of the main attitude survey were of interest in filling out this conclusion. Among the specific issues of personnel policy discussed, some produced very much higher levels of dis-

5. Scored on knowledge of the constitution and the readership of appropriate items in the Partnership journals.

satisfaction than others among both men and women. The figures are shown in Table 1.

Table 1 Levels of Dissatisfaction with Various Personnel Policies

	Men	Women
Proportion dissatisfied with:	%	%
Job security	17	7
Profit sharing	28	22
Consultation by supervisors	30	30
Pay	49	34

We have shown that in general job satisfaction in the Partnership reaches much the same level as that recorded in a national sample of the working population. These comparisons in themselves would therefore not be conclusive – other surveys have shown that pay is often the most frequent source of complaint among employees. But the actual comments by individuals in the interviews made it clear that, while the Partnership is rated highly as an employer concerned with their security and welfare, it comes in for a fair amount of criticism from the rank and file essentially on the grounds that they have not enough say in settling pay and working conditions. The greater value they attach to the Committees for Communication (in spite of their having no powers of decision) as compared with the Branch Councils and the Central Council, points in the same direction. The rank and file employees of the Partnership, as in other firms, seem to be most interested in participating in decisions made about their own jobs and the pay and conditions attaching to them.

The ideology of the Partnership is undoubtedly a barrier to the growth of any 'pressure group' type of democracy from below. Its principles preclude restrictions being placed on management by local groups of employees, although they may have perforce to be accepted in the union-organized segments of employment. Management derives its authority from and is accountable to the Partnership as a whole. The structure of representative institutions, while it serves to convey Partnership opinion to management, does not provide for sharing managerial authority by allowing representatives of the rank and file to participate in business decisions relating to matters of closest interest to them, like the determination of their pay. In terms of political theory the ideology rejects pluralism and rests on a unitary view of power and authority within the firm.

The long and complicated history of the discussions and decisions within the Partnership preceding the introduction of the five-day week, the personnel policy issue which we traced through the system, plainly revealed the consequent restraints on its internal democracy. This was a subject of considerable interest to the rank and file – and also to managerial employees as employees – because it affected their pay, work and leisure. Equally it had – as all such issues are bound to have – important trading and financial implications. In the evolution of policy management went to great lengths to ascertain the views and preferences of all Partners. No one reading our account could possibly doubt top management's sincerity in trying to find a solution which would meet with general consent. Debate was encouraged so that Partners could make a considered choice on how they preferred to dispose of revenue. Use was made of all the elected bodies to sound out opinion, supplemented at one stage by a direct questionnaire. Above all, local experimentation with different variants of the earlier Increased Leisure Scheme was encouraged according to local choice.

Yet eventually it had to be recognized for compelling reasons that this was not 'a question which should or can be decided by individual Branch Councils solely in accordance with local preferences'. And then a decision was reached, as we have said, by a process which 'was basically the normal one of management deciding what it wanted to achieve, and preparing the ground in such a way that orders issued were likely to be obeyed'. In the end even the Central Council made relatively little contribution to the formation of policy. To this general outcome there was one exception coming near the end of our study. At John Barnes the rank and file Partners appear to have had their say for the first time in deciding something which could affect trading policy. In a secret ballot its Branch Council rejected management's proposal for a five-day working and shopping week, and the Chairman accepted their decision.

Having summarized the results of our enquiry, we may return in conclusion to the initial problem we posed in the Introduction, the problem of combining managerial and democratic control. The first was defined as the system by which management controls the work behaviour of employees to further the objectives of the firm, and the second as the system by which employees control the behaviour of management to further their own objectives. Some integration of the two systems – or at least their mutual accommodation – is necessary in any business enterprise regardless of its form of ownership. What is unique about the Partnership, as we said, is that it has a management-conceived system of democratic control. Thus management provides, indeed imposes, its own solution to the problem of integration in accordance, as we may now add, with the principles of an ideology which also controls the behaviour of management. Since the ideology was created by its Founder, the Partnership is in every sense an experiment in industrial democracy introduced and sustained from above. What general conclusions about such experiments, if any, can be drawn from its experience?

One conclusion suggested is that they need not suffer from disruptive conflict and instability. Although, as we have argued, there is very little real sharing of power in the Partnership as between management and rank and file, the arrangements made for sharing gain and sharing knowledge, together with the existence of representative institutions however limited their powers, have made the employment relationship positively attractive for most employees, and especially for those who want to involve themselves in its institutions. Whether the system would preserve its stability outside the special circumstances of retail distribution – if it had, for instance, to contend with the challenge of strong trade unions – it is impossible to say. Such evidence as we were able to gather indicates that one strong source of discontent among the rank and file was their lack of any direct control over their pay and other working conditions.[6] But there were no signs of this discontent reaching proportions that would encourage a trade union to look on the Partnership as a good prospect for recruitment. The accountability of management, although it may not be strictly a democratic control, does serve, along with

6. It must be remembered that our main attitude survey was confined to the Partnership's eight largest department stores and included hardly any Partners covered by collective bargaining arrangements.

the other conditions we have mentioned, to legitimize its authority and make it responsive to the employees' human and social needs.

An objection which can be raised against introducing industrial democracy from above is that it may result in paternalism. This danger is certainly prevalent in the Partnership system for its ideology has a strong paternalistic flavour. Management, it is assumed, knows what is in the best interests of all the Partners. Though trading interests may not always be preferred to personnel considerations, the balance should be struck by those in authority and, in the last resort, by the Chairman. Democratic institutions are deliberately held within bounds which will prevent them from placing any formal restraints on the powers and discretion of management in these matters. All this, as we found in our interviews, is further reflected in a common ethos shared by a majority of top managers who are inclined to assume that in a system like that of the Partnership those who are best qualified to exercise authority come to the top.

Not everyone, of course, objects to paternalism when it is genuinely benevolent; least of all in industry where it has frequently been the reverse. Here we enter the realm of value judgements where there are conflicting opinions and personal choices have to be made. As long as alternative employment possibilities are available, the Partnership is entitled to say, as it does every week in the *Gazette*: 'No one partnership can hope to suit everyone and the John Lewis Partnership does not attempt to do so. It is intended only for those who, to be really happy, need to feel they are giving good service to the general community and whom its particular character and methods suit well enough in other ways.'

Reference

GRAY, D. H. (1966), *Manpower Planning*, Institute of Personnel Management.

Part Four
Contingency Theory

Until very recently the idea that it might be possible to match
a payment system and a set of circumstances in such a
way as to achieve stated objectives has not seriously been
canvassed. As we have seen, the literature either claims that
one system is better than another in all circumstances, or
shows how circumstances interfere with a system's
operation in a way that defeats its objects.

At the same time as Grinyer and Kessler (1967) were
preparing their paper I was preparing one for a conference of
OECD. This latter paper, which is not published here, formed
the basis of the later book by Dan Gowler and myself,
detailing a systematic procedure, extracts from which are
included. A similar idea – that as circumstances change, so
must the method of payment, and therefore must be
audited annually, is advanced by John Percival of a British
consulting firm. Already progressive firms in Britain are using
fruitfully the ideas and procedures outlined in these
two readings.

Reference

GRINYER, P. H., and KESSLER, S. (1967), 'The systematic evaluation of
    methods of wage payment', *Journal of Management Studies*, vol. 4, no. 3,
    pp. 309–20.

14 John Percival

Towards an Annual Wage Audit

John Percival, 'Towards an annual wage audit', *Enterprise* (the magazine of the PE Consulting Group), Spring 1970.

The problems of wage payment, of the right 'rate for the job', in situations constantly being influenced by varying economic, political and social pressures, are today increasingly receiving management attention by skilled specialists. The whole trend of present effort in the industrial relations sector is towards working out wage and salary patterns which will strike a practical balance between business and technological considerations on the one hand, and political and trade union constraints on the other.

There is a danger, however, that with the emphasis on the search for immediate solutions, an important long-term factor will be ignored. This is that any wage payment solution tends to lose by gradual and often unnoticed stages its relevance to the situation in which it is applied. When important commercial decisions in a trading organization provoke major distortions in the pay or employment situation, it is easy enough to see these and to take action accordingly. But it is not so easy to realise that commercial decisions often give rise to apparently quite small wage or employment adjustments which, so far as their effects on the total situation are concerned, remain largely unnoticed. Unnoticed, partly because the decisions which put them into effect may be taken at a low management level, and partly because they do appear to involve only insignificant changes or precedents. It is the gradual accumulation of such small decisions over a period of time which lead to incoherent and unworkable wage structures in many otherwise well-managed and successful organizations.

A typical case

The truth of this proposition is well illustrated in the following case history. Skilled fitters employed in the toolroom of a major engineering plant traditionally earned 30s. a week more than men similarly skilled working in the main factory. This had long been accepted, and the basic rate reflected this differential. But then a new product was introduced into the assembly line, and this caused the production men to argue for and eventually obtain more money. The settlement was very much in their favour, involving a loosening of bonus rates which enabled them to increase their weekly earnings by between £2 and £3. Soon the men in the toolroom, whose work had remained unaffected by the new product, complained that they had lost their differential, and so they negotiated with the management an increase in their *basic rate* of 70s. a week.

With the differential restored, all was well – for the moment. The factory men raised no objections so long as buoyant production and substantial overtime kept overall earnings high. But as soon as production dropped and overtime fell away, the result predictably was an explosive rejection of the basic skilled rate in the factory – now not 30s. but 100s. less than the rate for the toolroom.

It is in anticipating and forestalling such deterioration that an annual wage payment audit, carried out by independent outside specialists in much the same way as the annual financial audit required by law, can make an effective contribution. The basic idea of such an audit is to substitute for a four- or five-yearly re-think of the pay structure (often totally inadequate to deal with the chaos by the time management gets round to it) a regular review, subjecting the whole field of pay and related benefits to the kind of scrutiny that ordinary auditors apply to a company's finances.

An audit is particularly relevant to two situations typical of many forward-looking companies which in fact take particular care to devise well-thought out pay structures. The first is that in which senior management is unaware of the potentially erosive or distorting pay bargains being made at foreman and supervisor level; the second is where, even given such knowledge, management fails to relate this to the total wage situation, with the inevitable result that it tends to be always on the defensive. Pay is one sector of a whole wide front of problems which it has to tackle, and localized issues such as the toolroom demand may seem in a wide context petty and distracting. The shrewd union negotiator, on the other hand, can concentrate all his energy and attention on a narrow front, gaining one point at a time and then exploiting the anomalies thus created.

The audit in detail

A wage audit as applied in the writer's experience has two distinct elements. First, specific criteria are used as the basis of factual comment on the current situation (this may be compared in the financial audit with the balance sheet and profit and loss account). Second, informed comment is made to the board of a company based on an interpretation of the criteria and the ways in which these need to be changed in the light of devloping trends. If remedial action is then required, it will rarely not be within the competence of the company's own staff to effect this.

The actual criteria used in an audit must be constructed to suit the particular needs and circumstances of a company. The elements to which they are applied will normally include:

1. Unit cost of labour per hour
2. Percentage overtime worked
3. The average performance level achieved by operatives per month or similar period
4. Percentage 'covered' time, i.e. that time not worked under a bonus arrangement where bonus is applicable
5. Percentage shift premium in total pay
6. Percentage bonus in total pay
7. The spread of earnings between departments
8. The spread of earnings within departments
9. The principal items of unproductive time
10. Average earnings as related to the salary scales of first line supervision

Specific measurements of these elements, made usually in each department, are reinforced by and interpreted through selected interviews with key personnel. The resulting report to the board would typically incorporate the points which follow.

1. An analysis of the specific figures in the light of the criteria agreed with the company as appropriate for its needs

2. Comment on these figures with special reference to changes and trends observable

3. Comparison of total earnings with:
- other rates in the district
- the national growth in related earnings during the period

4. The continued effectiveness of the job evaluated wage structure where applicable

5. Comment on the prevailing industrial relations climate in the light of current wage policies

6. Comment on the continuing relevance of the company's training programme for hourly paid shop floor supervision and other personnel concerned

7. Comment on other shop floor factors arising from the specific figures, as for example, the effect of production planning on waiting time, the validity of the figures *per se*, or the booking system employed

8. Comment on the effects of plant investment programmes or other proposed technological changes.

Typically an annual wage audit based on sound data in a company employing 1000 hourly paid staff takes between four and five days. In the first instance, however, when the need is to establish in detail the quality and quantity of the information to be collected, up to three weeks may be necessary. Here, the precise definition of information requirements provides a sound basis both for future audits and for improved day-to-day control by management of the payment situation.

Problems of overtime and shift working

It is worth looking in more detail at typical situations in the two areas of overtime and shift working which are often brought to light when the wage audit procedure is applied.

On the question of overtime, a root cause of much industrial unrest is the presence of anomalies in the take-home pay packets of employees within departments, between departments, or between the company and its employing neighbours. Overtime, rarely spread evenly throughout an organization, has two main causes, both of which lead to its uneven application. It may, in the first place, be the outcome of a genuine need – temporary overload situation arising from an influx of orders, or perhaps a temporary imbalance in the capacities of the plant. In either case, it would be most unlikely for the extra work to be shared equally between different departments – production and service, for example. Second, and much more often, overtime may be used deliberately in order to raise a low wage to a rate which is implicitly accepted by both management and workpeople as reasonable. Rarely, if ever, is this official policy, but rather a *de facto* arrangement 'negotiated' at departmental level, which is not only bad in itself but also shows up management in an unfortunate light. From the workpeople's point of view, the arrangement will of course depend on their local bargaining strength with their own supervisors, and this, with corresponding levels of overtime, will vary from department to department. The wage audit procedure, by throwing the spotlight regularly on such situations, can contribute to getting both the uses and abuses of overtime into manageable perspective.

The impact of shift arrangements on overtime illustrates another distortion which a wage audit can often isolate. For example, in many industries the shift premium for three-shift working is still barely 10 per cent of the forty-hour pay of a day worker, and the day worker can easily exceed this additional inconvenience payment by working an extra four hours, say on a Saturday morning. In other words, the reward tends to be in inverse proportion to the degree of social disturbance in each case. Yet the rapid rise in the capital intensity of industry leads to the necessity for maximum plant utilisation through multi-shift working; in some process industries seven days a week, twenty-four hours a day working is essential. If shift premiums are not large enough to compensate for social disturbance – much depends here on the history of a locality in regard to shift working – the result is often a serious inability to recruit enough shift labour.

In such circumstances, overtime on a massive scale may be management's only recourse, though a disastrously costly one.

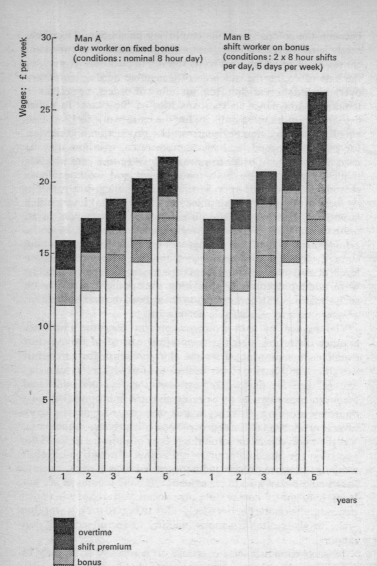

Wages: £ per week

Man A
day worker on fixed bonus
(conditions: nominal 8 hour day)

Man B
shift worker on bonus
(conditions: 2 x 8 hour shifts
per day, 5 days per week)

years

overtime
shift premium
bonus
minimum earnings increase
basic pay.

Here again a wage audit can not only help in pinpointing the situation, but in certain circumstances point to a valid alternative. In one recent case, a process works faced the problem of having to expand a two-shift to a three-shift operation for about three months in the year. Historically the company paid below average shift premiums, and this drawback allied to the difficulty in any case of recruiting shift workers on a temporary basis, led to the desperate expedient of working two twelve-hour shifts including substantial overtime. This in turn resulted in an absentee rate of up to 25 per cent for male workers, which only made the situation worse. However, analysis of the total wage situation showed that it was more economic as well as socially acceptable to smooth the production flow by pre-stocking of low labour-intensive products. This allowed a better plant utilization to be achieved with normal two-shift working throughout the year.

Benefits of a wage audit

What in summary are the principal positive benefits which emerge from the wage audit in practice? The conclusion from the

Figure 1 This chart very much oversimplifies the wage situation described since with the exception of overtime it ignores the effects of internally generated problems. Nevertheless, it effectively illustrates the kind of distortion that can arise over a five year period, taking the case of two workpeople, both of whom at the start of the period have 'equitable' pay. Such distortions include:
1 Pay differential has trebled.
2 Bonus as a percentage of total pay has dropped by one third and one half respectively (without justification?).
3 Shift premium has become approximately equal to four and a half hours' overtime (is this fair?).
4 In practice, inevitable changes in operation, with their effect on pay arrangement (mainly for workers on bonus), will lead to further earnings drift, thus accentuating all the above distortion.
Summary of wage history depicted
At end of year 1 Increase in basic rate.
At end of year 2 Increase in basic rate, plus minimum earnings increase not allowable for bonus, shift premium, or overtime calculations (a recent feature of engineering agreements).
At end of year 3 As end of year 2, but with Saturday a.m. overtime commencing for shift worker.
At end of year 4 As end of year 3.

situations already discussed is that management is much better briefed and therefore much less likely to be taken by surprise not only by problems of labour utilisation but also by disputes resulting from cumulative distortions or contradictions creeping into the pay structure. In one audit with which the writer was concerned, a factory with some 700 hourly paid operatives and no apparent pay troubles was shown, to the management's surprise, to have a basic pay too low for the district, which would cause trouble if not put right. The audit also showed that excessive overtime was being worked in sections of what was basically a two shift factory, that there was serious overmanning in some areas, and that piece rates were being badly eroded.

At an even more positive level, a wage audit implies a management which is demonstrably in control of its wage policies and therefore able to take the initiative instead of being always on the defensive. Trade union representatives in such a climate will be that much more ready to take a constructive view of management's pay proposals.

It should be said finally that the wage audit above all helps to establish awareness at senior management and board levels of the need to integrate pay and salary policies with total company thinking and planning. As described above, the audit is concerned mainly with hourly paid employees and only in one respect with front-line supervisors. But clearly in the future it will be increasingly necessary to include all types of clerical and management staff in the audit procedure. Apart from the fact that wages and salaries in these categories are often anomalous in themselves, there are increasing signs of an organised management 'backlash', which will force companies to pay much closer attention to salary policies at all levels.

15 Tom Lupton and Dan Gowler

Selecting a Wage Payment Scheme

Excerpt from Tom Lupton and Dan Gowler, *Selecting a Wage Payment System*, Kogan, Page, 1969, pp. 6–35.

The experience of generations of managers has shown that there are many different ways of relating effort and reward and many different kinds of effort and reward depending on what is being produced, by what processes, and by what kind of workers. There are many different kinds of payment systems; payment-by-results schemes of various kinds, systems that link time-related inducements to performance criteria, individual and group plans, bonus schemes related to plant output as a whole and so on. Some payment systems are observed to work well in some situations but not in others. We have observed a natural tendency amongst managers, not to seek reasons for success, and to attribute failure to one or two obvious factors. We think it unsatisfactory that managers' experiences with payment systems have not been assembled in a systematic way to indicate what payment systems are appropriate for what situations, and in the light of what objectives.

We have pointed already to some of the factors that have to be taken into account in choosing an appropriate payment system. These included product markets, labour markets, technology, Trade Unions, and the attitudes and expectations of workpeople. We shall presently introduce further factors that must be considered by the manager making decisions about modifying or changing a payment system. All these factors are present in every situation; every manufacturing company has customers and competitors, plant and machinery, procedures for organizing them to complete a task, and workpeople with attitudes and expectations; but the factors differ in their effects from situation to situation and from time to time in any one situation. If, as we intend, we are to assemble systematically research findings and the experience of management about payment systems, we need a method of measuring differences in these factors. We want to be able to say with some accuracy how the technology of one company differs from the technology of another, or from one period of time to another in the recent history and projected future of the same firm; how the conditions in the labour market and the product market may be accurately compared, and so on. To our knowledge this has so far not been done, but we will attempt it in this paper.

To systematize the experience of management also requires a method of classifying payment schemes in such a way that they may be matched to the circumstances as defined. This has not been done either, for although there have been attempts to classify payment systems the criteria for classification have not been designed especially to assist in selecting a payment system, nor in such a way as to make possible the design of novel payment systems especially designed to match unprecedented or unusual circumstances.

We shall be explaining later in greater detail what might seem at this stage to be a neglect of worker motivation in our scheme of things. It is true that we have concentrated so far on what may be called structural factors. We roughly define these as the factors external to the individual that influence his behaviour. It could be argued that different individuals might react in different ways to the same external influence, or that all individuals will try to shape their environment to give expression to their needs for interesting work, congenial company, scope to exercise personal judgement, and the desire to participate in decisions which affect their jobs; and that all individual human beings have similar needs to satisfy. It has been said that when certain basic needs are satisfied, e.g. for food, clothing, shelter, then higher order needs call for satisfaction such as the need for work which allows self-expression and involves recognition of one's personal contribution. All of this we accept. We would expect that management's part in providing opportunities for self-expression, etc., would be to re-define jobs so as to enlarge the range of skill and judgement required, and therefore the training needed, within the limits the technology imposes. The increased job interest which might be promised as a result could be regarded as an inducement to the individual to join the organisation and to perform well in response to the system relating effort and reward. Similarly, arrangements for worker participation in decision making might be regarded as an inducement to join, and stay to perform well.

We have dealt with all these matters; firstly, by classifying payment schemes so as to take into account workers' motivations; secondly, by including in our method of defining a situation an opportunity to provide for them in the design of the organization and thirdly by including them in the possible objectives that managers might set for themselves. We have *not* dealt with them by considering what payment system will move an individual to high performance, *given the characteristics of that individual*. Rather, we have taken the view that the behaviour of individuals which is what we are interested in, can only sensibly be considered in relation to the particular circumstances in which they are placed (indeed motives can only be deduced from observations of behaviour *in situ*). So the basic question that we shall tackle throughout this work is: *what combination of organization, environment and payment system is best fitted to satisfy a given set of objectives?*

Payment systems and the motives of workers – the debate

We have asked ourselves four questions about payment systems; and our method of selecting a scheme has evolved from trying to answer them. They are:

1. What should the objectives of a firm be when installing or modifying a payment scheme?

2. What payment systems are available to choose from?

3. How should a firm go about deciding which of the available schemes is best suited to its circumstances?

4. Which of the available schemes satisfies its objectives?

These questions seem the simple and obvious ones to ask. Yet they are not the questions that are usually asked. In our experience it is rare for a firm to state clearly and fully what its objectives are when installing a scheme; nor is it usual to scan the whole range of known schemes. Although a firm may have it in mind to look for something suitable to its own circumstances, it is also rare for these circumstances to be sharply and fully defined, let alone measured.

If, on the face of it, it seems odd that intelligent men have missed the obvious in such an important matter for them, a little reflection reveals the reason. The long debate about payment schemes – it has gone on for at least sixty years – has been for the most part inconclusively argued in terms of conflicting theories about human nature in general; about individuals and their motives for working.

Who has not heard the opinion strongly expressed, and backed by the 'evidence' of one man's experience, that the only way to raise the performance of workers who have been paid wholly by the hour, is to put them on payment by results (PBR)? It is almost accepted as a law of nature in many quarters that a worker on payment by results will work one-third again as hard or as effectively (or both) as a time worker. But the catalogue of exceptions to that particular law of nature is almost long enough to cancel it out completely.

Increasingly, in the last two or three decades, people in industry have observed and commented on the fact that payment by results schemes very often fail to motivate in the way expected of them when they are installed. Managers speak of the 'decay' and 'erosion' of payment schemes, and report that workers 'fiddle' and 'make bonus with the pencil'. In addition it has become clear that given a choice, workers will not, in all circumstances, work harder or more effectively to increase their pay. It begins to look as if payment by results schemes might rest on a too naive view of human motives, although some advocates of payment-by-results such as R M Currie (1963), have continued to insist that the pull of cash is the prime mover for workers. Such writers have attributed 'decay' to managerial neglect to use proper methods for deciding performance standards, and to 'gear' the slope of the graph relating pay and performance to the circumstances of the case. They also point out, amongst other things, the need to explain the logic of the scheme to the workers, and to enlist their cooperation in implementing and running it.

For all the persuasiveness of the arguments in favour of payment by results, and for all the ingenuity exercised in producing variations on the general theme (of which more later), scepticism about payment by results is increasing. The sceptics seem so far not to have had a marked practical effect, so deep rooted is the belief in the cash motive. Those who have turned against payment by results say that it is based on a much too simple view of human nature. They will allow that men go to work to make money; but they say when men are at work, they are not moved only by the desire for more money, but also by the need to be well regarded by their mates and their bosses, and the wish to be treated as fully adult and responsible human beings. Given the opportunity, and the encouragement, they will take a pride in what they are doing. They will also have, and are certainly entitled to have, so the argument goes, their own ideas about how much they ought to give of their time, physical and mental energy, and attention, in return for the pay they get. If a payment by result scheme does not meet their idea of a fair and proper bargain between effort and reward, they might well choose to adjust the bargain, by controlling, either individually or jointly with their mates, the effort or the reward; or even by leaving the job. If all this is true, and much evidence has been adduced (persuasively) in support of it, then it would seem that we now have to accept that some form of measured daywork is more appropriate than PBR.

Measured daywork, in its proper application as defined by its supporters, requires that Work-Study be used to help determine what the workers performance standard ought to be for each job. The rate of pay for the job is then established by negotiation. The worker is asked to perform according to standard in return for the regular weekly pay. It is the job of the manager now to see that the worker is provided with work. The manager is very interested in doing this because the wage bill has become under measured daywork a kind of overhead. Procedures have to be agreed as to what sanctions will be imposed if it can be shown that the worker deliberately performs below standard. Some advocate fines, some down-grading to a less-skilled job, some warning and eventual dismissal. Some argue that management should exert unilateral control, others that control should be jointly exerted. As may be seen, measured day work has its variants, and of this also more will be said presently. One general point here is that although measured day work, like PBR, is about the relationship between effort (in its broad sense) and money reward, it assumes that workers will give of their best if they freely agree to do so, and if the conditions in which they work are arranged so that they can do so. It assumes that the powerful human motive at work here is the moral obligation to keep contracts willingly entered into, and to meet undertakings freely accepted.

Unlike the advocates of PBR, supporters of measured day work do not agree that time workers will not give as much effort as piece-workers. On the contrary, they accept that if the conditions are right, e.g. the work properly measured, the contract and the rules to govern it properly and jointly agreed, and the administrative procedures well designed – then there is no reason for workers to do less than they are capable of.

There are many variants of both PBR and of measured day work, and all of these and many other payment systems will be described and classified [. . .] *We have at this point contrasted the argument for PBR and measured day work not in order to take one side or the other; this is the very trap we want to avoid.* Our purpose has been to show that, once it is accepted that the nature of human nature *in general* is the only ground on which payment schemes should be designed, it is impossible to do other than to accept that *one or other type of scheme must be best for all circumstances.* We believe that because individual motives in general have been accepted as fundamental to the argument, little attention has been given to defining the objectives of payment schemes and the circumstances essential for their success.

To us, it is evident that the environment of the works manager or production manager is much too complex to yield to explanation or improvement in terms only of ideas about human motives, or practices based upon them: and a moment's thought by the practitioner, or a quick look by the student at the research evidence, would we believe, amply justify our view. So we will now briefly contrast the speculation about motives with the practical experience of the manager and use the results of the comparison as a starting point for the development of our method for choosing a scheme.

The experience of management

The experience of managers is that however good a payment system looks in theory as a motivator, it is liable to get out of control. More correctly, it is liable to get out of the control of management. Take, for example, an incentive bonus scheme of the kind common in the engineering industry. Such a scheme probably rests on some formula that pays bonus for time saved on an agreed allowed time for the job. If there are a lot of changes of job, and method, if there are problems that come up unpredictably about shortage of work, or poor materials, or absence of parts, and labour is short and the shop stewards powerful, there will surely be pressure from the men to slacken the allowed times and an inclination on the part of management to give way. There will also be a tendency for special allowances for one thing and another to be asked for and granted. We heard recently of a 'frustration allowance'! It is also common for the effort side of the equation to be adjusted by the emergence of work group output norms – which are not the norms of management. It is easy for a scheme to become an administratively expensive way of handing out more money to help compete in local labour markets. A common response is to bewail the loss of pull of the cash incentive, and to look for some other system which seems likely to restore it. It is not so common to hear people define what it was that made control so difficult, and to see them trying to change those things.

A measured day work system is not in general any more insulated from the effects of 'erosion' than a PBR system. The classic objection to measured day work is that if people are given a regular weekly wage for a job which is related to a performance standard, the tendency under pressure of labour markets, and in coping with difficulties of work flow administration, is for workers' performances to slide downwards away from the standard. The administrative procedures for the installation and control of measured day work are likely to be complicated, and to maintain the scheme intact with the minimum of problems requires the skills of the really competent industrial engineer combined with highly effective departmental managers and foremen, as well as excellent procedures for scheduling and controlling the flow of production, and for reporting the performance of individuals and groups.

Defining the circumstances – the profile of a firm
Four kinds of influence on payment schemes

We have been trying to establish the point that there are external forces acting on the individual worker and the manager which affect their behaviour. These forces have to be taken into account as well as those factors that we infer from our observations of their behaviour and describe as motives. Managers are interested in influencing worker behaviour, and it would seem foolish for them to ignore or understress the structural factors and unduly stress the psychological ones. Yet this is what seems to have happened – otherwise what sense would it make to say that an incentive system is in 'decay'. Such a statement can only mean that a scheme which was based on an incomplete theory of individual behaviour has been undermined by the operation of factors that were, mistakenly, not considered as relevant. Either that, or there were factors that *were* taken account of but too difficult for managers to control, or were outside managements' control altogether.

Our own studies, our knowledge of current research findings, and our experience as consultants, have led us to believe that there are four groups of influences that affect the operation of a payment scheme. They are the influence of: technology, labour markets, disputes and disputes procedures, and structural characteristics. We have identified nine measures of technology, three of labour markets, four of disputes and disputes procedures and five structural characteristics. These are important parts of our scheme for selecting a payment system. We use them to define what the particular circumstances of a firm are. Before we go into this in detail, it is necessary to say something in general about the four sets of influence.

Technology

The machinery and equipment used to help people to produce goods and provide services, and the procedures for relating men and machines in production, make up our definition of techno-logy. Clearly, technology is a strong influence on the behaviour of workers, particularly as to their freedom to choose how the job will be done. For example, on the final assembly track of a vehicle assembly plant, the job is defined pretty completely by the technology – i.e. the movement of the conveyor, and the schedules governing the sequence of operations. It might be possible, if it were deemed desirable, and if sufficient thought were given to it, so to design the task of vehicle assembly that it would give the worker a little more choice and still be economical. But whatever one did would not make a great deal of difference. By contrast, the freedom to choose given to a skilled fitter engaged on the assembly of a large marine engine would probably be large. If it were not, why employ a skilled man who cannot use his skill?

These great differences in the extent of worker discretion are often, but by no means universally, sufficient to ensure that assembly line workers and skilled craftsmen are paid according to different systems. One way therefore of distinguishing the circumstances of one firm from the circumstances of another, or, indeed, of one workshop in a firm from another, is to find some way to measure the characteristics of technology. We have in fact defined nine such characteristics, and by measuring them for a particular firm, we are able to construct a *profile* for that firm, which defines its technology, and enables comparisons to be made with the technology of other firms. Our method of profile construction will be demonstrated shortly.

Labour markets

The labour market is a weighty influence on the operation of payment schemes. When workers are difficult to get hold of, firms may find themselves undermanned unless they are able and prepared to raise pay and having done so still remain in business. If they are undermanned, this may mean a good deal of overtime working and/or internal transfer from job to job, and the basis of the payment scheme might have to be altered to give people on unfamiliar jobs a chance to earn bonus if their services are to be kept. All these pressures can be intensified if the rate of labour turnover increases as a result of higher, and perhaps more stable, earnings becoming available elsewhere and their availability coming to the notice of workers. Workers who are in short supply can use their scarcity value to 'bend' systems of wage payment to their advantage, and to strike hard bargains about performance and pay. On the other hand, when orders are plentiful, and workers are fairly easy to get at the rate a firm is prepared to pay, and easy to keep, the pressure on the payment scheme will be less. There are three measures of the labour market that seemed to suit our purposes, and from these a labour market profile may be constructed.

Disputes and disputes procedures

The extent to which a payment scheme might get out of control; 'erode', 'decay', or whatever, will certainly be influenced by the effectiveness of the procedures that exist for settling disputes about pay arising from it. That is to say, if two firms have a similar technology and similar labour markets and a similar payment scheme, the one that has the most effective disputes procedures will, other things being equal, probably keep the scheme under better control. As a measure of the effectiveness of these procedures, we have two statistics. First, the amount of time lost in disputes in a given period, and second, the number of disputes. Here are two more profile items to add to the nine for technology, and the three for labour markets.

Structural characteristics

Where the central machinery for settling wages and conditions for an industry determines all, or almost all, of the take-home pay of the worker in each firm in the industry, then the scope for plant bargaining about bonus earnings is limited. When most of earnings is decided in the plant, in conditions, like those of recent years in engineering, where labour is scarce, shop stewards powerful, and payment schemes decayed, the scope for plant bargaining is extensive; when there are many Unions in a firm, each with a sharp eye on inter-union differentials; when there are many grades of worker, and many different departments in the firm, which might further encourage 'leap-frogging' and where labour cost is a significant proportion of product cost, then there will be difficulties in maintaining the pay scheme whatever it is. Obviously, our profile of the circumstances of a firm would have to include these items also, as well as the incidence of absenteeism (since high absenteeism disrupts job-allocation with consequences for payment *via* overtime working and job transfer), and the age and sex distribution of the working force (since some payment schemes might give an advantage to young men, others to older men, yet others to women). We have seen measures for these items.

The complete profile

So, adding it all up, there are twenty-three dimensions[1] on which to base a profile of the circumstances of a firm, or a department, or workshop of a firm, or even the job of any individual. There may be other ways of measuring and other measures. We have chosen these because they appear to be most relevant to the choice of payment scheme. There is nothing to stop anyone from adding other dimensions if they think them relevant, or striking out those they think irrelevant, if they have good reason to do so. Before we describe the measures we propose to employ to place particular firms on each of our profile dimensions, it might be useful to recall the place of the profile itself in our method of selecting a payment scheme. The reader will remember that the third of the three questions we posed at the outset asked how a firm might go about deciding which amongst the payment systems available would best suit its circumstances. This question cannot be answered without some systematic way of describing those circumstances of the firm that are relevant to the choice of a payment scheme. Hence the twenty-three dimensions; hence the profile. When we have given an example of the construction of a profile, we may then set about classifying payment schemes, defining objectives, and working step-by-step through a procedure for selecting a payment scheme appropriate to the circumstances.

The twenty-three dimensions[2] in the profile are given below.

1. Twenty-one profile dimensions plus two gate mechanisms (see p. 271 for a definition of gate mechanisms).
2. See pp. 271–6 for notes on the scoring of these twenty-three dimensions.

Technological dimensions

1. (*g*) Type of effort.
2. (*g*) Unit of accountability.
1.   Length of the job cycle.
2.   Number of job modifications per job.
3.   Degree of automation.
4.   Rate of product change.
5.   Recorded job stoppages.
6.   Average length of job stoppages.
7.   Percentage of job elements specified by management for operator.
8.   Percentage of material scrapped.
9.   Percentage of product/components declared defective.

Labour market dimensions

10.   Number of days required to fill vacancy, including training time.
11.   Labour stability index.
12.   Annual labour turnover.

Dispute and disputes procedure dimensions

13.   Number of stoppages due to pay disputes.
14.   Average length of such stoppages.

Structural dimensions

15.   Percentage of pay settled outside firm.
16.   Number of trade unions carrying on separate negotiations in firm.
17.   Number of job grades × number of work units, × number of shifts.
18.   Recorded absence as proportion of normal time.
19.   Average age of working force.
20.   Percentage of labour cost in total cost.
21.   Percentage of males in working force.

To show in a simplified way how a profile may be constructed, we pass over for the moment how the exact score on each dimension is determined. We shall use scales running through nine points, and draw profiles for an engineering firm *x* employing young semi-skilled females on the bench assembly of long runs of standard products, and a firm *y* employing skilled male labour on the machining and assembly of complex machine tools.[3] Firm *x* is assumed to be in a situation where female labour is plentiful. Firm *y* is assumed to be one of a number of firms competing for scarce skilled labour.

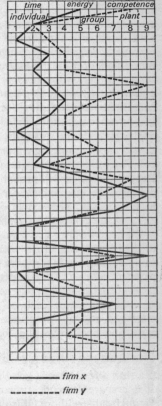

1 (g) Type of effort
2 (g) Unit of accountability
1 Length of job cycle
2 Number of job modifications
3 Degree of automation
4 Number of product changes
5 Number of job stoppages
6 Duration of job stoppages
7 % job elements specified by management
8 % material scrapped
9 % products/components rejected
10 Time required to fill vacancy
11 Labour stability
12 Labour turnover
13 Disputes about pay
14 Man hours lost in pay disputes
15 % earnings decided outside plant/company
16 Number of trade unions
17 Occupational structure
18 Absence (% normal hours)
19 Average age of working force
20 % labour cost in unit cost
21 % males in working force

———————— firm x
- - - - - - - - firm y

Figure 1 Examples of contrasting situation profiles

Referring to Figure 1 we see that the *length of the job cycle* differs between the two firms, the *number of job changes* is not very high in either. In each, the individual is the *unit of account-ability*, although it is possible that in the assembly shops of the machine tool firm a finished job might not easily be traced to an individual but to a small group, in which case the point on dimension 2 would go further to the right. In each the *degree of automation* is low; that is to say the work is done largely with hand tools and hand-controlled machines. The *rate of product change* is assumed to be high for firm *y*, low for firm *x*. *Job stoppages* are taken to be a little more frequent in firm *y* than in firm *x* and so is the average *length of such stoppages*. The *percentage of job elements specified* for the worker will clearly be much higher for the girl assemblers than for the skilled fitters and turners. Fitters will take *longer to recruit* than female assemblers, although training time might narrow the difference on the assumptions we made about local labour markets. *Labour turnover* is assumed to be fairly high in both cases. The men will have *longer and more frequent stoppages* about pay, less of their total *pay settled outside*, and *more trade unions*. Neither firm will have a complex job structure with many *grades* and many *departments*. Recorded *absence* will probably be higher amongst the girls than amongst the men and *labour costs* will be proportionately high in both cases. The scores on *materials scrapped*, *components rejected, age and sex distribution* do not call for comment.

We hope we have said enough to demonstrate that it is possible to distinguish any firm's circumstances from those of another, using dimensions in a profile that are relevant to the choice of a payment scheme. At an appropriate later point, as we elaborate the sequence of steps in our method of selecting payment schemes, we will show how each of the dimensions may be precisely measured, and how the profile is used. Our aim in the next section is to show how payment schemes may be classified.

Classifying and selecting payment schemes

If a firm already keeps good production and personnel records, or is prepared to collect them especially, for say six months, it should be able without difficulty using the scales for measurement that we have constructed (see page 271) to draw its own profile

---

3. This 'skill factor' determines 'choice' on the first dimension, i.e. (1(g), Type of effort, on Figure 1.

accurately along the twenty-three dimensions. If necessary separate profiles could be drawn for each plant, workshop or department or even individual. When this has been done the first short step has been taken in the method for selecting a payments scheme; but three of our four original questions still remain as yet unanswered, viz.: what should be the objectives? what alternative schemes are available? and what should be the procedure for deciding which of the schemes gives a 'best fit' to the circumstances of the firm?

Classification of schemes

All payment schemes, however different they may seem, are in essence similar. They may be described as sets of rules and procedures for relating some kind of effort to some kind of reward. This applies to managers' salaries as well as workers wages, but in this paper we shall concern ourselves very largely with the latter. Using a grid, we have worked out what appear to us to be all the logically possible relationships between types of effort and types of reward, *via* sets of rules and procedures. This is shown in Figure 2. It is necessary at this point only to explain summarily the meaning of the symbols in each box of Figure 2. Reading from top left across the rows we have:

		reward		
		reciprocal		non reciprocal
		immediate	deferred	
effort	time	TRI	TRD	TNR
	energy individual	ERI (ind)	ERD (ind)	ENR (ind)
	energy group	ERI (group)	ERD (group)	ENR (group)
	Competence	CRI	CRD	CNR
	status	X	X	SNR

Figure 2 Steps in selecting a payment scheme

Time effort

TRI Time–Reciprocal–Immediate

The rules in this case define a time period of attendance and the rewards for attendance are specified, in the expectation that the worker will be available for work as required during that period of attendance. Attendance outside the specified time is rewarded exceptionally and *immediately*,[4] by some kind of premium.

TRD Time–Reciprocal–Deferred

As in TRI above; save that exceptional reward for attendance outside specified hours is deferred; it may be cash, or time off.

TNR Time–Non-Reciprocal

In this case the rules do not distinguish normal or exceptional time periods for attendance. Rewards in cash or kind are related to a unit of time. A work contract specifies the number of time units of attendance, and the reward for each of these.

Energy effort (*individual or group*)

ERI Energy–Reciprocal–Immediate

The rules specify reward for separate measured units of expended muscular or mental energy. The reward follows immediately, i.e. in the agreed pay period.

ERD Energy–Reciprocal–Deferred

As above; save that the reward is deferred.

ENR Energy–Non-Reciprocal

A contract relating reward to energy expended. In this case the rules specify that ability to expend energy at that rate be demonstrated *prior* to the drawing up of the contract.

CRI Competence–Reciprocal–Immediate

In this case a generally recognized learned competence is rewarded immediately after it has been demonstrated in the performance of defined units of completed work.

CRD Competence–Reciprocal–Deferred

A generally recognized and learned competence is demonstrated in performance, but rewards for that performance are deferred.

CNR Competence–Non-Reciprocal

Once competence has been initially recognized, rewards are not related to demonstrated performance.

4. That which is paid within the recognized pay period.

SNR   Status–Non-Reciprocal[5]

Here the rules specify rewards for status; 'who you are' rather than 'what you do' – and not to recognized competence or to demonstrated performance or attendance.

Since all known payment schemes may, as we shall now show, be brought appropriately into each box in the grid (although there are some which might appear in more than one box) it might be as well to explain why it is necessary to construct the logical grid at all. There are two reasons:

1. Although it might seem that every possible set of rules relating every possible type of effort and reward will be reflected in some already tried and suggested payment systems, it is just possible that the grid used as part of a larger procedure will suggest other systems.

2. It may be that a combination of types of schemes may be appropriate to any company. A procedure is therefore needed which will indicate exactly which combination of types, before searching for known or possible payment systems which would, in practice, affect that combination. In short, although our grid contains 'pure types' there are real practical systems of payment to correspond to them, some of which are known, some possibly as yet unthought of.

Figure 3 shows the known and tried systems of payment which correspond to the boxes in the grid – and below is a brief description of the characteristics of each.

The time effort schemes[6]

For example:

TRI

A weekly time rate consisting e.g., of an hourly rate multiplied by 40, with shift and overtime premiums.

TRD

Again a weekly time rate. Monetary or other rewards for working

5. Since in this paper we are interested primarily in payment systems for manual workers we do not use this box of the grid further.

6. For a detailed description of all the schemes mentioned see Lupton, (1967).

		TRI	TRD	TNR
time		time rates, with, reciprocal payments, e.g. shift and overtime premiums	time rates, with reciprocal payments (or their equivalents) deferred, e.g. day off in lieu	pay hour by hour for the hour
energy	**individual**	ERI (ind) piecework incentive bonus schemes simple multi-factor schemes price lists	ERD (ind) individual productivity bonus personal contract schemes	ENR (ind) task work measured day work controlled day work
	group	ERI (gp) group piecework group incentive bonus schemes group simple multi-factor schemes price lists	ERD (GP) group productivity bonus Scanlon and Rucker type schemes profit sharing	ENR (gp) contract work
competence		CRI complex multi-factor schemes analytical estimating	CRD work simplification incremental scales with 'bars' based on performance	CNR full incremental salary scales professional fees
status		X	X	SNR fringe benefits ascription rewards

Figure 3

exceptional hours are paid later – say as an annual bonus, or monthly merit bonus.

TNR

Here, for example, a freelance worker will contract to attend for a given number of hours for an hourly rate.

Energy effort schemes

ERI

Straight Piecework
Incentive Bonus Schemes
Simple Multi-Factor Schemes   } Individual or Group
Price Lists

ERD (Ind.)

Productivity Bonus
Personal Contract Scheme

ENR (Ind.)

Task Work
Measured Day Work
Controlled Day Work

ERD (group)

Group Productivity Bonus
Scanlon Plan. Rucker Plan

ENR (group)

Sub-contracting

Competence effort schemes

CRI

Complex multi-factor schemes and schemes based on analytical estimating.

CRD

Work simplification schemes.
Incremental scales with 'bars' based on demonstrated performance or potential.

CNR

Full incremental salary scales.
Professional fees.

| | time | | | energy | | | competence | | | |
| | individual | | | group | | | plant | | | |
	1	2	3	4	5	6	7	8	9	
1 (g) Type of effort										
2 (g) Unit of accountability										
1 Length of job cycle	to 5	6-10	11-15	16-30	31-45	45-60	61-90	91-120	121+	mins.
2 Number of job modifications	0	1	2	3	4	5	6	7	8+	av. no. per month
3 Degree of automation	spt	pat	smt	cmt	stm	ctm	spo	cpo	ccp	
4 Number of product change	0	1	2	3	4	5	6	7	8+	av. no. per month
5 Number of job stoppages	0	1	2	3	4	5	6	7	8+	av. no per day
6 Duration of job stoppages	0	1-5	6-10	11-20	21-30	31-40	41-50	51-60	61+	av. no. mins. per day
7 % job elements specified by management	71+	61-70	51-60	41-50	31-40	21-30	11-20	1-10	0	%
8 % material scrapped	0	1-2	3-4	5-6	7-8	9-10	11-12	13-14	15+	%
9 % products/components rejected	0	1-2	3-4	5-6	7-8	9-10	11-12	13-14	15+	%
10 Time required to fill vacancy	1	2-4	5-7	8-10	11-13	14-16	17-19	20-22	23+	days

	81+	71-80	61-70	51-60	41-50	31-40	21-30	11-20	0-10	%
11 Labour stability	0	6	12	18	24	30	36	42	48	men %
12 Labour turnover	0	12	24	36	48	60	72	84	96	women %
13 Disputes about pay	0-4	5-8	9-12	13-16	17-20	21-24	25-28	29-32	33+	av. no. per month
14 Man hours lost in pay disputes	0-4	5-8	9-12	13-16	17-20	21-24	25-28	29-32	33+	% per month
15 % earnings decided outside plant/company	0-10	11-20	21-30	31-40	41-50	51-60	61-70	71-80	81+	%
16 Number of trade unions	0	1-3	4-6	7-9	10-12	13-15	16-18	19-21	22+	all plant
17 Occupational structure	0-3	4-6	7-9	10-12	13-15	16-18	19-21	22-24	25+	all plant
18 Absence	0	2-3	4-5	6-7	8-9	10-11	12-13	14-15	16+	% normal hours
19 Average age of working force		15-29			30-44			45+		years
20 % labour cost in unit cost	23+	21-23	18-20	15-17	12-14	10-12	7-9	4-6	1-3	%
21 % males in working force	0	to 10	11-20	21-30	31-40	41-50	51-60	61-70	71+	% all plant

Figure 4
Note see also Profile Dimensions, notes on scoring, page 270.

Status effort schemes

SRI $\Big\}$ Are practically speaking unlikely.
SRD

SNR

Covers fringe benefits and what one might call ascription reward, e.g. customary privileges that may go with a job whoever holds it and whatever his performance in it as long as he holds it, e.g. company car, dining room privileges, special discounts, deference.

This brief exercise in constructing the 'logical grid' and relating it to known payment systems gives us the answer to the second of our original questions, i.e. the one about available systems. We are now ready to answer the third question i.e.:

'how should a firm go about deciding which of the available systems is best suited to its circumstances'.

Selecting a payment system

We have already shown in a general way how a profile of the situation of a company might be constructed. We now show how such profiles may be used as part of the procedure for selecting a payment system.

In Figure 4 'The Profile Blank' each of the 23 dimensions is shown with a scale along which measurements may be accurately plotted. The complete 'plot' results in a 'situation profile' for each plant, department, workshop, etc. Instructions for 'scoring' are included in a note at the end of this section (page 270).

In Figure 5, which we have called the 'Master Block', the various types of *reward*[7] from our 'logical grid' have been 'strung along' each of the twenty-one dimensions, in such a way as to indicate what 'score' on each dimensions would be appropriate to each type of effort–reward relationship as derived from the 'logical grid'. For example, we have judged that 'reciprocal immediate reward' boxes are appropriate to short job cycles, and 'non-reciprocal reward' boxes to very long job cycles. Similarly, 'reciprocal immediate reward' is, in our judgement appro-

7. For identification of type of *effort* see Profile Dimensions – Notes on Scoring (p. 270).

priate to tasks when the operator has low discretion, and 'non-reciprocal reward' to tasks giving high discretion – and so on.

We are bound to stress that our procedure for distributing the various forms of reward along each dimension is based on informed professional judgement and admittedly incomplete factual evidence from research and consultancy. We cannot, therefore, promise pin-point accuracy. Our claim that the procedure is an improvement on any that have been previously suggested rests not on the ground that every point in it has been rigorously proved; it rests rather on the ground that the procedure includes a wide range of factors that are widely known to affect the operation of payment schemes, that it quantifies these factors where there is a considerable body of evidence from which an analysis can be made, and when such evidence is lacking it relies at least on informed judgement. More importantly perhaps, as we shall see, it offers a framework of ideas for the continuous monitoring of a payment scheme; to assess perhaps what steps need to be taken if e.g. technological changes are made, or a new system of job grades is introduced or changes take place in labour markets or product markets.

We hope that by now it has become clear what has to be done to select a payment scheme. If a transparency of the Situation Profile of the plant, workshop, etc., is laid over the Master Block, boxes from the Logical Grid will be 'picked up'. By referring again to Figure 3 (page 256) which for convenience we call the Payment System Classification and which identifies the known payment schemes that correspond to the 'pure types' in the Logical Grid, a scheme or combination of schemes is selected, or at the very least some payment systems or combinations are immediately rejected as completely inappropriate, and some alternatives left for final selection.

Alternatively, the Master Block could be used to construct a set of Ideal Profiles, i.e. profiles which characterize the situation which would be exactly appropriate to each of the categories of payment system represented by a box in the logical grid. The actual situation profile could then be tried for 'fit' against each 'ideal' profile. In this way the appropriate category or categories is identified.

1 (g) Type of effort →	time			energy			competence			
2 (g) Unit of accountability →	individual			group			plant			units
	1	2	3	4	5	6	7	8	9	
1 Length of job cycle	3ri	2ri	1ri	3rd	2rd	1rd	1nr	2nr	3nr	
	to 5	6-10	11-15	16-30	31-45	46-60	61-90	91-120	121+	mins.
2 Number of job modifications	3ri	2ri	1ri	3rd	2rd	1rd	1nr	2nr	3nr	
	0	1	2	3	4	5	6	7	8+	av. no. per month
3 Degree of automation	spt	pat	smt	cmt	stm	ctm	spo	cpo	ccp	
	3ri	2ri	1ri	3rd	2rd	1rd	1nr	2nr	3nr	
4 Number of product changes	0	1	2	3	4	5	6	7	8+	av. no. per month
	3ri	2ri	1ri	3rd	2rd	1rd	1nr	2nr	3nr	
5 Number of job stoppages	0	1	2	3	4	5	6	7	8+	av. no. per day
	3ri	2ri	1ri	3rd	2rd	1rd	1nr	2nr	3nr	
6 Duration of job stoppages	0	1-5	6-10	11-20	21-30	31-40	41-50	51-60	61+	av. no. min. per day
	3ri	2ri	1ri	3rd	2rd	1rd	1nr	2nr	3nr	
7 % job elements specified by management	71+	61-70	51-60	41-50	31-40	21-30	11-20	1-10	0	%
	3ri	2ri	1ri	3rd	2rd	1rd	1nr	2nr	3nr	
8 % material scrapped	0	1-2	3-4	5-6	7-8	9-10	11-12	13-14	15+	%
	3ri	2ri	1ri	3rd	2rd	1rd	1nr	2nr	3nr	
9 % products/components rejected	0	1-2	3-4	5-6	7-8	9-10	11-12	13-14	15+	%
	1	2-4	5-7	8-10	11-13	14-16	17-19	20-22	23+	days
10 Time required to fill vacancy	3ri	2ri	1ri	3rd	2rd	1rd	1nr	2nr	3nr	

Figure 5

(score codes)	81+	71-80	61+70	51-60	41-50	31-40	21-30	11-20	to 10	
	3ri	2ri	1ri	3rd	2rd	1rd	1nr	2nr	3nr	%
11 Labour stability	81+	71-80	61+70	51-60	41-50	31-40	21-30	11-20	to 10	
12 Labour turnover	0	6	12	18	24	30	36	42	48	men %
	0	12	24	36	48	60	72	84	96	women %
13 Disputes about pay	0-4	5-8	9-12	13-16	17-20	21-24	25-28	29-32	33+	av. no. per month
14 Man hours lost in pay disputes	0-4	5-8	9-12	13-16	17-20	21-24	25-28	29-32	33+	% per month
15 % earnings decided outside plant—company	0-10	11-20	21-30	31-40	41-50	51-60	61-70	71-80	81+	%
16 Number of trade unions	0	1-3	4-6	7-9	10-12	13-15	16-18	19-21	22+	all plant
17 Occupational structure	0-3	4-6	7-9	10-12	13-15	16-18	19-21	22-24	25+	all plant
18 Absence	0	2-3	4-5	6-7	8-9	10-11	12-13	14-15	16+	% normal hours
19 Average age of working force		15-29			30-44			45+		years
20 % labour cost in unit cost	23+	21-23	18-20	15-17	12-14	10-12	7-9	4-6	1-3	%
21 % males in working force	to 10	11-20	21-30	31-40	41-50	51-60	61-70	71-80	81+	% all plant

Note See also Profile dimensions—notes on scoring page 270.

To summarize the steps of the procedure that have been covered so far:

Construct from scores on the 23 dimensions a Situation Profile of a plant, workshop, or department.

Lay situation profile(s) on the Master Block to 'pick up' the labelled boxes from the Logical Grid.

Identify the appropriate payment system or systems by reference to the Payment System Classification.

or alternatively

Use Master Block to identify Ideal Profiles for each category of scheme in the Logical Grid.

Compare Situation Profile(s) with Ideal Profile(s) to select payment system(s).

This is not the end of the matter, for a company will already have a payment scheme or schemes in operation. Among the payment systems identified by the procedure as appropriate may be the existing system – or the existing system might be shown up as not very obviously inappropriate. Subsequent steps in the procedure which will be described in detail presently, include the possibility of changing the Situation Profile(s) so that it (they) will 'pick-up' the existing system(s) e.g. by changing the length of the job cycle, the operators' discretion or improving the system of production control and quality control. The question may then be asked whether the trouble and expense of introducing a new payment system would be greater or less than the trouble and expense of altering the scores on the relevant dimensions to produce a modified Situation Profile. We have also evolved a method for dealing with situations in which the situation profile 'picks-up' a mixture of boxes from the logical grid; a method which distils out what is common to them and allows a clear choice to be made. The method is best described by references to practical examples and will therefore be dealt with in Section 6 [not dealt with here].

There is a final step, and other problem of method to be solved, before the description of the procedure for selecting a payment scheme is complete. We have yet to discuss objectives, and to say something of how the profile dimensions might be 'weighted' according to their significance. This we shall do in the next section, after which we will work in detail through a number of examples to demonstrate the complete procedure.

Objectives, values and assumptions

Anyone following the steps in the method just outlined will probably be led to ask about the differences between (a) the Situation Profile as it currently is and (b) as it might be if management objectives on certain matters are realized, or (c) as it might be if certain factors outside the control of management change. This is a useful question because the payment system which best fits each of these profiles might differ. Further, a payment system selected only by the method of profile matching we have just described might be repugnant to some deeply held values and assumptions of management or workers, so another might have to be adopted, and perhaps some modifications of the situation made, to achieve a reasonable 'fit'. Finally, there is the question of implementing the changes indicated. All these questions will now be dealt with.

By following the steps in selecting a payment scheme, a management might decide after matching profiles that the present payment scheme would be adequate if certain modifications were made to the situation profile – but management might already be in the process of altering that profile by pursuing certain objectives, or certain changes might be taking place in the circumstances of the company that management is powerless to alter, e.g. in product or labour markets. For example: independently of anything they wish to do about payment systems, a management might be pursuing objectives such as to:

Reduce labour turnover by 25 per cent in the next six months.
Improve the machinery of bargaining, consultation, and disputes handling, so as to reduce the frequency and severity of disputes about pay.
Improve production control so as to reduce down-time.
Increase the level of mechanization.

One could think of other objectives which, if realized, would alter the shape of the situation profile. A management might wish, then, to construct a *modified situation profile* representing the situation as it would be if management's objectives were realized, including perhaps modified scores on labour market and product market dimensions based on predictions for say, a year ahead; and to select a payment scheme based on the modified profile. It would be unwise to leave the matter there, for the following reasons.

Presumably, the reason why a management might be pursuing objectives which will reduce down-time, or reduce the number and duration of pay disputes, or economize on material utilisation, or install labour-saving machines, would be to reduce the unit cost of the product, and gain greater control so as to meet delivery dates and quality standards. Some objectives might claim priority over others on the grounds that they offer worthwhile immediate gains in cost and control, for less than proportional cost in the resources and effort devoted to achieving them and these might be assigned first priority. So instead of just modifying the situation profile to take account of objectives all regarded as equal in their cost saving potentiality, and all having equal claims upon resources, the management should set out a list of objectives in order of priority. One simple method of doing this is to use a *Potentiality–Difficulty Grid* as shown in Figure 6.

The vertical axis is a measure of cost-saving control-improving potentiality. The horizontal axis is a measure of the difficulty of making the organisational changes necessary to reduce the cost or increase the control. Each objective may be assigned a box in the grid. All that is necessary now is to decide in the light of the resources available to pursue objectives – which ones are to be taken first, second, etc.; which may be tackled at the same time – and so on. The shape of the *modified situation profile* for say a year ahead is now affected by the priorities as determined by the management in the light of their judgements of the desirability and difficulty of pursuing certain objectives. The modified profile may now be used to select a payment system. If further re-shaping of the situation profile is required to accommodate the existing payment system, then management may wish to adopt new objectives and to re-assign its priorities.

To summarize the suggested steps to incorporate management objectives into the methods of selecting a payment system:

List all cost-saving control-improving objectives.

Express objectives as scores on profile dimensions and construct modified situation profile for end of time period.

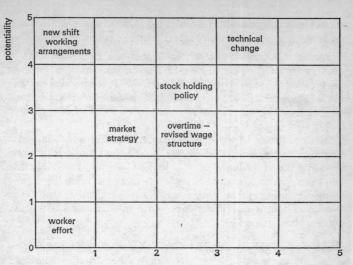

Figure 6 difficulty

Assign priorities to objectives using *Potentiality–Difficulty Grid – re-shape modified situation profile* for end of time period. Select payment scheme.

Identify the changes needed to re-shape the profile to match the existing payment system; or to introduce another. Re-assign priorities if necessary.

This procedure clearly has uses as a guide to the formulation of managerial strategy and tactics in implementing changes. Some of the difficulties that are shown up when constructing the *Potentiality–Difficulty Grid* might be identified as purely technical ones, impinging little upon existing patterns of expectation, values, and power. Those which are seen to arise from conflicting expectations, incompatible beliefs and the exercise of power, call for meticulous attention to questions such as: who ought to meet whom? when? and about what? with what objectives? and avoiding what anticipated pitfalls? It is not possible in this text to examine these questions in detail, because the answers depend too much on detailed knowledge of a particular firm or department.

Tom Lupton and Dan Gowler 267

Values and assumptions

So far we have dealt with those objectives that can be expressed as modified scores on the profile dimensions. However, there is another set of considerations to be taken into account, and we have called these *Values and Assumptions*. It is conceivable that the management of a company might raise more or less serious objections to a payment system selected by the methods we have elaborated so far.

It is not for us to say what values and assumptions managers ought to have, or for that matter what values workers or shop stewards ought to have. Nor is it necessary for us to disclose what our values would be if we were managers selecting a payment scheme or Trade Union officers passing judgement on it. We know, from our experience, how in fact some managers express their values.

A manager might say that he believes that workers should participate fully in deciding what a reasonable performance standard on their job should be. Another manager might claim that it is management's right or duty to decide these matters.

A manager might say that he wants to maximize the freedom of workers to choose how they will do their jobs (within the limits imposed by technology). Another might quite strongly disagree with a high level of discretion.

A manager might say that no payment system ought to be installed which is perceived by the worker to be inequitable, or to present difficulties for the worker in calculating the pay entitlement. Another view could be that if all the other features of a scheme offer great cost savings and increase managerial control then these two matters should be put into proper perspective – as practical difficulties to be tackled later.

Some managers believe it right that workers should be encouraged to make improvements in their jobs, to be trained to do so, and to be rewarded for the improvements they make. Others do not.

Some managers want to encourage a sense of commitment to the firms' objectives. Others believe this is a waste of time and money.

So one could go on. *Our advice is that managers embarking on the process of selecting a payment system ought first to make their values and assumptions absolutely explicit and clear.* Having done so, it is possible to determine what effect holding to a set of values and assumptions will have on the shape of the *modified situation profile*. For example, a belief in high job discretion might have implications for the length of the job cycle, or for the percentage of job elements that management prescribes. Some values, such as perceived equity and ease of payment calculation, are not easily translatable into profile scores. These values may counsel the rejection of a selected payment scheme however good a match it may be with the situation profile as modified in the light of the firms' objectives. For example, a multi-factor incentive scheme might be rejected on the ground that the worker would find difficulty in understanding it, or any payment by results scheme because it may give rise to unequal earnings, which is regarded as unfair. A scheme might be rejected because of the fear that it will be perceived by the worker to be unfair.

If a payment scheme is, in fact, ruled out because it is inconsistent with a set of values and assumptions, then two courses are open. The first is to ask whether one is prepared to change one's values and assumptions and re-adopt it; the second is to declare oneself unprepared to change one's values and assumptions, and then to calculate the costs of adhering to them. These costs may be assessed by examining the implications of the discrepancy between the *modified situation profile* and the *value-preferred payment system*, e.g. the costs of making the technical and administrative changes necessary to change job design and job cycles so as to increase worker discretion. One is really asking about the economic short-run costs and benefits of indulging one's values and assumptions. Presumably, one is only ready to bear costs if necessary in the belief that this kind of indulgence offers long-term benefits, e.g. in improved job satisfaction which may reduce costly labour turnover and absenteeism, and increase commitment to the firm and its purposes. There are those who think that this is pie-in-sky, jam-tomorrow stuff, and would prefer to jettison inconvenient values and assumptions.

The description of all the steps in our procedure is now complete. At this point a diagram (Figure 7) showing the sequence of steps in the procedure might be helpful.

The information needed to make this complex procedure possible will be drawn from many departments of the firm. The Work Study Department, the Planning and Scheduling Departments, and the Quality Control Department, will probably supply the technological data. Material on the labour market and the occupational structure will probably have to be supplied by the Personnel Department, on costs the Accounting Department, and so on. And, whatever decision is taken as the result of following the procedure, the consequences will affect many departments.

For these reasons we are firmly of the opinion that our procedure should be worked through not by the Personnel Department alone, or the Work Study Department alone, but by a team of specialists from all departments, including someone in touch with the product market. This team should, as we see it, be led by a very senior manager. If this seems to be building a steam hammer to crack a nut, it should be remembered that the payment system is a significant link between the worker as family man, consumer, and citizen, and the worker as producer. As such, it deserves equal attention with the links with shareholders, customers and suppliers, which usually get the attention of senior managers.

Profile dimensions – notes on scoring

Before scoring each dimension *decide which unit of production is being considered;*[8] an individual, a section, a workshop, a department, a plant, a company, and score consistently for that unit. It may be found necessary, or useful, to construct profiles for each department, so that similarities and differences are clearly shown up. The comparison will indicate whether one, or a number of payment schemes is appropriate. *It is also possible to derive from a number of profiles that effort/reward relationship which is common to each of the units considered.*

'Gate' mechanisms

Type of effort 1(g). It is necessary to identify the type of effort appropriate to the unit concerned, thus:

8. The 'score' on the Unit of Accountability dimension dictates whether individual or group reward in the Master Block should be picked up by the situation profile.

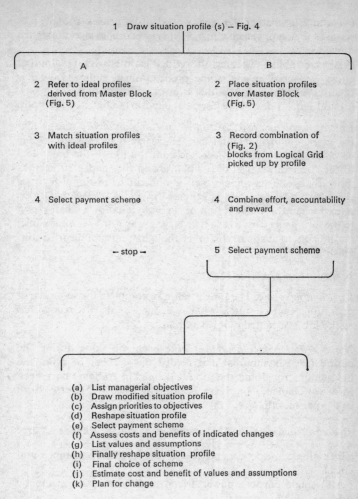

1 Draw situation profile (s) — Fig. 4

A

2 Refer to ideal profiles derived from Master Block (Fig. 5)

3 Match situation profiles with ideal profiles

4 Select payment scheme

— stop —

B

2 Place situation profiles over Master Block (Fig. 5)

3 Record combination of (Fig. 2) blocks from Logical Grid picked up by profile

4 Combine effort, accountability and reward

5 Select payment scheme

(a) List managerial objectives
(b) Draw modified situation profile
(c) Assign priorities to objectives
(d) Reshape situation profile
(e) Select payment scheme
(f) Assess costs and benefits of indicated changes
(g) List values and assumptions
(h) Finally reshape situation profile
(i) Final choice of scheme
(j) Estimate cost and benefit of values and assumptions
(k) Plan for change

Figure 7

(a) establish whether the work is skilled or professional. If it is score C for competence effort. If it is not competence effort then move to;

(b) and establish whether the effort is intensive, i.e., output effort measured against some predetermined standard. If it is then score E for energy effort. If not then move to;

(c) and score T for time effort, i.e. pay for the hour by the hour.

Unit of accountability 2(g). Individual accountability means that the work of an individual can be clearly distinguished. *Group accountability* is scored when the contribution of the individual to the cooperative task of a small group (i.e. under 20 persons more than one) is impossible, or difficult to distinguish (or is thought undesirable to distinguish). *Plant accountability* is scored when the contribution of the individual or a small group to the task being carried out by a large group (20+) is impossible, or difficult to distinguish (or is thought undesirable to distinguish).

Profile dimensions

Length of job cycle. The time it takes to complete the sequence of operations that comprise what is defined or usually recognized as the job.[9] *Scale* from 0–121 minutes.

Number of job modifications. Take each job done during the period (say six months) and record the number of times the instructions for doing the job (as defined in 1 above) have been formally changed, i.e. have been written down.[9] *Scale* from 0–8+ per month.

Degree of automation. The categories along the dimension are:

SPT: single purpose hand tools, e.g. handsaw, hammer and chisel.
PAT: single purpose power-driven hand tools, e.g. pneumatic drill.
SMT: simple machine tools, e.g. centre lathe, shaper, radial arm driller, circular saw.

9. Where there are a number of jobs involved *average* job-cycle times and modifications should be calculated.

CMT: complex machine tools, e.g. gear cutting machines.

STM: simple transfer machines, i.e. automatic sequence of similar operations e.g. drilling and facing.

CTM: complex transfer machines, embodying automatic sequences of dissimilar operations.

SPO: simple process operations, e.g. rolling mill and blast-furnace operations.

CPO: complex process operations, e.g. instrument controlled chemical process.

CCP: continuous complex process operations, e.g. a chemical process with on-line computer control.

Product changes. We define a product change as either the introduction of a completely new product into the range, or a change-over in a production unit from one product to another, both of which are already in the firm's present range. *Scale* from 0–8 + changes per month. (For example, in a garment factory an order for 500 dresses of a new fashion, or a re-order of a conventional garment would both be product changes. In a jobbing engineering firm every new order or repeat order is a product change.)

Job stoppages (number). Record the average daily occasions when work was stopped. *Scale* 0–8 + stoppages per day – for such reasons as:

(a) shortage of materials
(b) shortage of components
(c) poor quality materials
(d) shortage of tools
(e) absence of service
(f) shortage of labour
(g) absence of instructions
(h) ambiguous instructions
(i) machine/process failure

Job stoppages duration. The duration in minutes of job stoppages, as defined in 5, above. *Scale* 0–61 + minutes (average per day)

Percentage of job elements specified by management. State (on average) what percentage of the elements of each job is not at the discretion of the worker but is:

(a) prescribed by management, and/or
(b) controlled by machine
Scale $+71\% - 0\%$.

Percentage material scrapped. Sum all materials put into production/service *each day* and average for the period concerned how much has been recorded as wasted, i.e.

(a) has been spoiled by (i) poor workmanship, (ii) poor tools and (iii) poor organization, and
(b) has been scrapped necessarily in production (e.g. material lost by cutting and machining).
Scale $0\%-15\%$ + average daily waste

Percentage product/components scrapped. Record the percentage of all components and finished products, put into production/service each day, that were rejected as sub-standard (this differs from 8 in being concerned with what happens at points where work is checked for quality). *Scale* $0\%-15\%$ + average rejects daily.

Time required to fill a vacancy. Record for the period concerned the average time elapsed from the notification of a vacancy to the filling of a vacancy by a person competent to do the job.

Labour stability. The labour stability index (devised by Angela Bowey) is arrived at by the following formula:

$$\frac{Ln}{n \times N} \times 100.$$

N   is the total number of employees,
n is the number of months over which stability is being measured,
Ln is the total length of service in months of the employees concerned measured over the past n months.

This formula expresses stability as a percentage of the maximum possible stability.

Labour stability measures the ability of the unit to retain its employees, as distinct from labour turnover which measures the rate of replacement of employees. The significant difference between these two measures is illustrated, for instance, where a high labour turnover rate is due mostly to a small proportion of jobs in the unit being filled several times in the time period considered. High labour turnover in this example does not indicate low labour stability. *Scale* $+81\%-0\%$

Labour turnover. This is measured by the usual formula, i.e.

$$\frac{\text{total no. leavers} \times 100}{\text{average no. employed during period}}.$$

However, *it must be noted that leavers here includes all those transferred to another unit of production.*
Scale $0\%-48\%+$ men
$0\%-96\%+$ women

Disputes about pay (number). State how many disputes were recorded each month during the period concerned which were about the amount of pay. For example, a claim for a money allowance for some special circumstances, which is not admitted by management, is a dispute, so is a refusal of an operator to be transferred on the grounds that his bonus earnings would suffer, and so is a refusal to accept regrading. If no detailed records are kept, a 'straw-poll' of supervisors, shop-stewards and work study men, might suffice to produce a figure for a typical month *Scale* $0 - 33+$ disputes (average) per month.

Disputes about pay (duration). Record total hours lost through pay disputes as defined in 13 above, and express these as a percentage of total normal hours, *Scale* $0\%-33\%+$.

Percentage earnings decided outside plant/company. Take the average total earnings of the workers in the unit under consideration and state what percentage is the outcome of settlement made *outside the firm*, e.g. by an Employers' Federation and a Union Confederation nationally, or by statute. *Scale* $0\%-81\%+$.

Number of Trade Unions. This refers to the number of Trade Unions in the *whole* plant/company under consideration whose representatives bargain with managements representatives. *Scale* $0-22+$.

Occupational structure. Multiply the total number of grades in the plant/company by the total number of administrative units, by the number of shifts worked to arrive at a measure of the complexity of occupational structure

$$\frac{\text{grades} \times \text{number of admin. units} \times \text{number of shifts}}{100}.$$

For example: if a job evaluated grading structure has 4 grades, and there are; some 100 administrative units[10] in the plant/company, and 2 shifts are worked; we have

$$\frac{4 \times 100 \times 2}{100} = 8$$

This is intended as a measure of the potentiality of earnings movements to 'leap-frog'. *Scale* 0–25+.

Percentage absence. Recorded absence from the unit *for any reason*, including time lost through strikes, sickness, absence, days off, and lateness are included, but not lay-offs due to e.g., shortage of material, or managerial shortcomings, *Scale* 0%–16%+.

Average age of work force. Three point scale as Figure 4, i.e. 15–29 years, 30–44 years and 45+ years.

Percentage labour cost in product cost. Percentage of direct labour cost in the total production costs generated by the unit concerned.

Percentage males in working force (all plant/company). This is obvious from Figure 4 (page 258). *Scale* 0%–71%+.

Note on time period. We suggest that the data needed for the completion of a situation profile should be collected over at least six months previous to the exercise. The scales have been constructed with this time period in mind, but care should be taken to allow for seasonal fluctuations that might occur outside the period selected for data collection.

References

CURRIE, R. M. (1963), Financial Incentives, BIM.
LUPTON, T. (1967), 'Forms of wage and salary payment for higher productivity,' OECD, Paris, pp. 11–12.

10. The number of units administered by first line management.

Part Five
Salary Structures

In previous sections the readings have been largely concerned
with methods of wage payment. When we turn to salaries we
find little by way of empirical enquiry of the kind exemplified
by Dalton's account of the 'rate-buster' (p. 64) or Roy's
account of the control of time as practised by the work
group he observed. The salaried employee to an extent far
greater than the wage earner is interested in a career, so his
pay to-day reflects his success so far, and marks (hopefully)
a step on the way to higher pay. So with salaries we seem to
be concerned more with hierarchial pay grading *structures*,
than with methods of relating pay and performance. It will
be readily seen, however, that the promise of advancement is
itself an incentive, so that a salary structure is also a method
of wage payment.

The question arises of how to arrange jobs in a hierarchy
so that each individual's pay and position (and the efforts
called for by incumbency of position) are fairly matched, and
continue to be so as he advances through the grades. The
enquiry of the British Prices and Incomes Board describes how
the organizations it studied actually set up their salary
structures and attempted to classify types of salary structure.
Elliott Jaque's papers and the papers describing
T. T. Patterson's method, suggest how a salary structure
ought to be set up. Alan Fox's critique of Jaque's system
might be read as a comment on all simply based procedures
for evaluating and comparing jobs.

16 Prices and Incomes Board Report

Types of Salary Structures

Excerpts from 'Types of salary structures', *Prices and Incomes Board Report*, HMSO, Cmnd 4187, 1969, pp. 9–37.

Types of salary structures

No organization which employs MEPT[1] staff is entirely without a salary structure of any kind. But the structures which are found may vary in two ways. They may be more or less systematic up to the point where each job or group of jobs carries with it certain pay limits, whether these are in the form of a range or scale, a prescribed minimum or maximum for the post, or age/service pay guidelines related to the type of occupation. Secondly, there may be what can be termed planned structures, i.e. ones in which there is a system of evaluating or grading jobs. The distinction between a planned and an unplanned salary structure, is not however clear cut, being one of degree rather than of kind. In our national survey, the results of which are given in Appendix B [not included here], we sought first of all to find out whether firms had salary structures with pay limits. To this end, we asked firms to state whether they had defined salary guidelines or limits for any of their MEPT staff. Next we wished to gauge the extent of planning, and this was assessed indirectly by asking whether the pay limits for jobs in the company were associated with a job evaluation scheme and whether jobs of equal responsibility were grouped into grades.

The survey reveals that pay limits are associated with three-fifths of all MEPT staff jobs in the organizations employing 250 or more employees with which our enquiry was concerned. As was to be expected, a structure with pay limits is more likely to be found among the larger organisations, and in firms with more

1. MEPT is an abbreviation for 'Managerial, Executive, Professional and Technical.'

than 5000 employees, nearly three-quarters of MEPT staff have salary limits associated with their jobs. In terms of the number of firms, the proportion which have pay limits for at least some of their staff is therefore less, and amounts to only just over two fifths. Even so, the pay of a quarter of MEPT staff in companies employing less than 500 employees is determined within prescribed limits, and it is therefore evident that the need for systematizing salary structures is accepted in at least some of the smaller companies.

Size of firm is the predominant but not the only factor contributing to the likelihood of a firm having a structure with pay limits. An analysis of a sub-sample of firms by type of production (process, unit, mass) shows that the kind of production process also has an influence. Such structures are found most frequently in process production plants and least often among mass production firms. Research has shown that, in terms of the number of levels in the management hierarchy, the process industry has a more complex organization than firms specializing in unit and mass production. It may be therefore that structures are more likely to have pay limits when there are many management layers in the organizations.

Over four-fifths of the MEPT staff who are covered by pay limits are in jobs having both associated salary minima and associated salary maxima. This type of salary limit is favoured particularly by the larger firms with more than 5000 employees. Other types of pay limits are therefore more likely to be found amongst smaller organizations. The most common alternative is for jobs to have associated salary maxima but no prescribed minima. We also find single rates for jobs, salary minima for jobs but no upper salary ceiling, and limits in the form of guidelines related to the person's age or service rather than to the actual job the person is doing. In all only about 6 per cent of the staff with pay limits do not have some kind of prescribed salary ceiling related to their present position within the organization.

Firms with a systematic structure do not necessarily have pay limits for all their MEPT staff, for in these firms about 14 per cent of the staff are in jobs without related guidelines. In two thirds of such firms, however, pay limits apply to all MEPT staff. Where this is not so, it is sometimes the senior staff whose pay is not related to guidelines, but in some firms there are guidelines only for specific groups of staff such as production managers, technical grades and certain other staff. In the case of senior staff the absence of guidelines may reflect the view that the individuals concerned determine the scope and extent of their own job to such an extent that no general system can take the place of individual consideration of each separate salary. On the other hand, the fact that production staff are exceptionally likely to be covered by structures with pay limits may be associated with the existence of pay structures for manual workers whom they supervize. Structures with pay limits for technical grades and certain other staff may be attributed to the publication of recommended rates by unions or professional associations for these occupations.

[2] The salary practices of firms with pay limits can be divided between those where there is a single structure embracing all the MEPT staff in the enterprise, and those where there are a series of structures for different groups of staff identified either by their specialism or by their promotion potential. The returns made by firms for the national survey indicate that though smaller firms are likely to have a single structure for all their staff, many of the larger companies have more than one structure. Sometimes the structure distinguishes between different levels of skills. For example, some firms have one structure for technical and supervisory staff whose career horizons in the main are limited, and another structure for managerial and specialist staff whose potential for promotion is greater. In other companies, however, the existence of more than one structure is related either to the concept of separate labour markets for staff in different specialist fields and different geographic locations or, as in the case of sales staff and some production staff, to the different way they may be paid. In these companies the structural division is between 'market groups' or the ease with which performance can be related to targets, and not seniority.

Turning now to the degree of planning, in the sense in which we have defined it, the national survey shows that of the 512,000

2. [This is para. 27.]

MEPT staff (60 per cent of all MEPT staff jobs) for which there are defined salary limits, 444,000 jobs are associated with a graded structure (whether or not based on job evaluation) and a further 40,000 though not graded have been job evaluated. Thus the majority of jobs for which there are pay limits are also associated with a planned structure.

The rigour with which jobs covered by planned structures are evaluated can vary considerably. At one end there are systems which depend primarily on assessors' intuitive knowledge of jobs in the company. At the other, there are sophisticated analytic rating schemes in which an attempt is made, not only to show that one job is more complicated than another, but also how much more important one job is than another. Companies which use analytic job evaluation techniques to rank jobs of varying responsibility do not then necessarily group jobs into grades. In some cases they may translate the 'evaluation units' directly into individual salary ranges. The survey shows that the grouping of jobs into grades for rather more than half (55 per cent) of the staff covered by graded structures is based on a job evaluation process. Only 5 per cent of all MEPT staff covered by structures have individual pay limits directly related to job evaluation units. Among companies with graded structures, the larger companies are more likely to use job evaluation techniques but even among the smallest companies with 250–499 employees nearly a third of the staff salaries in graded structures are based on a formal job evaluation scheme.

Graded structures can be divided into those with few grades ('broad-banded') and those with many grades throughout the structure ('multi-grade'). As might be expected, the survey confirms that on the whole multi-grade structures are associated with narrow pay ranges and small overlaps between grades, while broad-banded structures, which incorporate fewer grades, generally have wider salary ranges and greater overlaps. The average width of the salary range associated with a grade (i.e., the difference between the minimum and maximum) is 43 per cent above the minimum for the grade, but the actual widths of ranges varies considerably. Amongst large firms a range width of 50 per cent above the minimum is favoured. But structures with average width of ranges anywhere between 15 per cent to 55 per cent are almost equally likely. The average overlap between grades (i.e., the proportion of a salary range which may be simultaneously covered by the range immediately below) is 18 per cent for all structures. Again, there are wide variations between structures; just over a tenth of all systematic structures have grades which do not overlap.

The widths of grades and the overlaps between grades reflect to some extent the management's philosophy on salary progression. An overlap between grades acknowledges that an experienced person doing a job carrying a certain level of responsibility can be of more value to the company than a newcomer to a job in the grade above. A larger overlap between grades and a wider salary range for a grade place more emphasis on the performance of the individual within the grade, whilst narrower widths and overlaps, especially when associated with a multi-grade structure, place more emphasis on the job level and promotion. We have shown how the practice regarding widths and overlaps varies between firms. The survey also shows that even within a single structure practice is not uniform. For instance although in the firms surveyed the width of salary ranges in percentage terms is approximately the same for all grades in about three-fifths of the structures with associated salary ranges, in a quarter of the structures the pay ranges are wider at the top. The structures with the wider ranges for senior jobs probably acknowledge that at these levels individual merit assumes greater importance.

In practice there may be less distinction between the two types of structure than might be thought at first sight. To some extent, the concepts of moving through a single wide grade and moving through a hierarchy of narrow grades can be so applied as to produce very similar effects for the organisation or for the individuals concerned. Much depends on the controls which exist in the organization. But where there are effective controls, narrow bands of salaries and ranges may cause some inflexibility. This is because narrow ranges of salaries for particular grades may lead to difficulty in distinguishing between variation in performance. Thus, organizations operating this type of structure may succumb to excuses for regrading jobs, not because of any alteration in the context of the work but more as a result of wishing to reward those staff whose performance is considered to be of sufficiently high quality.

It has been put to us by experts in the salary administration field, both practising salary administrators and management consultants, that all firms, regardless of size, would benefit from having systematic pay limits and some system for evaluating the relative worth of jobs in the organisation. The survey results suggest that a large part of industry and commerce would concur with this point of view, with the majority favouring a graded structure. The survey results, however, also show that the salary structures of organisations which have adopted a planned approach, in the sense that they accept the need for defined pay parameters and some system of job evaluation, do not then necessarily develop along the same lines.

We have shown that organizational factors such as the size of the undertaking and the type of job hierarchy may influence the basic type of structure chosen. But within this basic framework other structural divergencies occur according to the extent to which the organisation is subject to pressures which cause salary administrators to depart from what might otherwise be their aim of providing similar maximum awards for jobs with the same evaluation grading. Once such variations occur within the organization's overall structural framework the reasons for treating certain groups of staff differently and in particular for departing from the normal relationship between pay and evaluation gradings, should in our view be made explicit so that the implications for the whole payment system of choosing a particular type of solution are clearly understood. This is necessary to ensure that the particular method chosen does not have other unwanted repercussions and that the cost of the particular action can be measured. In this sense one function of a salary structure is to act as an information system.

A number of devices which can be used to meet particular pressures will be seen to have obvious dangers for the integrity and for the cost of the structure as a whole. Thus distortion of the grading system to enable higher salaries to be paid to particular individuals will undermine the whole rationale underlying the salary structure. Raising salary levels generally rather than making separate provisions for particular groups of individuals affected by a well-defined labour market is likely to prove unnecessarily costly for the undertaking and inflationary for the economy. On the other hand, penny-pinching activities may provide a short-term saving but be expensive in the long run in terms of morale and obtaining staff of the appropriate ability. But the kind of pressures which have led to differences in structural characteristics do have to be catered for to a greater or lesser extent by most firms. We, therefore, now look at our findings from the standpoint of maintaining the integrity of the structure, without loss of flexibility, and describe briefly the techniques we have found in use to meet some of the difficulties commonly encountered.

A difficulty which all companies are likely to meet is the need to maintain both a logical internal relationship between jobs at different levels within the organisation, and to match externally the salaries for highly mobile groups who, because there is a market shortage for their skills, can command higher salaries than their colleagues carrying out work at a similar level. [See page 281.] We showed that some companies have overcome this difficulty by developing separate structures for each labour market group, whether or not the group is in short supply. Other companies, who as far as possible prefer to have one structure covering all staff, have developed separate structures only for special groups, such as computer staff. But the survey also shows that many undertakings have only one structure for all staff, and from the case studies as well as from our survey we learnt of a number of other techniques for dealing with the special problems concerned.

[3] A number of companies pointed out that because staff in a particular occupational group could command high salaries early in their career, the same was not necessarily true for them as they progressed up the career ladder. These companies considered that many other organizations were too ready to assume

3. [This is para. 37.]

that special action was needed for the whole group. The former found that they could cater for mobile staff merely by adjusting their recruiting salaries and permitting the average salaries for these staff to be a higher point in the salary range for the grade than other staff groups. Many of these companies felt that they could offer staff good career prospects, and such firms might not need to adjust the salary maxima for individuals. Staff will often stay with a company because of promotion prospects even when they know that in the short-term they can obtain more money elsewhere.

Some companies have found it necessary to adjust the salary maxima for certain groups of staff. One company effectively increased the salary maxima for staff in short supply by permitting on a strictly monitored basis staff in certain occupations to be graded higher than would have been justified on evaluation points. Among companies who relate job evaluation points to salaries by multiplying the evaluation points by a constant we found instances of companies adjusting the constant for different occupational groups. Another technique was to leave the grading of jobs unaltered but to pay a special allowance to staff in recognized occupations. What distinguished these companies from organizations who responded to pressures in an *ad hoc* fashion was that the staff for whom adjustments could be made was predetermined and the extent to which the provisions were used was measurable and explicit.

The relationship of the pay of salaried staff with that of wage-earners in the same company raised a similar problem of devising techniques to respond to a particular form of pressure on the structure as a whole. We have already pointed out that a firm must maintain reasonable consistency in the internal relationships of its pay structure. This principle is also applicable to the relationship between wages and salaries. The need for this is naturally felt in practice most strongly at points where the two structures meet, for example where foremen classed as salaried staff supervise operatives classed as wage-earners. Another point at which the relationship commonly makes itself felt is where draughtsmen and engineering craftsmen are concerned, since in a typical situation both are recruited from among a common group of apprentices but the former are paid salaries whereas the latter are wage-earners.

[4] In recent years many manual workers have been able to obtain considerable improvements in pay as a result of productivity agreements. In so far as this has meant the abandonment of long-standing traditions and attitudes and the adoption of what are often termed 'staff' attitudes, there is nothing paradoxical in accepting a permanent raising of the structure of wages of these particular workers in relation to what of salaries. Indeed where conditions of service are concerned it is now widely accepted among progressive companies that customary distinctions between 'staff' and 'payroll' workers are becoming irrelevant and should in time be removed. But though it may be logical to narrow differentials between manual workers affected by a settlement and the company's staff as a whole, it will still be necessary to maintain reasonable differentials between a foreman's pay and that of the workers he is supervising.

It does not follow however that changes in the whole of an undertaking's structure are required. For example in the case of foremen, changed working methods resulting from efficiency agreements may bring about a radical re-organization of supervision. This has in some instances provided an opportunity to reduce the number of levels of shop floor supervision and upgrade the jobs of the remaining supervisory staff to reflect their increased responsibilities. We referred to an example of this in our recent report (no. 125) on an agreement covering salaried staff employed by BICC Ltd.

Where this situation does not apply, the remedy may well be found in having separate structures for draughtsmen, technical staff and supervisors. But if it is then found necessary to adjust one of these structures for special reasons, it becomes most important that these reasons be kept clearly in view and not be confused with, or disguised as, techniques which serve different purposes. In particular, if there is not a separate structure for such staff it is important that the extent to which they are being paid a special allowance is not confused with payment for

4. [This is para. 40].

'merit'. If adjustment of salary maxima becomes necessary for a special group, we have referred in paragraph 37 (see page 285) to some methods of achieving this.

Groups and companies with establishments at more than one location have to consider whether the pay for jobs in different areas are to be the same. At one extreme we found examples in our enquiries of market group structures in which the relationship between evaluation grading and pay could be varied both for occupational groups and for establishments at different locations. The majority view, however, seemed to be that extra pay pressures for professional staff occurred only for staff based in London, though some firms mentioned differences in local rates for staff based outside London at middle and junior levels. Companies who customarily move staff between establishments pointed out the advantages of having a national salary structure at the grade levels at which transfers took place. But even some of these firms had found it necessary to make a distinction between London and other parts of the country and paid staff a London allowance. Some firms make the level of salaries for the more junior staff, who are less likely to be transferred to other establishments within the company, a local responsibility so enabling establishments in different areas to relate the level of their salaries to conditions in their part of the country.

Another problem which might cause distortion of a structure arises from the need to recognise staff potential. The important thing is that the structure should not be distorted to accommodate employees whose performance is considered to be exceptional. The way to cater for such staff is to ensure that they progress more rapidly through the salary range for the grade. This, in conjunction with a planned career progression is a better way of dealing with outstandingly able staff. This will not always suffice, and it must be accepted that there will always be some good people who will wish to change their jobs because their interests and inclinations lead them to do so; making *ad hoc* payments will not change their minds. The firm may in the long run be the beneficiary as well as the loser from this type of mobility.

Graduate trainees are a special case of staff with potential.

Most companies consider that they require separate consideration, and it is, perhaps, sufficient in this context to note that they have either developed separate structures or made provision for adjusting salary maxima within the main structure until the graduate can be given a graded job which he will not outgrow in too short a period.

A problem of a rather different kind concerns staff who have less rather than more than the normal power to claim their proper rate of pay. Such a case may arise where middle managers have reached their salary ceiling, and who cannot expect further promotion. These staff may be in a weak bargaining position because they are unable to move to a different job by reason of their age. Though a proper evaluation scheme will ensure that such staff are not unfairly treated, many companies seek to reinforce the value placed on the services of these people by advocating a system of 'good performance' bonuses for them. This provides a continuing method of recognizing the contribution made by these staff.

A similar problem can arise where staff have little opportunity of changing their jobs because they form part of a very small labour market. Language translators may be a case in point. An effective internal evaluation scheme overcomes the difficulty of how much to pay such staff but they may also come into the broader category of staff for whom the salary ceilings for the most able are sometimes set too low. This can occur when it is particularly difficult to distinguish between a job well done and a job carried out in such a way as to warrant up-grading. For these staff wider salary ranges may be appropriate.

Finally we draw attention to awards which can be made to staff for a particular achievement or for temporarily carrying out work which warrants a higher grading. The latter may occur because of a superior's absence for a long period through illness, or because when someone leaves unexpectedly and internal promotion is not appropriate the senior position must be filled whilst the company is seeking a more permanent replacement. In such cases our findings were that most companies operated a scheme whereby a special payment could be paid to such persons.

We also found examples of firms' salary systems catering for 'once in a life-time' bonus payments for special achievements, sometimes directly connected with their work, in other cases to reward staff for obtaining a higher qualification relevant to their job. Occasionally bonus payments were made to staff who had to work an exceptional amount of overtime on the job over a long period due to factors outside their control. In all these instances it was company policy to recognize the nature of the special factors and to pay for them directly.

So far we have described our findings on salary structures as a whole. We turn now to a particular subject on which our enquiries have thrown some light. This is the extent to which salary levels in the organizations are negotiated with a union or procedures exist for unions to make representations about salary matters. We have shown in our survey that three-fifths of MEPT staff are covered by salary limits. The survey reveals that for the undertakings covered by the survey the level of salaries of 16 per cent of staff who have salary limits are subject to union negotiation and that in the case of a further 10 per cent of the staff with salary limits the level of salaries is subject to representations by a staff association or trade union. It should be noted however that our industrial coverage is confined to manufacturing industry so that the nationalized sector is under-represented. For MEPT staff in all fields, these figures would no doubt be greater (and they would be considerably greater still if weekly-paid technical staff were included). Union activities in the firms surveyed were confined mainly to staff in larger organizations: of the 81,000 staff reported as having their salaries subject to collective negotiations, 63,000 were in firms employing more than 5000 employees. The organisations most affected by negotiations are the nationalized corporations. Next come financial institutions, such as commercial banks and insurance companies. But even in the private sector of industry union negotiations do affect the salary levels of an appreciable proportion of MEPT staff.

We examined the returns of companies in which there is collective bargaining for staff to see whether union negotiations are more likely to affect the salaries of staff at a given level of seniority or in a particular occupation. Examples of negotiations affecting staff right up to middle and senior management levels are found mainly in the public and commercial sector. Collective bargaining on the whole, however, only affects staff at the more junior levels, and in manufacturing industry is particularly likely to affect draughtsmen, technicians and foremen. We also scrutinized the returns to see if there is a relationship between union activities and types of salary limits or fixed incremental pay progressions. Salary ranges for jobs – over four-fifths of the MEPT staff covered by a salary structure are covered by this type of salary limit – are the type most frequently reported whether or not the ranges are subject to collective bargaining. But we did find that in the small number of cases where there are only salary minima and no related salary maxima for jobs (2 per cent of all salary limits reported) the minima were more likely to be union negotiated rates. We did not find a clear relationship between incremental pay scales and collective bargaining. In the majority of companies in which unions play a part in salary matters management have flexibility over how individual staff should advance through their salary ranges. A higher proportion of incremental pay scales are found among companies affected by union activities but even so the salary progression of three-fifths of the MEPT staff whose salary levels are negotiated with unions remains a management responsibility.

Arguments put forward by companies that do not favour union negotiations at staff level, apart from concern about undue increases in the total salary bill, tend to centre around a fear that union activities will hamper management's flexibility to treat staff as individuals. These companies fear that unions will demand incremental pay scales related to age or seniority which inhibit pay being related to performance. In fact however the evidence of our survey is that this by no means follows. On the other hand, unions may have doubts about the objectivity with which increments based on merit are awarded. Our survey shows that review forms are used to help assess performance before awarding salary increases for less than half of all MEPT staff. Moreover even where review forms are used the documents in question might often be better described as personality rating questionnaires rather than performance review forms. Unions may thus have good reason to oppose performance review schemes in which assessments are almost entirely subjective.

Not all union intervention can be turned into constructive channels by appropriate improvement and rationalization of a salary structure. Unhelpful union attitudes may be dictated by considerations quite outside a company's control, and may indeed be based simply on traditional thinking which is difficult to change. We would consider a root and branch opposition to a system of pay linked to performance to come into this category. But in so far as rational responses govern union intervention we would expect their influence to be constructive in organizations having a planned salary structure combined with adequate techniques for its administration. A company without a defensible salary system does not have a framework or agreed starting point within which sensible negotiations can be pursued; nor is either side likely to have the information necessary for constructive discussions. It is clear to us that a salary system, if it is to be effective, must be acceptable to the staff covered by the system. If it is, then not only can unions play a valuable part in achieving this aim; they can also, if they adopt a constructive approach, help to improve efficiency within the organization.

We can now summarize our conclusions about the choice of salary structures by undertakings. The most obvious is that it is desirable for all firms even those which are quite small, consciously to adopt a systematic structural framework for the salaries of the MEPT staff whom they employ; and they need to do this having clearly before them the aims which their salary system is designed to serve.

In the systematizing of a salary structure a number of points are likely to need special attention. First, the process almost inevitably involves fixing salary guidelines or limits for MEPT posts. Secondly, consistency in the treatment of varying levels of responsibility and performance needs to be pursued; and to this end job evaluation and reasonably consistent methods of performance appraisal are tools of special importance. Thirdly, the system needs to be such as to enable the pressures of the labour market or the need to give individuals special rewards to be met without either undue cost or distortion of the structure as a whole; we have discussed the various techniques which can be used. Finally the choice of a broad-banded or multi-grade structure needs to be related to the organization of the company (and particularly the steps in the management hierarchy), to the need for mobility of staff and to the extent to which it is thought desirable and practicable to relate the pay of individuals to their performance in their existing posts.

Pay progression of individuals

Almost all salaried staff, on taking up an appointment, expect that the salary which at that point is offered to them will be increased over time for one of three reasons. These are:

1. The addition of increments, based either on length of service and experience, or on 'merit' in the sense of quality of performance;

2. Additions made to the salary because of a general increase in salaries in the undertaking as a whole;

3. Promotion to a higher grade or to a job of greater responsibility.

These three reasons are set out in terminology which applies to a planned salary structure in which individuals are appointed to salary ranges and in which there is some form of job grading. But even in the absence of a structure, the expectations of the individual employee and the treatment accorded to him will be in some way related to these three factors, albeit in a more informal and no doubt less predictable way.

Promotion, although it is included in the above list, is of less direct concern to us in considering the present reference than are the other two factors. For our purposes it is sufficient to note that promotion will probably play some part, and may occasionally play a leading part, in providing incentives for employees or in rewarding outstanding performance.

Our primary concern in the present reference is with the other two types of pay increase listed above, namely those concerned with incremental or other progression through a salary range and those arising from a general uplift of the level of salaries. As Table 15 of Appendix B [not included here] shows, the effect of these two factors on the employee's salary may not always be separated, or at least may not be made known to him separately, though there is a clear distinction of principle as we point out in the next chapter. The present chapter is concerned only with increases in individuals' salaries based on merit appraisals, on incremental progression through a scale, or on whatever equivalent is applied in practice in the more informal situations where the salary structure provides for no more than purely *ad hoc* adjustments.

Table 7 of Appendix B [not included here] shows the information obtained from our survey on the methods of salary progression which are applied. It will be seen that more than four-fifths of the staff referred to receive increases in individual salaries on the basis of some form of appraisal or assessment of personal performance. In those fewer cases where increases are paid on an incremental pay scale, the majority of undertakings introduce the proviso that increments may be withheld, or double increments may be paid, in cases where performance is above or below some normal limit of attainment. Taking all these points together, it is likely that the level of performance plays some part in over 90 per cent of all decisions whether or not to increase individuals' salaries, and though this figure is derived only from those undertakings which have salary structures with pay limits, we would expect the picture to be broadly similar throughout the industrial and commercial field, and in relation to MEPT staff generally.

This situation is in marked contrast to the position in central and local government where the usual progression through salary ranges is by fixed annual increments. Salary structures for such staff are outside our terms of reference, and we do not propose to comment on them, but as far as salary structures in commerce and industry are concerned we welcome the evidence of close association between individual performance and individual pay.

The reason for our view requires some explanation. In our enquiries we were sometimes told that pay increases based on an assessment of merit provide the best or indeed the only incentive for the individual employee to reach the highest standard of performance of which he is capable. Behind this attitude we have found the assumption that people work only or mainly for money, and that money is therefore the best or the only 'motivator'.

We do not subscribe to the extreme form of this doctrine. Evidence, both from our case studies and from our witnesses, as well as a considerable volume of published research work, shows that there are many different approaches to the general question of motive. Thus it may be argued that the factors which determine whether an individual is stimulated to a very high standard of performance are centred on the content of the job itself, and the extent to which it permits him to feel a sense of achievement which is held to be at least as important as the salary. Indeed salary is sometimes referred to as a 'negative' factor in the sense of one which may cause dissatisfaction if the salary system fails to recognize a high standard of performance, but which will not itself provide the incentive to bring such a standard about.

It would appear from an analysis of this sort that while the amount of dissatisfaction can be reduced by improving features surrounding a job, paying a very high salary will by no means necessarily lead to job satisfaction. If the work content of a job or the associated status or power provides the individual with scope to attain satisfaction and self-fulfilment he may be willing to forgo significant financial rewards which may be available from other less intrinsically satisfying jobs. Thus the extent to which money is an important reward depends largely on the nature of the job.

In practice, we found that the evidence from the case studies we carried out would fit in with these observations. Thus, one of the salary administrators whose company we studied has written 'where morale problems exist, they appear to spring mainly from feelings that motivating factors are inadequate. In particular, employees identify problems relating to lack of praise and recognition, training needs, staffing, budget control and work load – with its attendant effect on an employee's home life'. In another company which expressed the view that 'the key objective is to motivate superior performance by paying higher salaries to those who make the greater contribution', thus explicitly identifying the recognition role of money, we were also told that 'especially towards the top, it is felt that salary is not of primary significance. At these levels, salary has to be sufficient to prevent people from being dissatisfied but once this state is achieved, the more important and difficult issues of management development, career planning, and maintenance of a continuing challenge are felt to be of major concern'. In yet another undertaking, though the salary structure is designed to ensure that the employees are not dissatisfied with their salary levels, it was said that 'the most important motivating factor is not money alone, but rather a background of a structure in which the individual may proceed to the best of his abilities, and part of this system is a just reward mechanism'.

It is clear, and the point is well highlighted by the last quotation, that analysis in these terms does not detract from the importance of linking individual performance to salary. It may well be that it is mainly the nature of the job itself, the environment in which it is carried out and the social relations surrounding it which will determine whether an individual will give of his best. At the same time however, if in fact he is motivated to do so and is successful by whatever criteria are applied to gauge success, then he will in our view rightly expect recognition in money as well as in other terms. It follows that a salary system, if it is to be successful, should be designed to provide such recognition. Moreover, performance related pay will assist in creating a climate where greater emphasis is seen to be placed on ability and competence than on age and seniority. It is the climate which performance related pay helps to produce as much as anything else which will encourage the individual employee to give of his best. In our view these factors can only be catered for if the system provides a method of pay progression which is appropriately linked with the quality of the individual employee's performance.

It is necessary to examine some of the more common methods of linking pay progression to performance which we have encountered in our researches. These are:

1. Where progression takes place through the range of a scale to the maximum point on it but increments may be deferred or withheld.

However, we have found that in several organizations where this type of progression operates it is rare for a salary increase in fact to be deferred. It is even more exceptional for increases to be withheld altogether. This is not perhaps surprising since it would otherwise be a penalty rather than a reward which would be applied.

2. Where there are fixed increments on a scale but where individuals may be awarded two or more increments simultaneously.

This type of progression is to be preferred to (1) above as, in part, the onus is on the detection of good performance. There may be instances where this system is appropriate. But fixed automatic increases which form the major component of this type of progression undoubtedly reduce the impact of an appraisal designed to identify good performance.

3. Where there exist two (or more) parallel scales for the same series of jobs, the higher scale or scales being reserved for individual employees whose performance is considered to merit it.

This is again only a partial form of performance-based progression in so far as it is designed to detect and reward good performance whilst, at the same time, staff whose performance is considered less satisfactory still receive automatic increases. In some circumstances it may be rather difficult to operate, especially when previously exceptional performance has rapidly deteriorated.

4. Where progression takes place through a salary range where only the minimum and maximum points are fixed rather than a scale with a number of specified steps of pre-determined increases.

This, according to one large undertaking in the public sector, 'enables management to give greater recognition to variations in performance than is customary in a scale with fixed increments by giving the better man more rapid progress within the range'. This form of progression is valuable in that its operation presupposes the identification of both good and inadequate performance. But the decision on the amount of any increase may become a matter of arbitrary judgment. For this reason such a method of progression is likely to be seen as being fair only when it is linked with a sophisticated form of performance appraisal, preferably when indicators of performance are quantifiable.

5. A progression where an employee would normally move to a predetermined point of a scale, e.g., the mid-point. Further advances beyond that point are reserved for individuals whose performance is consistently above average. The top of the scale can only be attained by exceptional employees.

This contains many advantages provided that management can ensure that the apparent 'headroom' in the upper part of each scale is not misused. Clearly such a form of progression must be accompanied by rigorous controls to prevent its distortion. As with (4), this type of appraisal needs to be linked with an adequate performance appraisal scheme.

In conjunction with any of these forms of progression, there may also be lump sum bonuses based on performance. Such bonus payments are kept apart from salary increments so that it is possible to have a system in which both bonuses and increments are performance-based. The payment of bonuses is subject to some of the drawbacks already noted, namely that the emphasis is on the detection of good performance alone. This may lead to a lack of discrimination between those staff whose performance is adequate or satisfactory, and those whose performance is poor.

As noted earlier, there is no one universally good salary system which can encompass every type of organization operating throughout industry and commerce. On the other hand on the assumption that there should be a clear and close relationship between salaries and performance, it should be possible to distinguish between the various methods of performance-linked progression on the basis of the following criteria:

1. Systematic and regular performance reviews are a pre-requisite for operating any defensible system.

2. Such reviews should attach as much weight as possible to quantifiable indicators of performance.

3. The reviews should identify both good and poor performance.

4. It follows from the above point that performance-linked pay progressions should not simply reward good performance *or* impose penalties on poor performance: they should enable both to be done.

5. The various informal pressures which are often brought to bear on salary administrators to grant increases over and above or in addition to those allowed for in the system must be resisted. This implies that the position of the person responsible for salary administration in the organization should be at a sufficiently high level for his voice to carry the requisite authority. All too often salary administrators merely administer an already pre-determined system without the necessary authority to prevent its abuse.

The common feature of all desirable methods of progression is that they rely on some form of performance assessment. There are several methods which organizations can employ to distinguish between the performance of different employees.

1. The most common method appears to be an annual appraisal interview of the job holder by his superior. This interview, which is often based on a written report, is also used to discuss the employee's particular strengths and weaknesses in the light of his previous year's performance. The report which follows the interview is kept for future reference, and in some organisations shown to the employee whose own comments on the fairness and accuracy of the appraisal may be included. In other cases a report may be written but not shown to or discussed with the job holder, who therefore has no direct means of knowing why any increment has been given or withheld.

2. Less usual is a ranking system where all the staff under a common superior are ranked, normally in respect of pre-determined and closely defined qualities. A variation is to select those employees who represent average performance, thereafter rating others in comparison to this average. Such a method is open to two objections. First, it is difficult to apply where a large number of staff are being assessed by one superior. Secondly, any two ranking from different departments are strictly comparable only when the number and the ability of staff in the departments concerned are similar. However, correction tables may be calculated to rectify such a deficiency.

3. Another method is that of 'forced distribution'. In this method the superior is asked to allocate a fixed, pre-determined percentage of his subordinates to any particular point in a range. Thus, for instance, only 10 per cent of staff being assessed may be permitted to reach the top end of the range, whilst a further 10 per cent must be assigned to the bottom end of the range, with a variety of gradations for the remainder. As in the ranking method, the distribution can be based on predetermined and closely defined specific qualities.

4. More common than either of the last two methods are rating scales. Here the various qualities demanded by the job are specified and defined. Each employee is then rated on a scale according to his performance with respect to the characteristics which have been included.

5. Another increasingly used method is related to systems of management by objectives. Here the assessment of employees' performance can more readily be linked with the attainment of pre-determined targets.

The last four methods can, of course, be used as a basis on which to conduct an assessment interview.

Regardless of the particular method chosen by an organization to assess its staff, we believe that there are certain general principles which should be followed in any assessment of performance. First, the particular method adopted must be seen by the staff affected to be fair and equitable. This factor assumes increasing importance at a time when white collar unions are increasing their membership. Secondly, it is important (though often difficult in practice) to assess only those factors which are directly related to performance. More general personality traits unrelated to performance are irrelevant to the process of performance appraisals. Thirdly, whatever system is adopted, quantifiable indicators of performance should be included wherever possible as they reduce the possibility of bias on the part of the assessor. Although the performance of many MEPT employees will not be measurable, as the criterion for judging their performance lies in the area of qualitative decision taking, it should be borne in mind that qualitative decisions often lead to measurable results. Lastly, it is important to distinguish between assessments made for the purposes of awarding or withholding salary increments, and those which are used to discover promotion or development potential or help employees to improve their performance. In practice the same information may be contained in both assessments, but the separation is desirable for two reasons. First, appraisals whose purpose is to consider the career development of individuals and form a basis on which to discuss with staff ways of improving their performance tend to be distracted by the introduction of the short-term issue of the award of a salary increment. For this reason many companies advocate separating discussion of performance appraisal from the assessments made to determine increases in salary. Secondly, the qualities demanded for success in a particular occupation group or grade may be quite different from those demanded at a higher level. This is merely another way of saying that because an employee may be judged excellent in a particular job this is not necessarily an indication that he is suitable for promotion.

One aspect to which we wish to draw particular attention concerns the effect on any of these techniques of secrecy. Our case studies show that in most companies in the private sector of industry many aspects of salary administration are kept secret. This applies not only to the level of individuals' salaries, where we accept that the tradition of secrecy is at its strongest, but also to the salary ranges which are by no means always disclosed even to the employees to whom they are directly applicable. Table 16 [not included here] of the statistical appendix shows the position found in our national survey. About half the MEPT staff covered by salary limits cannot find out the maximum of the pay range on which they are paid or at best can only find it out on request and in certain specified circumstances. It seems to us that such secrecy weakens the useful effect of performance-linked pay. Unless an employee knows whether he is advancing quickly or slowly towards the maximum pay he can expect in his present job, it seems impossible for him to tell whether or not he is doing well and whether or not his services are adequately recognized.

Similar considerations apply to secrecy over the method of assessment of performance. In our view this is clearly a case where justice has to be seen to be done and we think it is desirable that companies should inform their employees of the method of appraisal used and, so far as possible, of the policy which is to be followed in linking particular levels of performance with particular financial recognition.

This is an area in which unions could play an important part. We found in our enquiries that some unions were opposed to performance-linked pay and we think it possible that in a large measure at least this opposition is brought about by doubts about the fairness of the procedures employed. If such doubts are overcome by full disclosure of company policy and practice, then the likelihood of securing union agreement or indeed union cooperation seems to us to be greatly enhanced.

Although we recommend a much greater degree of disclosure of information than is the practice in private industry at present, we recognize that this change can at best be introduced only gradually and moreover will always be subject to certain limitations. We have referred elsewhere to the fact that planned salary structures are by no means universal, but that their use is gradually increasing. We would recommend that as company policies are increasingly clearly formulated, and as planned structures are more widely introduced in salary administration, so, hand in hand with this process, there should be an increasing degree of disclosure of policies and methods. But to be successful a policy of disclosure requires, in our view, that the shaping of the system which is to be introduced and to be made known to the staff is itself fashioned with the knowledge, and indeed the active help and full acceptance, of those to whom it will apply. Such involvement of staff will help to deal with any difficulties which a process of disclosure may well bring. For the rest such problems must be solved by capable and strong management, and its existence is a further essential requirement for a successful policy of disclosure. There may always be limits to the extent to which information about salaries, and particularly about individuals' salaries, can reasonably be disclosed, but we think it important to emphasize again that the value of performance-linked increments and indeed the existence of a pay system linked to performance are endangered by a policy of unnecessary secrecy.

We now turn to an examination of the cost of individual pay progressions and consider such costs in terms of the requirements of an incomes policy. The simple statement that all incremental payments are additions to income and therefore must be directly related to existing incomes policy rules is based on a misapprehension. The position can best be illustrated in terms of a single group of staff paid within the same pay range. The normal movement of salaries for the individual members of such a group set up what might be described as a circular process. While some individuals progress upwards, others leave the group by retirement or resignation or promotion and are replaced by newcomers who usually start lower down in the pay range. This process of 'attrition' can mean that in certain circumstances the payment of increments is completely self-financing and leads to no increase in the salary bill. In the short run, e.g., where staff turnover is exceptionally heavy, it can even mean that the salary bill for the group as a whole will decrease. Where there is a clearly established pay range for a group of staff, the position can be measured by means of the device known as the comparative salary ratio (or 'comp-ratio'). This is the ratio of the actual average salary paid to a group of staff to the theoretical mid-point of their pay scale. It is usually calculated in the same way as a percentage; where the actual average and the mid-point of the scale are identical, the comp-ratio is said to be 100.

We have given this explanation because it is important for the Prices and Incomes Policy which excludes payment of increments from such limits on pay increases as may exist. We consider that such provisions should be seen in the light of the foregoing explanation. Their intention clearly is, and should be seen to be, to allow the normal process of salary progression to continue, but on the assumption that over large groups of staff, and certainly over the economy as a whole, the process will not add to the total level of income, but will be self-financing on the basis of attrition.

In the strictest terms, this should be the basis on which the provisions of paragraph 40 [see page 287] of the present White Paper are applied to normal pay progressions i.e. in the normal case to money paid out by way of merit increments. But the degree of attrition on which such a rule depends will occur only in very large units of staff, and exceptions must therefore be provided for in cases where changes in the staffing structure of an undertaking make this necessary. Thus, where staff turnover in a grade falls below the expected level, the cost of pay increments will make some addition to the salary bill though not in the long term a permanent one. But apart from such staffing considerations, any departure from the suggested interpretation of paragraph 40 [see page 287] of the White Paper means that there is a real increase in salary level. The considerations which then apply are discussed in the next chapter [not included here].

The distinction which we are seeking to draw is not always easy to make in practice, even where a salary structure is fairly well developed, and still less where it is not. In particular 'merit pay' only fits within our view of the strict intention of paragraph 40 [see page 287] of the White Paper if it is properly part of the pre-planned, or at least the intended, salary progression of the individual. But different considerations apply where a group of staff receive special pay additions – perhaps in the form of a bonus – because it is held that their efforts have led to results which are above the undertaking's expectations. Such payments also arise from good performance, but they are akin to 'productivity increases' rather than the normal operation of the salary system. Indeed if such payments are made without any revision of the guidelines on which the salary system rests, the system itself may be damaged.

The separation of the two aspects of salary budgeting we have mentioned in the preceding paragraph is necessary if an undertaking is to exercise normal cost control over salary expenditure. The effect of increased expenditure can be fully assessed only if account can be taken of, e.g., changes in the staffing structure resulting from an exceptionally high or low rate of recruitment.

As we have already indicated, to make the separation we suggest will also assist in interpreting paragraph 40 [see page 287] of the White Paper. We suggest that in future phases of the incomes policy the purpose of this paragraph should be more clearly explained. The exemption which it at present provides from the limits of incomes policy must be related to increases in the salary bill required for the purely technical purpose of operating the system and to meet its normal requirements, and not to allow an upward revision of salary structures.

17 Elliott Jaques

Equitable Payment

Excerpt from Elliott Jaques, *Equitable Payment*, Heinemann, 1961, pp. 99–119.

I

To summarize, we may define the *time-span of discretion* as the period of time during which marginally sub-standard discretion could be exercised in a role before information about the accumulating sub-standard work would become available to the manager in charge of the role. The *level-of-work bracket in a role* is stated in terms of the maximum time-span to the first review point – which gives the bottom of the bracket – and that to the fourth review point – which gives the top of the bracket.

II

In measuring the time-span of discretion, it is of the greatest practical importance to distinguish two different categories of role: *single-task roles* – roles with only one task to be carried at a time; *multiple-task roles* – roles in which a number of different tasks have to be carried through concurrently.[1] Shop-floor level manual roles are most often single-task roles. The operator is given a task to carry out. When he has completed it, he gets his next task, and so on. In the multiple-task role, the person has a number of tasks which run concurrently, each of which may have a different completion date, and some of which may not be required to be completed until a considerably longer time into the future than others which may call for nearly immediate completion.

The essential difference, from the point of view of level-of-

1. The term *role* refers to a position in an executive system – the position to which a person is appointed. A *task* is a specific responsibility allocated to a subordinate by his manager, which has a discrete completion point (see Jaques, 1951).

work measurement, between the single- and multiple-task roles is that the person carrying multiple tasks must exercise discretion on priorities in his work. He must decide when to push ahead with one task, and when there is a risk of his being late with another. He has it within his discretion to 'borrow' time from one task in order to finish another one with an earlier completion date. This borrowing cannot, of course, go on indefinitely. If a person is taking a bit too long on each of his tasks, the time will come when he will get behind in all his work.

This characteristic of borrowing time simply cannot apply in single-task roles. If a person is working too carefully and falling behind, he will fall behind on the one task he is currently committed to getting done. He has no other tasks against which he can borrow time. This is not to deny that a sense of timing is still very important in single-task roles. There are always different aspects of the task which have to be planned for. In the most complicated tasks, different parts may have to be got ready or worked upon, the order in which they are done perhaps significantly affecting the time in which the whole task is completed. But once each task is completed, it must be booked in, passed on, and the next task obtained and commenced. Because of this circumstance, systematic and complete information is directly available to the manager on the actual rate at which his subordinate is completing tasks. To obtain similar information about rate of work in multiple-task roles, the manager cannot rely simply upon the time of completion of individual tasks. He must obtain additional information on the rate of progress of all the other tasks which he has allocated.

This difference in the work organization characteristic of single- and multiple-task roles brings about a significant difference in the marginally sub-standard discretion which gives the maximum time-span bracket. In single-task roles, getting marginally behind in work will show up more quickly than will being marginally sub-standard in quality. Getting marginally behind often presents itself in the form of direct review to the manager; the evidence of the sub-standard work may be right there, on the site, under his own nose. His subordinate is not doing as much work as he is being called upon to do. If the work is of sub-standard quality, however, it may pass on to a next point without being directly reviewed by the manager, indirect review coming into effect in the form of complaints and returned work. Even if the manager himself directly reviews quality, that serves only to bring the review mechanism down to the same time-scale as getting marginally behind.

In multiple-task roles, the reverse holds true: being marginally sub-standard in quality shows up more quickly than getting marginally behind. If the manager is exercising direct review, work that is sub-standard in quality is directly observable, whereas review of whether a subordinate is getting his work done in time requires a comprehensive review of the total work schedule. If indirect review is being exercised, work that is sub-standard in quality will still show up earlier than marginally getting behind. While a subordinate may be borrowing time from the tasks with the most distant completion date, the tasks which he is completing are being passed on and used by others. Work which is marginally sub-standard in quality would begin to show up. The fact that his longer-term completion date tasks are marginally behind schedule begins to emerge for the first time only when the lateness of those tasks begins to hold up the work of other members who are waiting for them. This point in time is later than the indirect review of the quality of the already completed tasks, since every multiple-task role, even those with the longest time-span brackets, contain many small tasks which are completed and reviewed in very short periods of time.

In order, therefore, to measure, it is necessary to consider the time-span for marginally sub-standard quality in single-task roles, and the time-span for marginally sub-standard discretion on pace and organization work in multiple-task roles.

III

I shall illustrate the measurement of single-task roles by reference to manual work.

In *Measurement of Responsibility*, I reported that difficulties had arisen in assessing the time-span brackets of the shorter time-span manual role. The reason for this difficulty had to do with discovering the review mechanisms, especially in manual operations linked to each other as part of a production flow system. The longer time-span roles which I had analyzed had been more amenable to analysis because they happened to be roles in which the operator did a relatively comprehensive operation followed by inspection; as, for example, in machine-tool fitting, electrical installation work, and heavy duty turning in which one operator did all the operations on his lathe necessary to turn a rough casting into a finished product. I had, however, had the opportunity to carry out analyses of only very few manual roles at that time. Since then my experience has very considerably extended. The opportunity has arisen, for example, to analyze the allocation and flow of work in whole production departments on various types of hand tool and on automatic, semi-automatic and standard machine tools, as well as to analyze work in labouring and in such specialized manual work as tool making, millwrighting, inspection, electrical work, and storekeeping. What one finds is this.

If you take a production flow process, the review points are readily discoverable if you apply the construct of accumulating marginally sub-standard discretion. Take, for example, a simple machining sequence of turning, followed by milling, drilling and grinding. In the particular example I have in mind, if the turner did marginally sub-standard work, it would show up at the milling or drilling stage if a jig or fixture was being used for either of these operations which required the turning work to be within standard if the work was to fit. If no such jigs or fixtures were employed, then sub-standard work would not show up until the grinding stage. Marginally too much material would have been left on the parts being machined, with the result that the time for grinding would be materially lengthened. The supervisor of the grinding work would become involved, and sub-standard work would be passed back to the supervisor on the turning section. The other three operations – milling, drilling and grinding – were not dependent upon each other in the particular production process to which I am referring. If marginally sub-standard work were done on either milling or drilling or grinding, it would not affect subsequent operations, and would therefore be picked up only at the final inspection stage.

This example is correct in its essentials, although simplified for presentation. The point I wish to make is that review points can just as readily be discovered for manual as for non-manual work. It is a matter of analyzing each job to discover at what subsequent stage in the production process marginally sub-standard work would manifest itself. It is not at all the case, therefore, that just because a particular operation comes early in the production process, it necessarily has a longer time-span than operations which come later in the process. This belief had contributed to earlier doubts about the realism of time-span measures of such manual roles, since many of the roles intuitively judged to have the highest responsibilities came at or towards the finishing stages, whereas the earlier rough machining operations were judged to have a relatively lower level of responsibility. Analysis has now shown, in fact, that sub-standard work on these earlier operations shows up at very early stages in the subsequent process.

The time-spans on manual work become readily calculable just as soon as the real review points are discovered. It becomes a matter of analyzing the flow of work from each operation through to its review point, and assessing the time lapses up to the first and up to the fourth reviews. The time-span is taken from the beginning of an operation through to the time when the first batches or items of work done reach the next operation in the process where marginally sub-standard discretion would show, and begins to be worked on by the operator doing that operation for a sufficient time for the marginally sub-standard work to become apparent. It has turned out to be possible to measure down to very short time-spans indeed, the shortest I have so far encountered being a bracket of two hours to one-half shift (four-and-a-half hours). At the other end of the scale, I have analyzed manual roles the top of whose time-span bracket is up to three months. There may well be hourly-rated manual roles carrying time-spans longer than this.

The accompanying Figure 1 shows a typical analysis of the flow of tasks from one operation to the review point – in this particular case, from turning to grinding. The time between the work leaving the turning operation till it begins to be worked on at grinding is partly time when the work is waiting to go on the next operation, and partly time taken up on milling and drilling work in which the turning work is not reviewed.

Two important points may be noted on the chart. First, a

number of tasks may be carried out before any one of them is reviewed. For example, between review points t_2 and t_3, three tasks were completed; and none of these three tasks has itself reached a review point by time t_3. This point is characteristic of many single-task roles. Review does not necessarily take place at the completion of each task. Just because, therefore, a manual operator is working on tasks none of which individually takes more than a few hours, say, to complete, it does not necessarily follow that he is working in a short time-span role. The critical issue to be determined is, when do those tasks arrive at a review point?

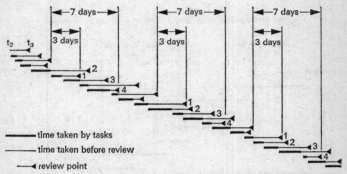

Figure 1 The maximum time lapse over which a person is required to exercise discretion

The second point is that the chart shows how the particular time-span pattern repeats itself. Search out the longest periods between reviews, and you will note that the three-day period keeps recurring. If, then, you begin with these three-day periods and count through to the fourth review point, you will note that a period of seven days recurs a number of times. Sample records taken as much as eighteen months apart, showed this same pattern to appear with great regularity. The maximum time-span bracket for this particular role, therefore, is 3 days to 7 days.

By way of contrast, Figure 2 shows a single-task role whose individual tasks require a longer time to complete, each task being reviewed on completion. This particular role is that of a heavy duty turning operator, making finished parts from rough castings. The review is carried out by a departmental inspector who does a final inspection as each task is done. It is of interest to note that the inspector may do some inspecting while the task is being worked on, but that in this particular role discretion has not actually been reviewed at that stage. The reason is that the intermediate inspection is carried out while the part being machined is held in the jaws of the chuck, and what the inspector cannot check at that stage is the operator's discretion in tightening the chuck – if it is marginally too tight there will be marginal distortion of the part which the inspector will not be able to detect until he checks the part on completion and out of the chuck.

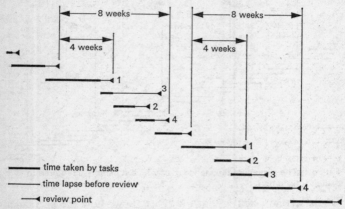

Figure 2 Equitable work-payment scale

In this instance, examination of the chart shows the maximum time-span bracket to be from one month (four weeks) up to two months (eight weeks).

The highest level of work I have found in a single-task role was a machine tool fitting role with a bracket running up to three months at the top. Some roles of longer time-span may at first on superficial consideration appear to be single-task roles, but in fact turn out not to be so; for example, research roles, or development work, where the work allocated seems to be composed of one single large-scale project extending over many months. In my experience, closer examination reveals that in addition to the one main project, numbers of other minor projects are carried concurrently, or fitted into the programme of work – smaller tasks, for example, which are required in a hurry and which must be carried out immediately.

IV

There is one important point, which applies equally to the measurement of single-task and multiple-task roles, which I shall briefly consider before turning to the measurement of level of work in multiple-task roles. I have observed time and again that when the pattern of work in a role begins to change, or undergoes a temporary change for any period of time, such that the time-span pattern is significantly affected, then managers begin to change the pattern of review in such a manner that the time-span bracket is retained unchanged.

For example, as the work in a shop began to pile up and the through-put time was lengthened because of longer waiting time between operations, the time-span of discretion also increased because it took longer for any given operation to reach the review point. In these circumstances, the direct review of work by supervisors and inspectors was increased, especially by means of spot checking of work that had been waiting for any length of time.

Similarly, as the time-span of projects in a development role began to increase, the manager responded by retaining more of the responsibility for projects at his own level. In due course, a reorganization occurred in which the manager's role was increased in rank, the manager promoted, and two new managerial roles created subordinate to him, to cope with the continued steady increase in the number of longer-term projects.

Such changes as I have illustrated were instituted on the basis of an intuitive awareness by managers that things had changed. There is pretty certainly a deep sense in most managers of the time-scale of the work they control – of through-put time, of time required for completion, of time targets, of things taking longer or shorter times to do. And they respond to changes in the movement of work through time, and in the time-scale of work planning so as to keep a steadying hand on the level of work in the roles they manage.

V

Let me turn now to the measurement of level of work in multiple-task roles. These comprise all roles other than hourly-rated manual roles and clerical roles – some hourly-rated and clerical roles being multiple-task roles as well. The general structure of tasks contained in these roles can be illustrated by reference to the role of manager of a department of about two hundred people in a chemical plant. He has myriad tasks which crop up daily in the form of specific problems, and which have to be dealt with as they arise. These include such tasks as getting out facts for the plant General Manager, giving decisions on production priorities, sanctioning special purchases of materials, settling individual wage appeals, etc., etc.

He also has a multitude of on-going tasks which may not be completed for weeks or months; for example, to complete certain training activities; to shift plant to increase the size of one of his process sections; to get certain new plant or tools modified; to revise the stocks in his general stores; to get new lighting installed; to introduce standardized process controls; and so on. Tasks of this kind are coming to completion nearly every day, and new ones are being added to his programme.

Finally, he has a small number of definable tasks, commonly referred to as his long-term projects, usually having to do with large-scale changes in plant and equipment; for example, to carry through the building, testing, and installation of newly-designed plant, making such modifications as are necessary in the light of the tests, and arranging the changes in organization and manning and in work-flow programming required by the new manufacturing methods; or carrying through the building of a new bay, getting plant installed, scheduling work, recruiting and training new personnel, and getting the process into production. Tasks of this kind may require up to two years from beginning to end.

The separation of these three categories of task – day-to-day, on-going, and long-term – is of course a fiction used for descriptive purposes. There is in fact a continuum from the day-to-day tasks to the longest-term tasks – some requiring an on-the-spot decision, some requiring intermittent attention over periods of days or weeks, some of a month, some a few months, some up to a year, and some few a year or more.

With regard to the long-term tasks, there is one confusion which commonly occurs, and to which I must refer. Many roles often appear to contain longer-term responsibilities than in reality they do, especially in connection with so-called responsibility for development work. Thus, an otherwise short time-span manual operator role is said to carry years of long-term responsibility for discovering short cuts and gimmicks for improving the efficiency with which the work is done. Or a research engineer is said to carry long-term responsibility for inventing new methods which will affect the Company's production methods for years hence; or a research chemist, new materials which will affect the Company's business for a similar period. Or a salesman is said to carry responsibility for the quality of the Company's relationship with an important customer for years to come. None of these statements has any substance, for the following reasons.

The operator's stated responsibility for development is nothing more than the normal development responsibility contained in any role, from shop floor to top management. It is the responsibility for intuitively finding better and quicker ways of doing work as a result of the experience gained in the course of doing that work. No allocation of special resources or expenditure is involved. No specific objectives are set. It is simply a fact that it is a human impossibility to repeat a particular task, or another one similar to it, without doing it a bit better (even if only minutely so) each time. If one employee proves very imaginative in this connection, he is most likely suitable for promotion. If another employee does his work, but with little or no imaginative development, he may not get promoted, but neither is he said not to be doing the job. To do the job is to complete the allocated tasks, with the material resources given and within the standards of quality and time set.

With regard to the engineer, the chemist, and the salesman, a related factor applies – one which refers back to the analysis of the concept of responsibility in chapter 3 [not included here]. They are given specific tasks to carry out. They are not responsible in some vague sense for inventions, or discoveries, or customer attitude towards the Company. The engineer and the chemist are responsible for tasks in the form of specified projects to be carried out. They are not University research fellows, following up lines of research which they themselves may have picked because of their interest in the topic. They are employees doing allocated projects. Capital (or physical resources and time) has been allocated for those projects, because someone higher up (and the Managing Director and the Board in the final analysis) has decided that it is in the economic interest of the Company for that work to be done. If an invention or discovery results, the credit lies higher up. If a lot of time and money are spent fruitlessly on projects which give no return, the discredit also lies higher up. The research worker is accountable for ensuring that the discretion he exercises in carrying out the project is not marginally sub-standard. The level of work in his role is set by the time-span of these projects, and not by the time-span of the possible effect of the results of these projects on the economy of the firm.

In the same way, the salesman has his own specific tasks to carry. The attitude of any customer to the firm is the resultant of an amalgam of factors: the salesman's behaviour, the quality and price of the goods offered, the quality of service given, the technical reputation of the firm, and many others besides. If, over a period of years, the attitude of a customer towards the company changes, either positively or negatively, the salesman cannot alone be held accountable for the change. He can be held accountable for such things as being overbearing or excessively compliant in negotiation with customers, or for visiting too often or too infrequently. The level of work in his role will be determined by the time-span of his allocated activities, and not by the time during which changes may occur in customer outlook.

Thus, returning to the department manager's role, when I record the longer-term responsibilities for the projects which I described (new plant and new building), I am referring to projects which he has actually been allocated. The policies for the new plant and building have been settled. The necessary capital has been allocated, and the department manager has been instructed to get on with it. He must, therefore, begin to get work under way – to commit resources and see that the work is kept going. There may of course be delays and hold-ups; these the department manager must overcome (or else report back to his own manager). Equally there may be periods when everything is progressing very smoothly according to plan; during these periods the department manager must keep his eye on things to make sure that they continue to run smoothly. These long-term tasks are thus not simply a generalized responsibility to 'develop' or 'go forward' or 'improve things'. They are concrete and specific activities with quality and time targets.

VI

The department manager's role which I have outlined may be seen to comprise a multitude of tasks, all of which he must carry along concurrently. He has a staff to whom he allocates many of the details of this work: his chief chemical engineer with his staff of engineers and draughtsmen; his chief process controller with his staff of process and stores controllers; and his four operational subordinate managers, each responsible for a production bay employing anywhere from twenty to sixty employees on three shifts. In addition, he draws upon services from the chief personnel manager, the chief works engineer with his millwrights, electricians and builders, the buying department, and others.

It is the department manager's responsibility to keep all these activities going. He is constantly faced with the problem of just how much time he himself ought to spend on any one task and how high a priority to give it. Equally, he must decide how much of the resources under his control to deploy on to these activities. For example, should he have one of his chemical engineers taken off a longer-term development project on which he is engaged, and have him spend a few weeks trying to sort out an immediate difficulty with a certain type of process? Should he play safe and increase the amount of overtime work, increase his night shift, or try to get over a production bottleneck without doing either? Should he get a piece of equipment thoroughly overhauled by the millwrights, or do a minimum repair to keep it running and direct his efforts towards getting sanction for replacement equipment with additional features? Should he carry out more frequent inspection of the discipline in the shops, or forget about that problem for a while and spend more time with his chief process controller investigating the planning and flow of work? Or should he get down into his stores and see for himself whether a new layout is necessary? Or should he get on with the necessary series of discussions with his shop stewards on the outstanding wages issues which have already been hanging fire too long?

There is inevitably never time to do everything which might be done, as he might wish to be able to do it. Everything must be done to some extent at the expense of something else. The art of effective management is to be spending one's time on the most relevant and urgent issues at any given time, and to keep one's subordinates oriented in the same way. The decision as to which are the issues most requiring attention and which are the ones which can be left to one side, is a matter calling for nice judgement indeed. To be able to use his discretion effectively in this way is one of the essential qualities in a good manager. It is equally one of the esential qualities in anyone who is to discharge successfully the responsibilities in any multiple-task role.

The multiple-task situation demands constant intuitive attention – and intermittent conscious attention – to be paid to the balance of activities. Sufficient time must be devoted to the immediate tasks to do what is necessary. At the same time, other longer-term projects must not be allowed to lag. They must not be forgotten about, overlooked, lost. A balancing and juggling performance must be carried on, with judicious attention to just the right work at just the right time, to keep the whole complex of tasks progressing in a satisfactory manner.

This balancing of activities and sense of importance and priority, must also take into account the shifting in priorities which occur over time. Of two longer-term projects, A and B, A might have been of greater importance at the start. But with changing circumstances, B may become increasingly important and A less so. The exercise of discretion in a multiple-task role calls for a good sense of the dynamics of the work situation, without the manager in charge of the role having to point out explicitly every change in priority and importance of tasks.

In general terms, we may note that from the moment any longer-term task is allocated, it comes into conflict with every succeeding task which is allocated, especially those with an earlier targeted completion date. This point can be illustrated in the accompanying Figure 3. The time and effort applied to the tasks, $ta_{2, 3, 4, 5}$, all have to be weighed against intermittent preoccupation with ta_1. Tasks, $ta_{7, 8, 9, 10, 11, 12, 13, 14}$, must jostle with both ta_1 and ta_6 and $ta_{13, 14}$ jostle with ta_{12} as well. Thus by the time its completion has been achieved, ta_1 has had to have had sufficient attention – but not too much attention – paid to

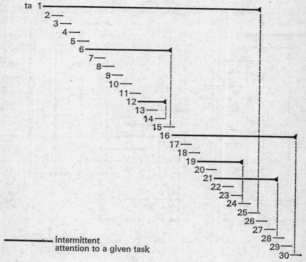

intermittent
attention to a given task

Figure 3

it against the competing demands of all the succeeding tasks down to ta_{25}. Once ta_1 and ta_{25} have been completed, it is then ta_{16} which the subsequent tasks are competing against for priority and attention in the manager's mind. I shall use the phrase *extended task* to refer to tasks like ta_1 and ta_{16}, which extend beyond the targeted completion times of all previously allocated tasks.

In the case of the department manager role which I have described, analysis of the task content of the role revealed the following pattern of extended tasks. In July 1951, he was allocated a large-scale equipment installation project for one of his bays, targeted for completion by the end of May 1952 at the latest. The next project to extend beyond that date was the establishment of a new type of production allocated in October 1951 and to be completed by the Spring of 1953. The next was a programme of special training, allocated in May 1952 to be completed by May 1953. The next was an extensive bay alteration and modification plan, allocated in September 1952 for completion by the same time the following year. There then followed

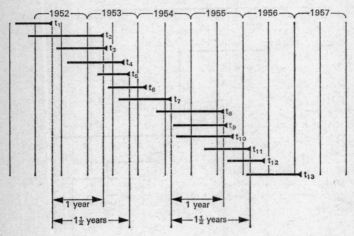

Figure 4

projects allocated for the periods March 1953 to October 1953, July 1953 to March 1954, and on, as shown on the accompanying Figure 4.

In between the allocation of these extended tasks there were, of course, literally hundreds of other tasks of shorter duration which had to be organized within the frame of the longer-term tasks. Marginally sub-standard discretion would accumulate in the longer-term projects. The maximum time-span bracket is shown in the sequences beginning at t_1 and t_7, with first reviews at t_2 and t_8, and fourth reviews at t_5 and t_{11}, giving a bracket of 1 year to $1\frac{1}{2}$ years.

VII

I shall further illustrate the time-span measurement of multiple-task roles by taking a short time-span role and a medium one.

An export documentation clerk was responsible for checking export documents for accuracy and completeness. Between 30 and 40 documents per day passed through his hands. Of these, three to four were priority, in that if they were not completed, shipments would be held up. The clerk had to exercise discretion on how much time he spent checking individual documents. With experience, a sense of the accuracy of documents is obtained so that a rapid scanning allows those which appear correct to be distinguished from those which are either obviously incorrect or at least give the feeling of being not quite right.

The sense of a document which feels not quite right is derived from variegated clues, such as: this customer usually orders larger quantities; these prices appear a bit odd; this customer does not usually order this type of product; these seem unusual terms of sale for this customer; something seems wrong about the mode of shipment, or insurance. Each of these impressions needs following up. It may mean a search in the files; or a phone call; or a visit to the Sales Officer. It is a matter of discretion whether to pursue these questions immediately or to set the documents aside until later in the day in order to complete more urgently required documents and get them out of the way first. It is equally a matter of discretion how much time to spend on any single document. A false sense of timing, and over-carefulness, will hold up the pace of work.

This sense of timing is of the greatest importance in the role. The documentation check is part of a highly geared flow of documents. A hold-up at any point of the flow creates a hold-up in succeeding steps through to the sending out of accounts. The priority documents must be checked and passed on the same day. They cannot be left overnight. The least urgent can be set aside for up to two days, but if held longer will create a bottleneck at the succeeding step in the flow. The first review point is thus just over two days. From then on, accumulating marginally sub-standard discretion would show up each succeeding morning through the failure of some documents to reach the next point.

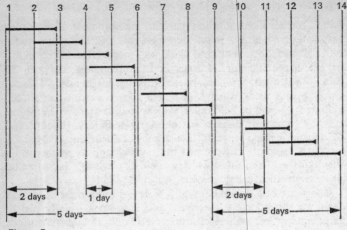

Figure 5

The fourth review point falls on the fifth day. The time-span bracket is two days to five days (one week), as shown in Figure 5.

The medium time-span example is that of a development engineering role. The balance of work comprises projects ranging from day-to-day trouble-shooting to carrying through development projects for which up to six weeks may be authorized. These development projects are phasic: there may be periods of looking up literature, or writing away for samples, or getting sample tools or fixtures made, with waiting periods of days when nothing can be done on any particular project.

The discretion in the role comprises deciding on the diagnosis of particular problems, deciding what special investigations might be needed to explore the matter, deciding what steps to take to put the difficulties right, deciding what steps to recommend to his manager if his own authority does not cover what he judges to be necessary, plus discretion in the application of his engineering knowledge. In exercising this discretion he must equally have a sense of the importance to the firm of the problems he is tackling, for it is easy to get lost in a technically interesting problem and to spend a lot of time getting an elegant solution for it when an *ad hoc* improvisation would have sufficed for the time being.

A sense of the priority and significance of each individual task is made more important by the fact that requests for all the shorter-term trouble-shooting tasks come directly to him from production managers, without having to go through his manager. He must assess for himself their priority in relation to each other and in relation to the progress of the projects directly allocated by his own manager which run on for weeks.

Analysis of the extended tasks showed a six-week task, followed nine days later by a five-week task, followed three weeks later by a four-week task, followed two weeks later by a four-week task, followed two weeks later by a five-week task. If this pattern is plotted it will be seen to give a time-span bracket of six weeks to twelve weeks, or $1\frac{1}{2}$ months to three months, as shown in Figure 6.

VIII

In summary, the level of work in roles in employment organizations can be measured by obtaining from the manager in charge of the role, information about the tasks he allocates into the role, their prescribed and discretionary content, and the review points at which marginally sub-standard discretion will declare itself. If the role is occupied, the manager may find it helpful to refer to the person in the role for a detailed description of what he has been doing.

When the role description in these terms has been completed, it is referred to the manager-once-removed and, if approved by him, becomes the officially authorized and established role.

The first step in measurement is different for single-task roles and for multiple-task roles.

1. Use the method of successive approximation to determine the standards of quality or completion time, and:

(a) *for single-task roles*, plot a sequence of tasks as straight lines in such a manner as to show the time of beginning the task and the time of arrival at a point where marginally sub-standard *quality* will first declare itself in each task (do not plot non-working days such as Sundays and holidays);

(b) *for multiple-task roles*, plot a sequence of extended tasks showing the beginning of each task and the *completion time* which

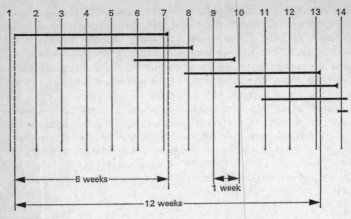

Figure 6

is marginally sub-standard with respect to its targeted completion time.

Then, for both single- and multiple-task roles:

2. Discover and mark out the two consecutive review points with the longest time lapse between them; the first of these points is called the start of the time-span sequence, and the second is the first review point; there will usually be found to be a number of such consecutive points with a roughly equal time lapse;

3. By trial exploration, discover that pair of the long time lapse review points which is followed by the longest time lapse to the fourth review point;

4. The time-span from the start of the sequence to the first review point measures the bottom of the level-of-work bracket; and from the start to the fourth review point measures the top of the bracket.

That the instrument can be applied consistently in practice, I now have reasonable evidence to demonstrate. It should be added that the technique is not an especially easy one to learn. The difficulty lies in the great trouble experienced in getting away from looking at level of work in terms of the skills and experience required in a person to do the job, and dealing with level of work in terms simply of activities and managerial review. This change

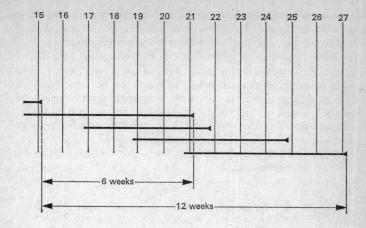

in outlook is harder to accomplish than might at first be realized.

Moreover, it has become perfectly clear that the carrying out of time-span analyses does not give only a measure of level of work. It can give a systematic method for revealing and describing the main facts of the real responsibilities to be carried in a role, as well as for revealing and describing the main mechanisms, many of which usually go unrecognized, by which a manager exercises control over the discretion used by his subordinates. A solid foundation has thereby been achieved for job analysis in terms of the content of the work done, without any reference whatever to the skills, experience, training, and other psychological characteristics of the person required to do the job. And, it might almost seem paradoxically, by carrying out the analysis in terms of work, a solid foundation is achieved for constructing a profile of the knowledge and skills needed for the job. The prescribed content outlines the necessary knowledge and experience, and the discretionary content points to the skills and *nous* required.

Moreover, I find that I use time-span analysis as a basic aid in carrying out analyses of executive organization. I merely mention these facts in passing. To go further would take us too far afield into questions of executive organization and manning, questions to which we may return on another occasion. (See Brown, 1960.)

Most important for our present purposes is the question of whether time-span of discretion can really be said by itself to give a measure of the range of level of work in a role. I have already explained that I would not wish to be interpreted as saying that no other factors than time-span are important in work. I intend to state only that the time-span scale, used in the manner described, does by itself constitute a yardstick for measuring purposes. Let me now turn to the evidence for this statement, to be found in people's feelings about payment in relation to level of work measured in time-span.

References

BROWN, W. (1960), *Exploration in Management*, Heinemann.
JAQUES, E. (1951), *Changing Culture of a Factory*, Humanities Press.

18 Elliott Jaques

A System for Income Equity

Elliott Jaques, 'A system for income equity,' *New Society*, vol. 2, no. 63, 1963.

The British are currently suffering the troubles attendant upon a state of growing affluence. It is not the affluence *per se* which is the trouble. It is the grab through organized power groups, when there is no just and approved way of sharing in plenty, to make sure you get the whole of your share. The potential enjoyment of affluence and security is spoiled by recurrent unrest about payment levels, and by the inequity of income distribution which at the extreme shows poverty side by side with plenty.

Who shall receive how much income is one of the key social problems of all democratic societies. Its solution is one of the necessary components of a solid foundation for society. No democratic nation has yet solved the problem in accord with principle and law. Every democratic nation has suffered social tension ranging from disunity to outright revolution, as a result. We are currently in process of squandering one of the rarely occurring opportunities to solve it. We shall be the weaker for having missed the chance.

There are two fundamental and separate issues in settling income policy. The first is that of the *absolute level of incomes;* I shall refer to it as *general income level*. The second is that of *income relativities or differentials* – the level of income of each member of society relative to every other member; I shall use the phrase *income differentials*.

Our practice as a nation has been to leave the general income level to settle out where it is pushed by the interaction of the social and economic forces active at the time. At the same time income differentials are handled by negotiation and collective bargaining for most manual wages and some staff salaries, with consequential adjustments to other salaried managerial, technical and commercial staff, mainly in the form of merit increases which have the dual function of recognizing individual merit and maintaining differentials.

A well-recognized difficulty with these crude and primitive techniques is that, once the smoke has cleared on each annual round of negotiations, very little adjustment of the differential pattern has been achieved. The general level of incomes has been increased, with a few slight differential shifts here and there, especially a relative worsening of the position of those whose bargaining position is weakened by unemployment, those with fixed incomes, or those such as teachers and nurses whose income levels are dictated by the fact that it has been held to be inappropriate for them to use militant power in bargaining. Moreover, another fillip has been given to rising prices, by both the general increase in income levels, and the drift in incomes caused by consequential adjustments to wages and salaries alike.

Recently, because of the resulting inflationary trend, it has become the fashion to seek a national incomes policy which will overcome the chronic undermining of our economic health caused by this inflation. The weakness, however, in our approach to a national income policy is that only half the problem is being taken into account. The setting of policies in terms of guiding lights, whether of 2 per cent or 5 per cent, deals only with the general income level; it does not touch the question of income differentials.

This halfway approach to the problem would not be unsatisfactory if we could assume that the differential pattern of incomes was sound. But there is strong evidence that the income relativities are not sound – and never have been sound – and that there is need for constant adjustment of the differential pattern of income awarded to different stata of society. In the event, current half measures may prove to be worse than nothing at all, since their silence on the issue of differentials seems to imply that the differential distribution of income is regarded as satisfactory, or at least that it is satisfactorily dealt with by negotiation.

The thorniest question in incomes policy is the question of differentials. Perhaps just because it is so thorny, it tends to receive the least attention. It is summarily dealt with in economic theory by treating labour as a commodity to be bargained over, so that the differential payment pattern becomes merely a matter of supply and demand at any given time.

Unfortunately, however, our feelings about how the national pie should be distributed are not so easily satisfied by this bargaining approach. Feelings of fairness, or equity, simply do exist, whether we like it or not. There is a sense of rightness or wrongness about the pattern of income distribution, regardless of supply and demand, and regardless of tradition, or of the special bargaining strength or power position of this or that employer or trade union or group of technologists at any given time.

To go on treating labour as a commodity subject to bargaining and to the vagaries of the market, is to go on allowing the use of power as the mode of regulating how we fare economically relative to each other. To the strong go the spoils. In such a setting, it is no use having national policy which merely guides everyone's income up by, say, $2\frac{1}{2}$ per cent. The disaffection and discontent which exist arise from those groups and individuals who consider themselves to be positioned wrongly in the economic scheme of things, and who are seeking not just to get an increase like everyone else, but to come higher up the economic ladder.

During the past ten years I have had what I think is probably a unique opportunity to have a close range look at these problems, as part of my work on the Glacier Project.[1] This particular aspect of the project has been reported in detail. From the findings, one thing at least emerges with great force. There is evidence not only that we are powerfully influenced by feelings of fairness with respect to differential payment, but that in a most remarkable way we share common norms of what constitutes equitable payment for any given level of work regardless of occupation.

What is responsibility

The most striking finding, and the one which is basic to this article, is as follows:

1. The Glacier Project is an applied research into all aspects of its organization and industrial relations, carried on by the Glacier Metal Company, a light-engineering firm with headquarters in West London. Systematic work has gone on continuously since 1948. The results are reported in: Brown, 1960, 1962 and Jaques, 1951, 1956, 1961.

Employed persons whose work is shown by measurement to be at the same level of responsibility, privately state the same wage or salary to be fair for the work they are doing: this finding holds regardless of a person's actual earnings, of occupation, of current market values, or of income tax levels.

These results were obtained once it became possible objectively to measure the level of work (level of responsibility) in jobs (not to evaluate or assess as a matter of judgement or opinion, but to measure). The measure – called the *time-span of discretion* –

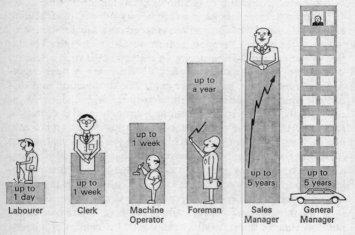

Figure 1

is the maximum time lapse over which a person is required to exercise discretion in his job without that discretion being reviewed.

In broad outline, the technique of time span measurement is to discover the longest tasks which may be allocated by a manager to his subordinate. It may, for example, be one manual task or a sequence of manual tasks, which is worked upon before any of the work is directly or indirectly reviewed. Or it may be a task which is to be worked on intermittently, along with other tasks which are simultaneously carried; such as, for example, six months to work up the material and write an article, or two years to introduce a new production method, or twelve months to carry through a given training programme, etc.

Two points must be made. The first is that it is objective measurement in the full meaning of measurement ordinarily associated with the natural sciences, and not mere job evaluation; indeed, I hope it will help to advance the solution to the problem of genuine measurement in social science. Second, there are many others besides myself who are now able to use the instrument: it has been applied to many kinds of employment work, and in many other countries besides the United Kingdom.

To illustrate, here are a few of the measured ranges of time span of discretion that have been obtained for various jobs.

Labouring jobs and lower level clerical work: a few hours up to a full day.

Machine operator jobs and ordinary clerical work: a few days up to a week or more.

Machine tool fitting, electrical installation work, secretarial work, book-keeping: one week to a few months.

Foreman positions: six months to a year, depending on the responsibilities connected with work throughput, forward orders and forward planning for work input.

Teaching positions: six months to 15 months, depending on the periods for which the teacher is accountable for progressing the teaching programme of a class.

Research technologist jobs: weeks, months or years, depending on the maximum length of the project assigned to the research worker.

Sales management: months to years, depending on the time allocated to cover territories, to open markets, to introduce new products.

General Manager positions, school principals, hospital superintendents: two to five years (and more for some managing directors) depending, for example, on the scale of capital or technical development projects.

As a result of analyzing some 3000 jobs – including many other companies besides Glacier, in different industries in both the private and nationalized sectors – it has become clear that there exist intuitively known norms of fair payment, and that these norms are shared in common among all people in employment work. The jobs studied have been of all kinds and with earnings ranging from 5s. 6d. per hour to £18,000 per annum. Putting together these findings, it has been possible to construct an *Equitable Work-payment Scale*, current at a given time.

When the results are set out in graphic form, they show the striking fact that a curve of the same shape has been obtained in work carried out independently by others using the time span instrument in Holland, the United States and Canada. That is to say, the relativities in payment experienced as fair or equitable for different levels of work measured in time-span are the same in other countries as in the UK.

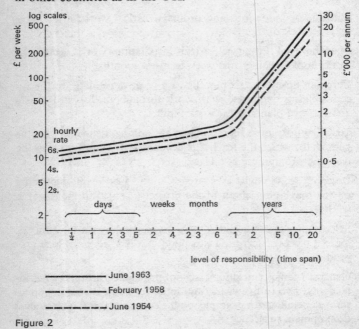

June 1963
February 1958
June 1954

Figure 2

332 Salary Structures

It is noteworthy that individuals paid in accord with the scale for their level of work state that they feel fairly paid. If paid above the scale, they describe their jobs as being 'very favourably' paid, and feel uneasy. And if paid below the scale, they describe their jobs as underpaid and push for more. The greater the deviation between actual and equitable payment, the stronger the feeling of disequilibrium.

It is this equitable work payment scale, used in conjunction with the time span instrument, which can be used for constructing a national incomes policy. This policy is intended to govern payment in all employment jobs, at all levels from top management to office and shop floor and to

1. Maintain full employment and a buoyant economy: exert every effort nationally to maintain full employment, so that there is opportunity for each one to obtain employment in work at a level consistent with his capacity, and to gain an increasing level of work as his capacity grows and develops.

In other words, although the policy proposed can be applied under varying economic conditions, it definitely does not require the minimum of two to three per cent unemployment which appears to be necessary to mitigate inflation under our present procedures. Indeed, the policy proposed really comes into its own only under conditions of complete abundance of employment opportunity.

2. Relate payment structure to level of work in jobs: establish the current level of work for the job by measuring its time-span, and then fix the equitable payment bracket for the job in accord with the equitable work-payment scale, so that all jobs of the same level of work carry the same payment bracket regardless of job title, industry, 'productivity', or any other such factors. An important feature is that all jobs would be measured by precisely the same instrument: whether manual workers, teachers, clerical staff, nurses, senior executives, etc.

3. Recognize individual performance by merit increases within the job payment brackets: as an individual's performance improves, pay him merit increases within the equitable payment bracket for the job. When his capacity becomes greater than the top of the bracket, he must seek a job with a higher level of work,

and consequently a higher payment bracket, in order to make further progress.

This policy would require that every employer has adequate procedures for periodic review of the performance and progress of his employees, the aim being that he should progress each individual in his work, and consequently in his payment, at a rate consistent with his progress in capacity.

4. Make national adjustments to the total payment pattern, if necessary: if the total national product should increase and the state of the economy become such as to make desirable the distribution of larger incomes (for example, to keep a proper balance between the general level of profits and of incomes), then do so by increasing the whole of the equitable work-payment scale by the same percentage amount (leaving the differential pattern of payment intact).

5. Never allow differential change in job rate except with change of level of work: the rate for a given job can be changed relative to other jobs only when it can be demonstrated that its level of work has moved up or down: when level of work goes down, ensure alternative employment for the occupant at a level consistent, with his capacity; when level of work goes up, keep the occupant in his job if his capacity is up to it, or transfer him to appropriate alternative employment if it is not. (By and large, it is a fair assumption that the total level of work in the nation remains pretty constant; therefore, the total wage and salary bill would not be affected by these differential adjustments.)

6. No wage or salary increase to be allowed for scarcity value: no employer whatever would be allowed to depart from the equitable work-payment scale; for example, payment above the scale to attract scarce labour would be contrary to the national policy. (It is this feature of the policy which attacks wage-drift inflation.)

7. Mobility of labour: the fundamental policy is to get new work into unemployment areas. As a subsidiary policy, labour mobility to expanding areas of the economy would be produced in a natural manner, owing to the fact that individual progress with growing capacity would depend upon finding the opportunity to progress in level of work – an opportunity provided more readily in conditions of expansion. Contracting areas would

drive out those seeking progress, and expanding areas would attract them. (Removal allowances would be paid as such, leaving the differential wage and salary structure intact, and so not inducing wage-drift.)

8. Special rewards: if for any other reason it is necessary to grant special rewards to individuals or occupational groups, then do so by means of explicit *ex gratia* payments, and not by manipulating the wage and salary structure. (Again leaving the differential pattern of payment intact.)

From scale to policy

The implications of this policy are many. The differential pattern and level of wages and salaries can be held constant in relation to level of work in jobs. The whole pattern can be moved in explicit and described ways so that what is happening can be known: equity is not only served, but can be seen to be served.

Full employment, economic expansion and full use of individual capacity are an integral part of the policy and not in conflict with it. Managers would be accountable for initiative in progressing individuals in their work, and in watching the dynamics of work organization so as to pick up changes in level of work which might be occurring in various areas. By fixing firmly the general structure of payment for level of work, the policy makes possible readjustments within that structure to cater for changes in level of work and in the capacity of individuals. It is these changes which stimulate wage-push and wage-drift inflation when there is no payment structure within which to grip them. The application of the policy would depend on:

Examination of the means of measuring level of work by employers, trade unions and government and acceptance of these measurements.

Agreement of these bodies to substitute power bargaining by using the results of measurement as a means of deciding differential wages.

Training of a sufficient number of Government officials, union officers and work study personnel in the technique of work measurement.

Legislation to establish and regulate the differential payments levels.

It is abundantly clear that our present bargaining and negotiation methods stimulate the wholesale expression of group rivalries and jealousy, and contribute to bitterness and social conflict. My experience leads to the impression that equally strong constructive forces of social cooperation lie waiting to be released if income were equitably distributed.

I believe that the policy outlined has deeply democratic roots, since it is based upon discoverable norms of equity, and can be administered in a manifestly lawful manner. It is this point which is of the greatest importance. A sound national incomes policy is not just a matter of controlling inflation. The democratic sharing of the national income is an essential component of sound national morality and social health.

References

BROWN, W. (1960), *Exploration in Management*, Heinemann.
BROWN, W. (1962), *Piecework Abandoned*, Heinemann.
JAQUES, E. (1951), *Changing Culture of a Factory*, Humanities Press.
JAQUES, E. (1956), *Measurement of Responsibility*, Tavistock.
JAQUES, E. (1961), *Equitable Payment*, Heinemann.

19 T. M. Husband

How to Evaluate Jobs

T. M. Husband, 'How to evaluate jobs', *Management Today*
July 1968.

A major breakthrough in company wage and salary administration is promised by an entirely fresh approach to the problem of job evaluation. This new approach, called the 'decision band' method, allows jobs at all levels in a company to be evaluated in terms of a common yardstick. The wage structure evolved by the use of this analysis is in a much more convenient form for collective bargaining and wage administration than that provided by any existing technique.

The purpose of any job evaluation is, of course, to provide an equitable scale of payment for jobs in relation to their value to the organization. Its application should, in theory, enable a company to set equitable wage differentials within its own wage structure; equitable wage differentials between its own wage structure and those of other companies in the community; and equitable wage rates for new jobs in the company. But the four conventional methods of job evaluation – ranking, classification, points, and factor comparison – are unable to meet these requirements. They rely to a large extent on purely subjective measures of essentially personality factors (education, experience, initiative, etc.) and ignore real assessment of the characteristics of the job itself.

The greatest shortcoming of all, however, is the fact that the conventional methods cannot compare unlike jobs. It is impossible to compare the job of plumber in a company with, say, a sales clerk simply because characteristics such as working conditions, skill and so on vary across job families. Companies using the conventional methods invariably have a wage plan for the blue-collar workers and a quite separate plan for their white-collar employees, which exacerbates the already invidious distinction between shop floor and office. Further, the conventional methods do not lend themselves to evaluating middle and senior management jobs, so emphasizing the difference between 'we' and 'they'. There should be no difference between wage and salary. There should be only pay.

There is an obvious need in industry today for a plan which can determine the equitable pay for *all* employees, from shop floor to board room. Consider the recent [1968] problems of the engineering employers when trying to establish a just wage for their draughtsmen. They found it very difficult to compare the worth of a draughtsman with that of, for example, a fully-skilled boilermaker. They had no common yardstick. Similarly, imagine how much better disposed employees should be to a wage plan if they know that the same plan is being applied in precisely the same manner at all levels, including top management. There would be less opportunity for accusations of double standards – one for managerial staff and another for 'the worker'. In fact, Jaques (1956) saw most of these advantages as far back as the mid 50s, but his approach has not been accepted as a practical proposition by industry.

There is as yet no hard evidence to show that the 'decision band' method would be acceptable in the great bulk of industrial situations – such as a large engineering works. However, the inherent logic in the technique, and the research carried out to date, suggest no basic reason why it should fail. Its validity has been under research at the University of Strathclyde, where it was developed by Professor T. T. Patterson. The method is being used on a day-to-day basis by the entire Rhodesian Civil Service, and the concept has been recommended by the PIB for application to the salary structure of nurses. Decision bands apply, as a common yardstick for all jobs, to the type of decisions required to carry out the job. Jobs are analysed and graded in terms of decision levels. The 'higher' the quality of decision required, the greater the value of the job to the company.

The hypothesis is that all organizations unconsciously tend to reward their members in terms of the decisions they make. The theory of decision levels flows from Patterson's theory of organizational grading. It postulates that there are only six basic kinds of decision, which define the whole range of jobs existing in the enterprise, and can be classified separately, as follows:

Band E. Policy-making decisions are made at the very top of the hierarchy, *top management*. They are associated with board level management. The word 'director' suggests the function of directing or guiding the enterprise, and the board does this by taking decisions on company policy. The limits set on the choice of decision tend to be wide and, in many cases, are specified only by the laws of the state. Designation as 'top management' does not necessarily put a man's decisions in this band – we define 'policy-making' as rigidly as possible, characterized, for example, by final decisions committing the entire company on significant issues.

Band D. Programming decisions are typical of those made by *senior managers* such as divisional managers, works managers and chief engineers. The decision is made within the limits set by the policy decision of Band E. It is a plan or programme for execution of the policy. In Band D no execution of decisions takes place.

Band C. Interpretative decisions are made by *middle managers*, by departmental heads such as a machine shop manager or a foundry superintendent. The decisions are made within the limits set in the programme at Band D. At this level there is still no execution of decisions.

Band B. Routine decisions are made by skilled workmen. These are decisions concerned with the *execution* of the interpreted policy decided at Band C. The craftsman or tradesman does not decide 'why' something must be done, he is concerned with the way it is carried out, the process.

Band A, automatic decisions, the *semi-skilled worker* also does not have to know 'why' he performs his operation. He need only concern himself with 'how' to carry out the instructions of 'what' to do, and 'where' and 'when' to do it, the operations within the process.

Band O, vegetative decisions, are made by an *unskilled worker* who is typically left with the most limited discretion, e.g. speed of working.

Consider the decision procedure in a typical engineering company. Imagine that the board of directors decide (Band E) that, as a matter of policy, the company will aim to double the market share of a product in the next year. To achieve this, the board decides that it is necessary to reduce the selling price, increase marketing expenditure and increase production by 150 per cent. To meet the increased output requirement, the works manager (Band D) has to establish a programme. He programmes, in broad terms, perhaps, the increased capital equipment required, the extra labour force needed and the rate of flow of parts through the production system. Similarly, the sales manager (Band D) develops a sales programme for the execution of the new policy. He establishes, say, a revised regional sales organization with an augmented staff of representatives in the key areas, a new quota of target sales per area, and so on.

At Band C level, several middle managers in both the sales and production functions interpret the programme of the new policy. For example, the machine shop superintendent decides which key machines must operate on a three-shift basis to meet the programme requirements. Similarly, in interpreting the sales programme the regional sales manager for, say, the West Country, decides that his most intensive selling effort must be directed at three specific outlets. At this level, decisions are taken as to the 'best' option among possible choices to meet the programme.

At Band B, the decisions made by fitters, turners, electricians and other skilled tradesmen on the shop floor are not affected by the new output programme. Their decisions are carried out by set routines. They do not decide 'why' a batch is made up of a certain number of components or 'why' a machining tolerance is 0·005 inch and not 0·01 inch. In the sales department, senior clerical staff in the sales office (Band B) will not have to change their routine as a result of the new sales target programme. At Band B the worker carries out some routine required to execute the policy, but the policy is interpreted for him in terms of his regular routine.

The Band A production workers are given even less discretion. They are left only to decide on operation, on 'how' to carry out a set of clearly specified tasks. The radial driller, for example, can decide perhaps on how to clamp the workpiece to the machine, but not on which drilling procedure or set of tools to use. Similarly, the ordinary clerical staff worker in the sales office (Band A) is not concerned with 'why' she marks certain column totals and sub-totals in sales documents in a specified manner. She decides only on 'how' this clerical task is carried out – for example, to process one set of figures in one document at a time or to process one document completely before moving on to the next. At vegetative level (Band O) in the sales office, the copy typist in the typing pool is allowed, virtually, to decide only on how fast or slow she will type. She does not even decide 'how' to copy, for example, invoice data on to a file card. In the production area, the shop labourer (Band O) is similarly allowed to decide only on his working speed. The equipment and task are clearly specified.

This concept of decision bands can be used to illustrate the organization structure. Each decision band (except Band O) is divisible into two levels or grades – upper and lower. The upper-level job holder in any decision band coordinates the work of the men in the lower level of the same decision band. He is the 'line' or 'structural' manager of the lower-level worker. Thus the upper level of Band B is the decision level of the shop foreman. His function is to coordinate the work of his subordinates and he can therefore be seen as a manager in the accepted sense. The foreman is often not widely accepted as a manager for the simple reason that he does not decide on 'why' certain action should be taken. The single-level Band O plus two levels in each of Band A through to Band E show jobs in these eleven grades to be of increasing status or importance in the hierarchy in relation to their value to the company.

In the engineering company example the shop labourer and copy typist are Grade O; the sales clerk and the radial driller are Grade 1 (the lower level of Band A); the shop floor tradesmen and the senior clerical sales staff are Grade 3 with the shop foreman and the senior sales clerk or section leader at Grade 4; a machine shop superintendent is Grade 5, several superintendents perhaps being coordinated by a departmental manager, Grade 6, reporting to the works manager, Grade 7. District sales managers, Grade 5, may be coordinated by a regional sales manager, Grade 6, responsible to the sales manager, Grade 7. He, the works manager, and their equivalents report to the general manager, Grade 8. The managing director is Grade 10, coordinating the sales and works directors, both Grade 9.

This decision grading is relevant to 'staff' functions as well as to the 'line' functions mentioned in the above progression. The quality control chemist, in an engineering example, may conclude that a certain temperature increase at a specific stage of a die-casting process will increase the process efficiency. To reach this conclusion he requires to draw upon his specialist knowledge of the physics theory underlying the process. If the foundry manager who has structural authority over the plant is advised by the quality control chemist to increase the process temperature, he feels obliged to act accordingly. He accepts this as 'good' advice.

If the process efficiency then shows a sharp decrease due to an error of calculation by the quality control chemist, the foundry manager can be held only partly responsible. He cannot be asked to question the expert conclusions of a specialist in such a highly technical area. That is to say, the quality control chemist is also held responsible at this decision level because his conclusions were wrongly drawn and, therefore, his decisions and advice were 'bad'. His job can be compared by 'decision band theory' since he bases his advice on his anticipation of the developing situation, and is therefore faced with the same degree of difficulty as the foundry manager. Indeed, he may save the foundry manager from having to make a deep assessment of the situation.

But what if two jobs are slotted into the same decision grade, but call for different levels of discretion in the sense that one is more 'difficult' than the other? This was the experience of the present writer when experimenting with decision bands at shop floor level in the engineering industry. A toolroom miller with a range of tasks that included milling very complex die blocks required Grade 3 decisions as the highest level for his function. In another workshop, a production milling operative (a fully skilled turner) required Grade 3 decisions to carry out his milling tasks. But the toolroom miller, in his typical task made about twelve Grade 3, thirty Grade 1 and fifty-eight Grade 0 decisions for every 100 decisions required. The production miller made only some three Grade 3 decisions for every 100 decisions required.

That is to say, Grade 3 discretion was required about four times more often by the toolroom worker. Is it therefore fair to pay both men at the same rate?

This is a matter for individual firms. They could adopt a basic rate for each of the 11 grades and build upon this, say, on a three (or five) point scale – for example, Grade 3 (a) most difficult jobs, Grade 3 (b) medium difficult, and Grade 3 (c) least difficult, assessing the (a), (b) and (c) levels as a percentage rate of total decisions made (our toolroom miller had a percentage rate of $12/100 = 12$ per cent). By so quantifying the decision analysis, greater objectivity can be introduced into discussions regarding the value of similar jobs. Alternatively the company might want to have only the eleven basic wage rates and apply, in addition, a merit rating scheme based on criteria appropriate to its own organization. Obviously another strategy would be to let collective bargaining decide the wage levels *within* a decision grade.

Significantly, in the decision band method shop floor jobs are analysed without reference to manual skills (such as the degree of machining accuracy), or years of service, or working conditions. This should not in any way invalidate the method. To base job evaluation on measures of machining accuracy or knowledge of tools and equipment is usually quite misleading. Often the most accurate finish is required from workers who happen to operate the most accurate machinery, which tells nothing of the discretion or skill required in doing the job.

Similarly, length of service and working conditions are considerations which should be left out of job evaluation. Unavoidably bad working conditions must be met by special payment, which is the subject of regular bargaining. This is especially important in cases where the worker is not exposed to the hazard on a daily basis. For example, it is common to hear of maintenance personnel being granted, as part of their basic hourly wage rate, 3*d*. or 6*d*. to compensate for working conditions which are occasionally unpleasant. They are regularly paid an allowance for working in conditions of intense heat when in fact they may only do so twice a year. Length of service is a matter which applies entirely to the individual doing a job and has no bearing on the value of the job to the enterprise.

When companies use one of the conventional methods they

may well introduce labour relations problems which previously did not exist. For example, when a company defines the degrees of education required for various jobs it often uses terminology such as 'degree 1 – requires professional status; degree 2 – requires technician status', and so on. Now, when it comes to evaluating the job of a draughtsman, who decides if he is a professional or a technician? If he is defined as a technician there will be many disillusioned draughtsmen who had always thought of themselves as professionals. Similarly, if the draughtsman is ranked as a professional, then the laboratory technicians will, in many cases, insist that they also be re-classified. The point is simply that the conventional approaches tend to lend themselves to dangerous terminology, which in turn tends to lead to invidious comparisons. Decision-band theory seeks to avoid this pitfall by concentrating on the only characteristic that matters, the type of decision required, and the responsibility that automatically goes with it.

Perhaps the most fascinating aspect of this whole research, however, is the apparent logarithmic relationship of existing wage rates to the different decision grades. In all tests of the theory to date, in several hundred thousand jobs in many different industries, the pay differential between each decision grade has been found to increase exponentially. That is to say, when the current pay rates were plotted on a log scale against the 11 job grades, the scatter points on the graph did not form a perfect straight line, but fell sufficiently close to indicate clearly that the line of best fit was straight. It appears that there is an unconscious tendency by enterprises to reward employees, or decision-makers, according to this specific linear relationship.

In 1960 Paterson made a sample analysis of jobs in a range of Ministries in the Civil Service. The minimum pay at that time was approximately £360 per annum for Grade O employees. Very simple mathematics established the gradient of the curve, that is, the angle of climb in pay from bottom to top. Thus, knowing the pay value at Grade O, the gradient of the curve, and the number of workers in each job grade, it is easy to establish the total *equitable* payroll for an organization. Similarly, any firm using the method could approach the problem from the opposite angle; by specifying how much money it wished to spend on payroll, it could establish the equitable wage value for each grade. It would also have to establish (and doubtless negotiate) the value of the minimum wage. It is then a simple matter to draw the wage curve at the appropriate gradient from the minimum wage point.

Of course, there will have to be some departures from the straight line. It would be foolish to attempt to thwart the forces of the labour market. For example, pay rates of computer personnel at the moment distort more company pay structures than those of any other single set of employees. Here again bargaining should take place to establish by how much above the 'decision band' payroll line scarce skills should be paid. This extra payment should be bargained for every year. The point is that the inflated payment should not be built into the basic structure as a permanent value.

This raises an interesting point. The value of the gradient of the pay curve appears to vary between industries and regions, very probably because of the effects of the local labour market and varying degrees of profitability. At Strathclyde, we are now trying to establish gradient values for various types of industry, e.g. printing as against shipbuilding as against a department store. We intend also to correlate the gradient of different individual company pay structures with indices of business success or market share, etc., within the same industry and region. It is tempting to think that a national, or at least regional or industrial, pay structure could be founded on this approach. If it were possible to establish payroll equations for each industry within each region as a function, say, of sales turnover, it clearly would be much simpler to calculate equitable payment for each grade of job within each industry.

The band method, then, approaches the problem of equitable payment objectively, yet without any need for elaborate committees to discuss degree definitions and the weightings of mental skill against physical skill, as is so typical of the existing techniques. The common denominator from tea boy to chairman is quality of decision. There is no need to have a staff salary plan separate from an hourly paid wage scheme along with a top executive payment scheme. A single criterion is the basis for a comprehensive wage and salary system. In addition, when the grading analysis is applied to a firm it becomes obvious where craft, clerical and managerial skills are being misused. The method of analysis of jobs into decision bands and grades is extremely simple and easily taught. A standard questioning procedure can be used for analysis by interview, but in almost all cases it is also necessary to observe the job being carried out. The advantages are obvious. But to get the method properly launched we need still more researching. At Strathclyde we are now experimenting with decision bands in foundries, and the method certainly needs to be streamlined further before it can be sold to industry in a big way.

It would obviously be naïve to imagine, for example, that the trade unions would accept the principle overnight. Would the same union which insists on maintaining wage differentials solely on the difference between workers with a five-year as against a three-year apprenticeship be eager to accept a pay plan based solely on the decisions required to do the job and ignoring the length of apprenticeship altogether? Nevertheless, many of our craft unions are yielding to levels of flexibility and manning that were undreamt of just a few years ago. Hopefully, the attempts at stream-lining the decision band method will meet with success in the not too distant future. There can be no doubt that British industry needs its advantages – and the sooner the better.

Reference

JAQUES, E. (1956), *Time Span of Discretion Methods*, Heinemann.

20 Alan Fox

Time-Span of Discretion Theory: An Appraisal

Excerpt from Alan Fox, 'The time-span of discretion theory: an appraisal,' Institute of Personnel Management, 1966.[1]

I

Discretionary and prescribed responsibilities

'What is it,' asks Jaques (1961) 'that enterprise seeks when it employs a person to work in its executive organization – what is it that it pays a wage or salary *for* . . .?' The answer involves a definition of work which distinguishes between two major components: '(a) the discretionary content, comprising the discretion, choice or judgment which the person doing the work is expected to exercise; and (b) the prescribed content, comprising the rules, regulations, procedures and policies, the custom and practice, and the physical limits of plant, equipment or tooling, which set external limits within which the discretion has to be exercised.' All jobs contain both elements, though the proportions vary enormously.

This distinction between the discretionary and prescribed content of work is so crucial to the theory as to call for close examination.

The individual can be in no doubt when he has satisfactorily discharged the prescribed elements in his work 'because the result to be achieved or the regulations to be adhered to have been established in objective terms such as that anyone would know when the work had been done as required'. Examples of prescribed content are: 'follow this routine; get such-and-such records out each Friday; use British standards in drawing; keep double-entry books; use the Matrix intelligence test; travel via trunk road A3; keep below the speeds, as shown on a speedometer, specified for each curve on a railway; confine yourself to

1. This work was originally commissioned for the Prices and Incomes Board.

air ejector systems in designing these machine tools; advertise only in the national daily newspapers; see that a random 10 per cent of all goods is inspected before dispatch; visit all customers with more than a given turnover at least once a month'. The language of the prescribed content is always concrete and specific in the sense of having an *external objective reference* by which the individual can check his performance. A departure from instructions and regulations is immediately apparent without the exercise of judgment.

Any aspect of the job which does not have this objective reference is discretionary. The individual has to use his own discretion in deciding when he has pursued the particular activities to the point where the result is likely to satisfy his superior. Examples are: 'make sure you buy enough stamps; use the best method in the circumstances; design advertisements with public appeal; keep a satisfactory standard of finish; select the most capable of the applicants'. Such instructions tell the individual that he must do *something* about stamps, best methods, appealing advertisements, satisfactory finish, or capable applicants, but exactly what or how is left to his personal judgment.

All jobs contain both prescribed and discretionary elements. 'It is impossible for any manager to issue an instruction that has no prescribed limits. There are always prescribing policies, limits, results, to be achieved.' Similarly, it is impossible wholly to exclude discretion, even from the most tightly 'programmed' work. There is always some residual aspect of behaviour remaining within the discretion of the operator.

The distinction may be pursued further. The performance of the prescribed aspects of a job demands knowledge. 'The person . . . must have been taught, or must otherwise have learned, the particular routines, or the signals, or the tests, or the policies, or the techniques, which he has been instructed to use in carrying out his assigned activities.' For the discretionary aspects, the individual 'must decide, choose, judge, feel, sense, consider, conclude just what would be the best thing to do in the circumstances, the best way of going about what he is doing'.

We may now return to the question which began this section – what it is that an enterprise seeks when it employs a person. 'First, it employs that person's capacity to carry out the prescribed responsibilities and to conform to them: he must know enough to do so. Second, it employs his ability to exercise sufficient discretion on his own account to cope with uncertainties, the vicissitudes, the unknowns, in the job: he must have enough capacity and experience – the know-how or the *nous* – to do so.'

Discretionary responsibilities and the 'level of work'

But where, asks Jaques in effect, does the real pressure of a job lie? His answer is vital to the whole theory. In an earlier work it is boldly unequivocal. 'What is experienced as one's level of work has only to do with the use of discretion and judgement, and has nothing whatever to do with the prescribed content of one's work.' (Jaques, 1956, p. 85.) Later formulations are more cautious. 'We appear to derive our sensation of level of work or responsibility from the discretion we are called upon to exercise, and not from the regulated or prescribed actions which have been set and which we have learned and can carry out automatically.' It is 'the exercise of discretion ... which is mainly connected with the sensation of the amount of responsibility in a job.' (Jaques, 1961, p. 81.)

Why is this? Why do we 'react to the regulated aspects of our work as though there were no great effort required in doing it, whereas carrying out the discretionary aspect imparts the sensation of personal responsibility'? The answer is that 'conforming to regulations feels like doing work which someone else has already decided about, and if it goes wrong it is 'his' doing and not your own. When required to use your own discretion, however, it feels like doing your own work, it is you yourself who carry the responsibility, and it is to yourself that you turn if things go wrong, for it feels as if you yourself are to blame.' The 'essence of the effort in work is to be found in the anxiety engendered by the uncertainties which are part and parcel of the exercise of discretion.'

In these arguments, level of work = effort in work = degree of responsibility in work = degree of discretionary content in work. For Jaques, the definition of work must encompass the notion of responsibility. 'For no sooner do we consider the question of the value of different types of work in terms of payment differentials than we find ourselves in the field of argument about the relative degrees of responsibility in the various types of work under consideration. Payment in the sense of value of labour or work is intimately associated with felt weight of responsibility carried.' Thus what the individual is really being rewarded for is the level of work as measured by the degree of discretion exercised. Jaques asserts that 'the principle that payment should be directly related to the level of work done' receives 'widespread endorsement' in the slogan 'the rate for the job'. (Jaques, 1956, p. 5).

The time-span of discretion

But 'the large question that remains is how to measure the job'. Intuitive judgements are too coarse and in any case are often based on insufficient knowledge and on differing criteria and frames of references. Systems of job evaluation are no improvement, for much of it 'is based on such judgement – although the largely intuitive basis is often obscured behind the apparent, but simulated, objectivity to be obtained by using rating scales that give varying numbers of points to various aspects of a job.'

The answer lies, as already implied, in measuring the time-span of discretion. This is defined as 'the maximum period of time during which the use of discretion is authorized and expected, without review of that discretion by a superior.' The notion of 'review' is less straightforward than may seem. 'The occasions when a manager himself *directly* reviews the results of the work of his subordinates are much rarer than the occasions when he does not.' (Jaques, 1961, p. 85.) What usually happens is that the manager allows the work to continue on the assumption – sometimes unconscious – that in the absence of complaints from elsewhere the performance is satisfactory. This is 'indirect' rather than direct review. Many situations giving the impression of direct review contain nothing of the kind. Shareholders allegedly scrutinizing the discretion exercised by the board during the preceding year are doing no such thing; neither is a designer who has full confidence in a subordinate draughtsman's work and gives it only a cursory scrutiny. The time-span of discretion must therefore be measured in terms of 'how long it would be possible to exercise inadequate discretion' – i.e. do substandard work – before that fact came to the attention of the immediate manager.

The techniques and mechanisms of review are thus crucial for the application of the time-span method, and in his earlier book, *Measurement of Responsibility*, Jaques reported difficulties in identifying the review points of manual operations linked to each other in a production flow system. For this reason it had not 'been found possible to use the time-span of discretion form of measurement with any consistency as a measure of level of work in manual jobs.' In *Equitable Payment* such qualifications have gone and 'the level of work in both manual and non-manual jobs can be measured objectively by a common yardstick.' He reports having had 'the opportunity . . . to analyse the allocation and flow of work in whole production departments on various types of hand tools and on automatic, semi-automatic and standard machine tools, as well as to analyze work in labouring and . . . tool making, millwrighting, inspection, electrical work, and storekeeping.' Review points for these and other manual jobs can be identified as easily as for non-manual work. 'It is a matter of analyzing each job to discover at what subsequent stage in the production process marginally substandard work would manifest itself.' Jaques points out that 'the technique is not an especially easy one to learn. The difficulty lies in the great trouble experienced in getting away from looking at level of work in terms of the skills and experience required in a person to do the job, and dealing with level of work in terms simply of activities and managerial review. This change in outlook is harder to accomplish than might at first be realized.'

Jaques realizes of course that such an emphasis violates many received opinions. Jobs are being analysed solely in terms of responsibility measured by time, thus excluding the type of responsibility, its importance, the consequences of sub-standard use of discretion, and many other factors commonly assessed in conventional job evaluation systems, such as skill, experience, training and qualifications, and necessary psychological characteristics. His earlier statement of the method attracted considerable criticism on these grounds.

He seeks to disarm much of it by saying that he does not 'wish to imply that either the time-span of a role or its level of work is the most important thing about that role.' But just as a thermometer can measure our body's temperature without telling us anything of its structure and functioning, so his method can scientifically measure the level of work by focusing on the time-span of discretion to the exclusion of other characteristics of the job. And for Jaques it is the level of work, so defined and measured, from which we derive our sense of the weight of responsibility we carry. Implicit throughout *Equitable Payment* is the belief that this is the element for which the individual seeks reward. This received explicit formulation in the earlier *Measurement of Responsibility* in the statement that 'the principle that payment should be directly related to the level of work done . . . is commonly stated in the slogan "the rate for the job".' (Jaques, 1956, p. 5.) This brings us to the whole question of how Jaques validates his theory.

Validation of the time-span measure

Apart from the simple assertion just quoted, Jaques seeks to validate his theory by reference to analyses carried out with the occupants of some 3,000 jobs in a heavy engineering firm, a food factory, a bank, a woodworking concern, a chemical works, and other companies in different industries in both the private and nationalized sectors. (Jaques, 1963.) This research, extending over many years, stemmed from enquiries pursued at the Glacier Metal Company which threw up 'the totally unexpected finding of a regular connection between time-span and the sums of money which individuals stated would, in their estimation, constitute fair payment for their work. Regardless of the actual wage or salary they might have been earning, regardless of type of occupation (accounting, engineering, shop management, manual or clerical work, purchasing, research, etc.), regardless of position (from shop floor work to top management), and regardless of income tax paid, individuals in jobs whose range of level of work as measured in time-span was the same, privately stated a very similar wage or salary bracket to be fair for the work they were doing.'

The method by which this evidence was secured is an unusual one in social science. 'These analyses . . . were conducted within a social-analytic relationship (which) gives access to private aspects of a person's feelings, judgements and attitudes, which have most likely gone unrecognized by himself.' Responses emerge which are unlikely to be expressed in 'discussion between a manager and a subordinate; and ordinary conversation or public discussion between friends, working colleagues, fellow trade unionists, etc. For in such discussions, the deeper-lying personal feelings and views are never able to come to the surface. Even if he has become conscious of these views and verbalized them – a most improbable circumstance – their expression is blocked by stereotypes of what others will expect one's views to be, or by the desire to influence other people's views in some particular direction.'

These 'special methods that must be used to make . . . contact with these private reactions' suggest the existence of 'an unrecognized system of norms of fair payment for any given level of work, unconscious knowledge of these norms being shared among the population . . .'. We return here to those 'deep unconscious . . . norms of fairness' referred to earlier. They relate directly to the concept of equity in wage and salary payments. Equitable payment is the payment which is 'felt to be fair' for the level of work as measured by the time span of discretion.

The consequences of diverging from equity payment

Deviations from equity which exceed 3 per cent in either direction create psychological disturbance. The reaction to payment below equity passes from feelings of unfairness at 5 per cent to 'explosive disequilibrium' at 20 per cent. Above equity the response becomes increasingly uneasy; 'guilt may be warded off by a devil-take-the-hindmost attitude' until eventually 'greed and avarice may be stimulated.' Jaques observes that such propositions 'posit a high degree of intuitive sensitivity in people . . . about the level of work they are discharging and the rates of pay appropriate to that level.' (Jaques, 1956, p. 119.)

As can be seen, Jaques is here describing the dynamics of disequilibrium in purely individual terms, and he is at pains to emphasize the futility of asking 'whether manual workers, or professional workers, or physicists, or the working classes, or the middle classes, are over- or under-paid.' (Jaques, 1961, p. 137.) Whether or not payment is equitable can be decided only in relation to the level of work in particular roles, and 'not in terms of generalized groups of roles'. Both over- and under-equity paid roles will be found within any given occupational group.

Elsewhere, however, he speaks of deviations which are widespread and which affect 'socially connected groups of individuals', causing 'signs of social malaise and instability' to ensue. The discrepancy is only apparent, for in a society where the regulation of payment is not based on equity, rivalries and anxieties are aroused to the point where power-bargaining by organized groups takes over and man's destructive impulses swamp his more cooperative nature. Such groups exert pressure to get their payment either increased to equity level or brought into line with other groups who are enjoying over-equity payment.

Thus 'in the absence of manifest and explicit equitable regulating mechanisms, the forces of anxiety, greed and envy are strengthened . . . It would require explicit and open recognition in society of an equitable differential pattern of payment . . . for the socially cohesive sense of economic equity to be openly manifested.'

In practical terms, this would mean the elevation of the time-span method of measuring work into a national principle and the abandonment of power-bargaining employers, unions and government. Government officials, union officers and work study personnel would be trained in the appropriate techniques, and legislation would establish and regulate the differential payment levels which were to attach to the differential time-spans of discretion. (Jaques, 1963.)

Such a policy, Jaques argues, has 'deeply democratic roots, since it is based upon discoverable norms of equity, and can be administered in a manifestly lawful manner.' It would 'give no favoured individuals or groups the opportunity to exploit either tradition or disequilibria in the labour market in order to enjoy or accumulate wealth by means of over-equity payment. The moral fibre of the nation would be toughened.' (Jaques, 1961, p. 286.)

This and other quoted references from Jaques may give the impression that he sees his theory as being applicable to income-receivers of every sort. In fact Jaques carefully defines certain limits of application. There is economic work, directed to the creation and distribution of goods and services, and non-economic work, which Jaques excludes from his theory directed to artistic, charitable and household tasks. But even some economic work has to be excluded, namely 'shareholding work', 'directorial work', and self-employment. Jaque's analysis is therefore confined to 'all contractual employment positions' in organizations directed to the production of goods or services.

He uses this selective application to support his argument that the risks of shareholding and investment work should be kept 'separate from the contract of employment, and from the issue of the equitable distribution of wages and salaries.' The use of time-span excludes, of course, such considerations as profitability, productivity and cost of living from the pay-fixing process. The relationship between dividend and income distribution would be regulated by legislated changes in the equitable work-payment scale.

This concludes the statement of the most significant aspects of Jaques's general theory. The remaining features can be briefly summarized. Full employment and a buoyant economy must be maintained, so that there is opportunity for everyone to obtain employment at a level of work consistent with his capacity, and to progress to higher levels of work as his capacity develops. It is an important part of management's function to organize this progression.

Considerable attention is given in the theory to an attempted justification of the whole principle of differential payment. This is done by asserting a 'direct correspondence' between each person's level of capacity in work and his 'capacity for discriminating expenditure'. Thus payment above equity (i.e. above that indicated by the time-span of discretion) brings no lasting satisfaction because the recipient is incapable of the appropriate level of discrimination in his spending. Payment below equity results in a mode of expenditure which is 'anxiety-ridden, ungratifying and unfilling, and leaves quantities of unused capacity for discriminating spending.'

Jaques is more modest about this proposition than about the others. 'It appears ... to be a justifiable hypothesis, and one worth testing.'

II

Jaques's theory can be reviewed on two levels. Jaques himself intends it as the answer to the whole problem of income distribution among the employed population, and as a means by which we can evoke social cooperation, strengthen social cohesion, and pursue society's moral redemption. But clearly it can be seen simply as a device which can be used by individual industrial and commercial organizations to rationalize their payment structure. It will be examined first from this standpoint.

Jaques' definition of work

The question which creates immediate doubts about the time-span measure relates to its theoretical basis, which is extremely vulnerable.

Jaques's definition of work contains something of a sleight-of-hand manoeuvre. Work is first analysed into prescribed and discretionary responsibilities. Thus work is responsibility. But the prescribed element in our work is really someone else's responsibility. It is work 'which someone else has already decided about.' There is 'no great effort required in doing it.' The discretionary element, on the other hand, is strictly our own responsibility: it 'feels like doing your own work'. Thus, by a simple process of deduction: since work is responsibility, and prescribed work is someone else's, one's own work is limited to the discretionary content. Payment for work is thus payment for the exercise of discretion: measure the discretion in terms of time-span and an objective standard exists to which payment can be related.

The ingenuity of this logical sequence need not blind us to its shortcomings. The perfectly valid analysis of work into prescribed and discretionary *responsibilities* does not entitle Jaques to reason as if work is only *responsibility*. The execution of both the prescribed and the discretionary content calls for the exercise of innate and acquired abilities, skills, aptitudes and forms of dexterity which of course vary widely from job to job. These may or may not require a previous investment of time, effort and money in a course of training or the acquiring of qualifications. Work requires physical or mental effort or both, under conditions which range from the highly congenial to the extremely punishing. It may fulfil a man's personality or stunt it. Those prescribed responsibilities which Jaques dismisses so lightly may indeed feel like 'work which someone else had already decided about'; they may on the other hand burden a man heavily with the feared consequences of a moment's absent-mindedness. In the discretionary field, responsibility may be for very different things – for materials, for tools and equipment, for output, for the health and safety of others, for major decisions on long-term objectives. No elaborate analysis of work is needed for Jaques's simple equating of work with responsibility to arouse initial misgivings.

Discretionary responsibility and 'felt-fair' pay

Even less persuasive is Jaques's proposal to reward only the exercise of discretionary responsibility, which alone is to be the measure of payment. The puzzle in accepting this arises from the abundant evidence that men insist on other aspects of the job being taken into account. Jaques refers to the 'widespread endorsement of the principle that payment should be directly related to the level of work done. This principle is commonly stated in the slogan *the rate for the job*.' Bearing in mind that for Jaques 'level of work' means 'time-span of discretion', this is a simple mis-statement. One may assert with some confidence that trade unionists pressing the principle of the rate for the job would examine, in their process of job-comparison, not only discretionary responsibility, but also the tools or machines used, the training required, physical working conditions and various other factors. Craft unionists might not examine the job at all, which removes them even further from Jaques's suppositions. They might argue that an apprenticed compositor who is a fully paid-up member of the appropriate union must get the full compositor's rate however humble the task on which he is employed. Job content would not enter into this comparison, which would rest upon the trained, specialized skills possessed by the man rather than upon the way in which the employer chose to utilize them.

Doubts are further fortified when we turn to the alleged association between the measured time-span of discretion in a job and the level of payment felt to be 'fair' by its incumbent. Jaques always returns, rightly from his point of view, to the crucial finding, drawn from diverse industries in diverse places, that 'individuals in jobs whose range of level of work as measured in time-span was the same, privately stated a very similar wage or salary bracket to be fair for the work they were doing.' His explanation is that they intuit norms of fairness in relation to payment for work; that such norms are present and accessible to introspection within us all, and that they result in the consensus which he describes.

Three points suggest themselves for examination: (1) the method by which the individual formulates for himself these 'felt-fair' norms of pay; (2) the research method by which Jaques discovers them; and (3) the nature of the consensus which results.

1. Jaques observes that the existence of the inner norms which result in such remarkable agreement seems to assume 'a high degree of intuitive sensitivity in people . . . about the level of work they are discharging and the rates of pay appropriate to that level.' Even this is surely a considerable understatement. Jaques is at pains elsewhere to argue that the measurement of time-span is a sophisticated technique requiring the abandonment of many conventional assumptions, and is not 'an especially easy one to learn'. He talks of the 'great trouble experienced in getting away from looking at level of work in terms of the skill and experience required . . .'. These are not mere self-inflating gestures. His chapter in *Equitable Payment* on Review of Substandard Discretion shows admirably the careful analysis of managerial review that is required for time-span measurement.

Thus although we need not take seriously the alleged declaration by 'one of Dr Jaques's ablest disciples' that 'it requires three years of study with Dr Jaques to understand it properly' (Patterson, 1963) a certain expertise is clearly demanded. Jaques's own estimate is that between four and six weeks' specialist training is necessary for the would-be practitioner. How, then, does the common man fare? His judgements are 'based upon unconscious intuitive awareness, the awareness of experience.' (Jaques, 1961, p. 223.) This would seem of doubtful reliability even in relation to his own work, yet the theory assumes him to build up accurate knowledge and judgement about other people's pay and work – people whom he never sees and whose work he never examines. For since 'fairness' is essentially a function of comparisons, how can the individual feel fair without comparing his work and pay with others?

Jaques's reliance upon intuitive awareness in this process is curiously at odds with his complete rejection of it in relation to conventional job evaluation systems. These he dismisses as being too subjective to be of any use when 'numbers of people in widely distributed establishments' are involved. A passage in *Measurement of Responsibility* where he enlarges on this theme strikes an unwitting but destructive blow at his own theory. He is concerned here to argue the need for purely objective measurement and the failure of conventional job evaluation systems to provide it. They rely overmuch on intuitive judgements about work, and these are 'too coarse for such a purpose'. Worse, the 'making of intuitive comparisons between jobs as a means of settling rates of pay suffers from other very great defects as well: people do not look at jobs in the same way; nor are they equally familiar with different jobs; nor, since jobs change, do they necessarily know a job today because they have done so at some time in the past; nor are they necessarily even talking about the same job, since the same job title can often cover a multitude of different kinds of work.' (Jaques, 1956, p. 6.)

All these weaknesses of intuitive judgement may be conceded, but it is precisely this method by which the untrained individual builds up his norms of fairness upon which Jaques places such massive reliance when his theory requires it. We have here no mere debating-point, but a major inconsistency concerning the very social process by which the alleged consensus on 'felt-fair' norms is supposed to be constructed. The implications for Jaques are uncomfortable. If the intuitive judgements upon which he depends for the individual to form his equity payment norms are reliable, they can serve equally well in implementing conventional job evaluation systems, which he argues are qualitatively inferior to his own through their lack of objectivity. If, on the other hand, job evaluation *is* weakened by its inevitable reliance on intuitive judgements, what is the validity of the individual's convictions about 'felt-fair' pay, which rest, as we have seen, upon intuitive notions about other people's pay and work?

In the hands of a trained enquirer the time-span measure is indeed objective, but the process by which the individual assesses his own time-span in relation to pay and compares it with that of other people is crude and imprecise. Any social psychologist would dismiss the results as being open to biased perceptions, social stereotypes, divergent frames of reference and simple ignorance. For Jaques, of course, it is crucial to demonstrate otherwise and he devotes three full pages of *Equitable Payment* to the task. Significantly, perhaps, his rejection of job evaluation in this later volume does not use the phrase 'intuitive judgements', which had been the basis of the earlier attack in *Measurement of Responsibility*.

2. Difficulties also arise with respect to the 'special methods' used by Jaques in bringing to light the intuitive judgements which people make about equity norms of payment. They emerge, we are told, 'within a social-analytic relationship (which) gives access to private aspects of a person's feelings, judgements and attitudes which have most likely gone unrecognized by himself'. There is reference to 'deeper-lying personal feelings' and responses which are unlikely to be voiced in ordinary conversation or public discussion. (Jaques, 1961, pp. 123–4.)

One may feel it odd that such mysterious reactions should be thought to exist on the subjects of work and pay, about which men are commonly vociferous if not shrill. Jaques does not elaborate the point, except to say that even if the individual has become conscious of these deep-lying feelings and has verbalized them – 'a most improbable circumstance' – their expression is blocked by 'social stereotypes of what others will expect one's views to be, or by the desire to influence other people's views in some particular direction.'

'Stereotypes' begs an important question – perhaps the blockage is provided by widely-accepted social *values*, which Jaques would find less easy to disparage than 'stereotypes'. If this is so, then the usefulness of equity payment norms derived from barely-conscious and rarely-verbalized intuitions which clash too sharply with social values to be openly expressed becomes somewhat dubious.

But the important point here is that we cannot judge this issue for ourselves because the research method precludes any scrutiny by independent observers. All forms of social investigation contain a subjective element, but this one more than most. Clearly the process involves probing and 'teasing-out' the required notions, and it may be that this can be kept completely free of unwitting prompting and suggestion even in the hands of rapidly-trained enquirers. By the very nature of the method, however, we cannot know.

3. Doubts about the method raise doubts about the consensus allegedly revealed by it. Men's feelings on fairness of payment are said to be determined by one single criterion about which they are unanimous – that time-span should be the arbiter of differentials.

This is a very surprising discovery. It flatly contradicts the commonplace finding of many experienced observers that there are conflicting criteria of fairness and that it is this very fact which makes the problem of income distribution so profoundly complex and intractable. One or two examples will suffice. It is currently thought fair for a constable in rural Dorset to receive the same rate as a constable in Oxford, or for the porter in Cornwall to be on a par with the porter in Coventry. This is the belief enshrined in the slogan 'the rate for the job'. Yet the constable in Oxford and the porter in Coventry are the poor relations alongside their highly-paid neighbours in the car industry. They feel it unfair that an unskilled labourer can make the same pay or more by the mere accident of a job in profitable mass-production. Yet the redress of grievances of this sort in Oxford and Coventry would only transfer them to Dorset and Cornwall, for why should porters and policemen be fobbed off with less simply because they live in the country? 'So long as the general public holds contradictory notions of fairness, it will be impossible to erect a consistent system of remuneration on the basis of fair comparisons which would prove generally acceptable.' (Clegg, 1961.)

One may take the argument further. It is a mistake to suppose, as Jaques's theory requires us to, that feelings of fairness are always related to job content. They may relate to general status and standard of life in relation to other groups. A change in a long-established pay and status relationship between two groups may leave the disadvantaged group feeling resentful about their relative decline simply because it is felt to be undeserved, fortuitous, caused by no misdemeanour or failure of the persons concerned. Arguments directed at job content or changes in it do not easily come to grips with this source of felt unfairness. It may not submit to the logic of technological or economic rationality because it derives from a totally unlike universe of values – 'the primacy of human values above the values of the market place'. (Wiseman, 1956.)

It is in this sphere that management's view of fairness and that of employees may clash very sharply. The 'ethical rationale' of the former may derive from strongly-held beliefs about the social desirability of maximizing efficiency, pursuing change and minimizing costs. A technical change which increases an operator's output but requires less skill may seem to management to justify a lower wage. The operator, however, sees no reason why, in the absence of any misdemeanour or failure on his part, he should be penalized because of a technical decision made by somebody else. Fairness for him lies in an increase – in getting a share of the greater output now being produced by the organization of which he is a member.

Practical application of the time-span method

A summary of the argument so far confronts us with a number of initial misgivings about the theoretical basis of Jaques's theory. It abstracts from work the single aspect of discretionary responsibility which alone is to determine payment. It seeks to validate this principle by reference to judgements formed by the individual through intuitive methods which Jaques strongly – and convincingly – disparages in another context. The intuitive judgements themselves are brought to light by a research method which is left mysterious. And, finally, they are said to reveal a consensus on there being one and only one criterion of fairness in payment – namely, the correspondence of differentials with the differing time-spans of discretion contained within jobs.

It is an important factor in understanding Jaques's position, however, to realize that theoretical criticism of this sort leaves him wholly unmoved. Indeed, to a considerable extent he disarms it. He does not profess to know precisely *why* the measurement of time-span gives – as he asserts – an unerring indication of what the individual feels to be his level of work. He simply presents the experimental finding that it is so. He compares the time-span measure with a thermometer, which can tell us the temperature of the human body – and thereby serve an indispensable purpose – without telling us anything of its structure or functioning. His reply to all the arguments that the time-span measure cannot be expected to work is therefore simple – try it and see.

He returns a similar reply to innumerable critics who have racked their brains and practical experience to think of examples which, as they believe, prove his theory to be nonsense. Of one he wrote: 'He (typical of all these critics) takes a number of jobs, and proceeds to assume – without using measurement – that the time spans are shorter or longer than the payment levels he himself assumes would be fair. But his figures are all mere conjecture. He does not in fact know either the time span or the individual felt-fair pay.' (Jaques, 1963.)

This rejoinder is perfectly legitimate. Jaques's theory is not to be demolished by concocting imaginary examples designed specifically to make the theory look silly. The test must be a practical one. With this in mind, we return to Jaques's plea to try it.

Has it been tried? The short answer is yes. Twenty or thirty companies in this country are using it, as are others in the United States, Canada, France and Switzerland. One of the central employers' organizations of Holland, where incomes policy has made use of a job evaluation system, has after long study recommended it to members, some 20 of whom are using it in the determination of management salaries.

This affirmative answer requires, however, a more precise definition. We need, for reasons which will soon become apparent, to ask a further question. How far is the time-span measure being applied as a grading or ranking device to staff and management levels whose salaries are determined unilaterally by higher management, and how far is it accepted by groups which are accustomed to act collectively through negotiation or discussion with management in the fixing of their rewards?

The answer is that in all known instances,[1] the former situation prevails. This in turn needs qualification. In none of the 20 or 30 firms in this country which are applying it in varying degrees to their staff systems is it officially declared company policy. In the Glacier Metal Company the staff salary structure is based on it, but top management have failed to secure agreement with staff

1. This was the case up to March 1966, when the writer of this report met Professor Jaques to ascertain the current position.

representatives on the works council that time-span should be recognized as the final arbiter on salary levels.

Its rejection by organizations and groups of employees who engage in collective bargaining is absolute. No trade union or employers' association in this country has agreed to make use of it, and the hourly-rated workers at Glacier, among whom the method has been tested with reported success, have vetoed any systematic research into it.

Time-span and the bargaining process

The reason is not far to seek. The time-span method excludes bargaining. Jaques is correct in asserting that, whereas conventional job evaluation systems involve judgements which are negotiable, time-span is an objectively measurable entity. Any negotiator who accepted it as the determinant of differentials would be surrendering his place to technicians trained in time-span measurement. The implications are explosive and gingerly reactions are readily comprehensible. The more evidence emerges which seems to validate the method, the more vigorously work groups and their organizations may be expected to resist it.

This rejection of his method by all organizations and groups who participate in bargaining is seen by Jaques as stemming from 'an unconscious persecuted feeling of loss of personal freedom – the loss of the freedom to look after one's own interests in a situation where one is suspicious of the other's envy, avarice, and desire for selfish exploitation.' (Jaques, 1961, p. 280.) It is inequity in payment differentials which fosters the projection into bargaining of 'unconscious greed, envy, hate and destructiveness'. Jaques is obliged by the logic of his theory to take this unflattering view of bargaining. He is, after all, assuming an inner consensus among all men as to the criterion of fairness in pay. If this is taken as given, there can be no legitimate objection among the parties involved in a pay question to objective measurement along the dimension jointly accepted as *the* one criterion. Where there is such objection and a determination to retain bargaining it automatically becomes suspect – as being due to fear or the desire to preserve privilege.

But of course it is perfectly possible to stand Jaques's logic on its head, and argue that the very determination to retain bargaining supports our other evidence that there are *conflicting* criteria for settling rewards and that bargaining is necessary if they are all to enjoy the right of expression. We can readily accept Jaques's assertion that men have a strong sense of fairness about pay differentials, but instead of supposing that this is trampled underfoot in the bargaining process, we could just as suitably argue that it needs a bargaining process if it is to receive effective expression as against different criteria of fairness held by others.

References

CLEGG, H. A. (1961), 'Fair wage comparisons', *J. indust. Econ.*, July.
JAQUES, E. (1956), *Measurement of Responsibility*, Tavistock.
JAQUES, E. (1961), *Equitable Payment*, Heinemann.
JAQUES, E. (1963), 'A system for income equity,' *New Soc.*, 12 December.
PATTERSON, T. T. (1963), 'The Jaques system: impractical?', *New Soc.*, 19 December.
WISEMAN, S. (1956), 'Wage criteria for collective bargaining,' Ind. and Lab. Rels. Rev., January.

Further Reading

William F. Whyte, *Money and Motivation*, Harper & Row, 1955.

R. Marriott, *Incentives: A Review of Research and Opinion*, Staples Press, 1961.

Tom Lupton, 'Money for Effort', HMSO, 1961.

R. Currie, 'Financial Incentives', British Institute of Management, 1963.

Tom Lupton, *Management and the Social Sciences*, Penguin, 1971.

G. Baldamus, *Efficiency and Effort*, Tavistock, 1961.

ILO, 'Payment by Results', 1951.

OECD, 'Forms of Wage and Salary Payment for Higher Productivity', Report of 1967 conference.

S. Cunnison, *Wages and Work Allocation*, Tavistock, 1961.

Elliott Jaques, *Equitable Payment*, Heinemann, 1961.

Elliott Jaques, *Measurement of Responsibility*, Tavistock, 1956.

National Board for Prices and Incomes, 'Payment by Results Systems', Report 65, HMSO.

National Board for Prices and Incomes, 'Job Evaluation', Report 83, HMSO.

Acknowledgements

Permission to reprint the Readings in this volume is acknowledged to the following sources:

1 Harper & Row Publishers, Inc.
2 Harvard University Press
3 University of Chicago Press
4 University of Colorado
5 American Management Association
6 Harvard Business Review
7 Pergamon Press Ltd
8 *Management Today*
9 Institute of Work Study Practitioners
10 Harvard Business Review
11 *Fortune*
12 Industrial Relations Counsellors Inc.
13 Faber & Faber Limited
14 P. E. Consulting Group Limited and John Percival
15 T. Lupton and D. Gowler
16 Her Majesty's Stationery Office
17 Heinemann Educational Books Ltd
18 IPC Magazines Limited
19 Management Today
20 Institute of Personnel Management

Author Index

Subject Index

Recent books in the Penguin Modern Management Readings series:

Modern Marketing Management

Edited by R. J. Lawrence and M. J. Thomas

This volume of Readings contains twenty-one articles on many important aspects of marketing management. The editors take the view that 'marketing is the system within the firm responsible for the interface between the organization and the outside world, considered as customers or potential customers'. This is only one way of looking at the topic: Part One contains Readings which explain the marketing concept in other dimensions. Part Two deals with information as an input to the marketing system (Ackoff's key article on mis-information systems appears here). Product mix and considerations which affect plans to extend, develop or cut back the product launch are discussed in Part Three. These aspects of information processing and decision making are vital to marketing. Management of the outward flow from the company to its environment, and particularly to its customers, is examined in Part Four.

R. J. Lawrence is Professor of Marketing at the University of Lancaster.
M. J. Thomas is Senior Lecturer in Marketing at the University of Lancaster.

Organization Theory

Edited by D. S. Pugh

The editor of this volume of Readings defines organization theory as 'the study of the structure, functions and performance of organizations and the behaviour of groups and individuals within them'.

From the point of view of organizational behaviour, the task of management can be considered as the organization of individuals' behaviour in relation to the physical means and resources to achieve the desired goal. In Part One the continuing activities of task allocation, coordination and supervision, which constitute the organization's structure are discussed. A theoretical analysis of what managers have to do and by what principles they have to do it is given in Part Two. Part Three describes behaviour in organizations. Included here is a section of Elton Mayo's key Hawthorne studies – the human relations approach. Some of the research by Lewin on group dynamics, attitude change and leadership style is also examined.

D. S. Pugh is Professor of Organizational Behaviour at the London Graduate School of Business Studies.